This book should be returned to any branch of the
Lancashire County Library on or before the date shown

Lancashire County Library
Bowran Street
Preston PR1 2UX

Lancashire
County Council

www.lancashire.gov.uk/...

LANC

30

D1424858

.1(A)

summersdale

DASH

Summersdale Publishers Ltd
46 West Street
Chichester
West Sussex
PO19 1RP
UK

www.summersdale.com

Printed and bound in Great Britain

ISBN: 978-1-84953-118-4

Substantial discounts on bulk quantities of Summersdale books are available to corporations, professional associations and other organisations. For details contact Summersdale Publishers by telephone: +44 (0) 1243 771107, fax: +44 (0) 1243 786300 or email: nicky@summersdale.com.

for
Sarah and Dash
(in that order)

Contents

Acknowledgements...7

Prologue..9

September...11

October..42

November...70

December..98

January..122

February..144

March..163

April...188

May..211

June...230

July...248

August..263

September (again)..285

Afterword...316

Acknowledgements

I'd like to thank the following for letting me sketch them in too few strokes: the Dilger family, Peter Bailey, Ron Bicknell, Kate Moore, Sarah McCloughry, Tony Ledger, Michael and Lesley Jennings, Jenny Berrell, Lynn Ward, Rebecca Vincent, the Nduka family, Sam and Soraya George, the Ashley family, Mel and Rich Hare, Ben Glasstone and Mark Espiner.

I'm also particularly grateful to Ian McCarthy and Anthony Godber for early greyhound advice; Chris Hartley for a tip-off that won me time; Tom Cox for a pointer about a photo shoot; Alastair Lane, Madelaine Levy, Georgia and James Styring, Simone Foster and Sue Kay for constructive criticism; Isobel Dixon and Jennifer Barclay for their keen noses in sniffing out a good story.

Prologue

Dash was standing on the table, panting feverishly. It was two o'clock in the morning. The door was scratched, the chair-backs gnawed, a plant pot smashed to pieces and an electric flex bitten clean through. Dirt was strewn all over the floor – the floor that just an hour ago had been so pristine you could have eaten off it. Now it looked like someone, or rather something, *had* eaten off it. A standard lamp leant precariously against the wall, like a boxer out on his feet. The table and chair legs were covered in a rash of bite marks, with several chunks completely missing. The scratches on one side of the door looked like they'd been made by a sabre-toothed tiger. Or a T. rex. It took just an instant to take all this in, my eyes were so wide with horror and fear. It also didn't escape my notice that the only item to escape the onslaught, the only thing in the whole room to have been left untouched by this ferocious, whirlwind attack was the dog bed in the corner.

I had always wanted a dog. Dogs were freedom, a passport to running through the fields and staying out all day. They were friends but also toys – something you could mould into the perfect playmate, a feral bond with the outdoors,

with what really mattered in life. Obedient and faithful
from first to last. Tail going like a windscreen wiper, tongue
a pink strip, wet-nosed, bright-eyed – what boy wouldn't
want such a force in his life? But a man of thirty-seven? And
an ex-racing greyhound? Well, I was about to find out. The
first thing I knew was that I didn't know a thing.

September

So how come a greyhound was wrecking the house at two in the morning? Well, first and foremost I blame work. After four years as an editor at Oxford University Press, I'd just quit my job to go freelance. I would now be at home for all the foreseeable days ahead. Why not finally get that dog I'd always wanted – a canine co-worker to curl up under my desk?

Work was also how I'd met Sarah, my girlfriend. It was Sarah who'd first seen the poster for the greyhound; it was Sarah who'd brought the poster back home; it was Sarah who'd wanted to help me fulfil my boyhood dream.

As much as I'd like to, however, I probably can't blame work. And I certainly can't blame Sarah – she's simply too lovely. When we first met, I'd never been so charmed by a woman before. I couldn't believe she was single. She wasn't, quite. She was also out of my league in terms of looks, with the kind of petite nose and high cheekbones to keep any bachelor awake at night.

No, the blame for the whole fiasco lies fairly and squarely with me. I was the fool who'd so badly wanted a dog – who'd wanted a dog but ended up getting a champion greyhound.

Strangely, perhaps, the name arrived before the dog. I had an idea it should be short and snappy – something you wouldn't feel embarrassed about shouting in the park. Among those on the shortlist were Spook, Nelson, Ace and Titus. All very butch-sounding names (if a little too much like fighter pilots) but in the end, I settled for what the *Oxford English Dictionary* defines as both 'to rush hastily' and 'a horizontal stroke in writing or printing'. Dash. Another dog book advised against something monosyllabic (difficult for a dog to pick up at a distance) but I figured shouting 'DA-ASH!' would work. I even practised in the garden, yelling it and asking Sarah to check audibility. The neighbours must have wondered what kind of invisible pantomime was going on but it got the thumbs up from Sarah standing in the vegetable patch. Now, in a marvellously back-to-front way, all I had to do was find the dog to fit the name.

The choice seemed simple: buy one or rescue one. But how much did a dog actually cost? A pedigree was bound to be more expensive than a mongrel, but were we talking a difference of tens or hundreds of pounds? I knew mongrels were healthier and generally more fun, but still couldn't shake the impression that pedigrees had history, lineage, family. In short, they had *pedigree*. The idea of rescuing rather than buying one had a philanthropic feel. It was also free, something which recommended itself to my new state as a sole trader hustling for work and watching the pennies.

Then the next conundrum: was it better to get a puppy or an adult dog? Being the last of three boys, I'd got used to growing up with hand-me-downs. From toys to clothes to friends, nothing had ever really 'started' with me. Here was my chance to be the bona fide first and only owner in one dog's life. What exactly was involved in bringing up a puppy? How difficult could it be? I talked to a friend who'd taken on a cocker spaniel puppy a few months earlier. After hearing about a summer of pee-sodden and poo-stained carpets, as well as everything from shoes to receipts ending up chewed, I decided there was enough on my plate without putting my new business in the dog bowl. I would adopt an older dog and give it a new home. It was cheap, charitable and if it meant losing out on a few years of puppyhood, then there was the consolation of being able to start off straight away with a dog in its prime. We'd be running through the fields before I knew it.

So now the breed – this was going to be the best bit. They say a dog looks like the owner or, worse, vice versa. So what did that make me? A notch under six feet tall, bald with bright eyes and a button nose, sinewy not to say scrawny… I didn't imagine there were any breeds like that out there. Or at least nothing that looked like it would survive a winter. I considered my personal circumstances. Although freelance I still planned to work full-time, which meant a dog that needed no more than a couple of modest walks a day. So no spaniels or terriers. There were also practical considerations. The terraced house which now doubled as my workplace was small. It had a cute, grassy garden but it was barely long enough to lob a tennis ball in. So no retrievers. I thought the dog would probably be most comfortable in the little conservatory – warm in the morning, cooler in the afternoon. In fact, I'd already earmarked a spot in the corner by the radiator for its bed. It also gave easy access to the garden, had a tiled floor (for accidents) and was bright and airy with a full-length glass door. A nice view if the dog proved the sedentary sort.

Of course, the choice of dog would have to be approved by Sarah, too. The symbolism of taking on such a shared commitment wasn't lost on me. We were already living together... next a dog and even – yikes! – marriage. Not that I had anything against marriage. I'd just managed to reach the ripe age of thirty-seven without it ever happening to me. In fact, I really quite liked the idea – especially the idea of getting married to Sarah. Women like her didn't turn up often, and she was definitely worth holding onto. All I needed to do was summon up the courage and decide on a suitably special way of proposing. The fact that she was thirty-five herself and might not actually want to get married never even entered my head.

So back to the breed. Quite early on in our conversations, the issue of 'hair' had come up, closely followed by that of 'smell'. Sarah was keen that our new pet would be nothing with hair longer than hers and which also, when wet or muddy, wouldn't stink the place out. So no Afghan hounds or anything Tibetan (shih-tzu, Lhasa apso, etc.). This was fine by me since I couldn't imagine making a habit of trimming a dog's hair or giving it daily baths.

I consulted the *All-Colour Book of Dogs* – a childhood favourite and useful guide to just about every canine under the sun. After a couple of days of head-scratching, the choice was narrowed down to three candidates: the Weimaraner, the basenji, or the good honest whippet.

The Weimaraner is the Rolls-Royce of the dog world. Or more specifically, the Rolls-Royce Silver Ghost. A noble gun dog with phantom-grey fur. An old art teacher of mine had two of them – one with amber eyes and one with blue. She'd let them muscle around the school playing field and I remember thinking how distinctive they looked. But quite big too – apt to knock a small child clean off its feet. The *All-Colour Book of Dogs* advised that 'no walk is too far for these highly strung dogs which often wear out their owners'. I didn't want to be worn out; I wanted to be refreshed.

Candidate number two. The basenji, by contrast, was a more modest size. Unusual, certainly, with pricked ears and a tail as tightly curled as a Danish pastry. This dog was so bizarre it didn't actually bark. Instead it made a yodelling sound and groomed itself like a cat. The book had it down as 'active, energetic but somewhat aloof'. Did that mean it was downright unfriendly? Would it turn its nose up at substandard food or, worse still, at a first-time dog owner like me?

Bring on candidate number three, the whippet. I'd always liked it due to the associations with the north of England where my parents hailed from. Flat-caps, coal miners, 'the poor man's racehorse' – this little hound had clear affiliations. It was also quiet, gentle and surprisingly easy to house-train. Then the clincher: 'happy to spend much of the day asleep'. I had my breed.

The only question remaining was that of gender. Of course, it had to be a boy. If not exactly a 'he-dog', it'd always been a boy in my imagination. I'd grown up reading about and watching such doggy heroes as Gnasher, Mutley, Shep, Old Yeller and Hong Kong Phooey. Even a dog as flowing and feminine as Lassie was a boy. Yes, I could see us now: two rascals with only each other for company from nine to five. Then off round the neighbourhood parks or tearing through local woodland, the home office miles away in every sense.

What I'd failed to consider, of course, was that all this planning was about to come up against the realities of what a real rescue home had to offer. The search began in the Cotswolds – convenient since I was dropping Sarah off for a friend's hen party nearby. Since we'd agreed on the selection criteria together, she was happy for me to go to the rescue home on my own. Sneakily, I was rather looking forward to being the first one to clap eyes on our brand new dog. I duly did the chauffeur bit, greeted Sarah's friends without intruding, and then sped off in the direction of the rescue home. On the way, I passed a woman walking a trio of white-and-tan whippets, which I took as a good omen.

I arrived and completed the initial paperwork at reception. Then, my first disappointment. Even if I found 'the one', it might be a fortnight before I could bring him home. All sorts of checks would have to be done. Would my partner and I be responsible owners? Would our house, garden, even our lifestyle suit the dog? Did we have the long-term interests

of the dog at heart? In my naivety, I thou[...]
slip a collar on the lucky mutt and take him awa[...]
afternoon. Well, I'd just have to be patient. The kennels [...]
down a path behind the main building. After getting more
instructions about protocol from a young woman helper –
'Don't feed or tease the dogs', 'If you see a dog you like, just
note down its name and number' – I strode into a kind of
paddock with half a dozen wooden and concrete buildings
ranged about. Here then, was where it would happen, the
theatre of dreams.

After half an hour, all I'd seen were various mongrels (most
of which looked like they'd been crossed with Alsatians)
and a dozen out-of-sorts Staffordshire bull terriers. Two
or three greyhounds had also loped up shyly to the bars.
They seemed more like deer than dogs. Way too bony and
way, way too tall. It would be like taking a climbing frame
for a walk. The other dogs all had names already – either
bestowed on them by previous owners or given by the
rescue home if they came in anonymously. There weren't
many that seemed playful or in the least part happy. And
absolutely no whippets. Was I willing to rehabilitate a
nondescript loser? A dog that might take months before it
stopped moping… or maybe never? I reached the very last
cage. For some reason, I had a good feeling.

There were two dogs, both of which came up to the bars.
The taller one, a long-haired red setter soon loafed back
to its bed. The shorter one was a bright little cross-breed
terrier. Mostly white but with a black eyepatch, it hovered
and shimmied, licking my fingers and seeming delighted that
I'd even stopped to say hello. I watched it for some minutes.

...de and did a good job

...nd up for fun. Every now

...ound the edge of the kennel.

...my fingers it instantly sprang

...og obedience stuff was easy. Here

...the software pre-installed. He wasn't

a w...   ...as neat, responsive and would obviously

work ...   ...e. I didn't mind the name either: 'Midge'.

Feeling th...p had been worthwhile after all, I jotted down Midge's number and went back to see the helper and stake my claim. The young woman duly returned with a folder from the office.

'We like to give adopters a bit of history before they agree to rehome the dog.'

Great, I thought, perhaps we had the same star sign.

'Midge has been rehomed twice,' she said, 'and really needs an attentive, experienced owner...'

My heart sank. Midge had 'issues', it appeared. Snappy with most other dogs, destructive at home, prone to chronic separation anxiety and jealousy. In short, *The Hound of the Baskervilles* in miniature.

'But he seemed really sweet,' I said.

'He *is*,' the woman replied confusingly.

I knew my limitations – I might be attentive but I certainly wasn't experienced. Thanks to my dad, the closest we'd ever got as kids to owning a 'proper' pet was keeping guinea pigs. Or rather, we collected bagfuls of dandelion leaves and carted them back to the garage. Three large hutches were filled with no fewer than fourteen high-pitched squeakers – every shape and size from smooth water rats to multicoloured fashionistas with hair slicked into spiky rosettes. We sometimes took one out and let it bustle round the garden. But as for coping with behavioural problems, well, they were guinea pigs. Guinea pigs were either chirpy or sick. If they were sick, you left them alone and they got better. If they didn't get better, there were thirteen others to console you. I knew for a fact that Sarah wasn't exactly experienced with animals either. Her only childhood pet had been a white nanny goat which doubled as a lawnmower for the village bowling green.

I pondered the prospect of rehabilitating little Midge and had to confess that something in me came up short. He wasn't Dash, or at least not enough of him to give me a head start. I walked slowly back to the car park. Perhaps this search was going to be harder than I'd thought. But I wasn't about to be put off so easily. Whippet, terrier, Irish wolfhound if need be. A dog with my name on was out there somewhere – all I had to do was find him.

A few days later the search resumed. This time, Sarah and I went as a couple. I hoped it would present a united front and increase our chances as adopters. Who could resist such well-balanced would-be owners? We chose a rescue home closer to Oxford on the same basis. On arrival, we discovered that despite the kennel being open to visitors, the dogs were not at home. Every last one had effectively been quarantined due to an outbreak of kennel cough. We sat in a grim prefab office and leafed through a ring binder with pictures of the doggy internees in plastic wallets. Every half-decent animal seemed to have a 'reserved' sticker on it.

'Do you ever get any whippets?' I asked the woman behind the desk.

'No, not often,' she replied. 'The odd greyhound maybe – you know, ex-racers.'

We drove back home under a cloud. I slouched in the passenger seat and wondered just what it took to find the right dog... or any dog, in fact. Time to change tack perhaps – back to the *All-Colour Book of Dogs*. If there were no whippets out there, what was the next best thing? Size-wise, perhaps a foxhound would do. It was a hound after all. I read up on it but was unimpressed. Besides, the foxhunting angle bothered me. My ethics had always been pretty flimsy, but I certainly didn't want to look like someone who spent his weekend tearing up the countryside.

Then I came across the smooth collie. Short coat, medium height... and smart. According to the *All-Colour Book of Dogs*, it was 'easy to train, easy to please and easy to live with'. Not hard to spot the key trait there. The book also described it – somewhat in the style of Gerald Durrell – as 'good with children and other animals'. Was this the breed we'd been looking for? I could already see myself saying 'No, no, it's a smooth collie', putting an enigmatic emphasis on the word 'smooth'. The search was back on. That same afternoon, I located a rescue home that specialised in collies and was only an hour's drive away. There you go. My patience had paid off.

Sarah and I had arranged to visit on a Saturday morning and just after nine we found ourselves in a reception area with a round table, a few chairs and a host of leaflets and collie-related paraphernalia. We filled out a form; we listened to the advice. Like a menu to hungry restaurant customers, the folder of resident dogs was presented to us. We flicked through – plenty of charming pictures but no smooth collies. Perhaps there was a 'Specials Board'?

'No,' the woman advised us flatly. 'Every dog we've got is there.'

I looked at Sarah questioningly. Fate can take an unusual turn and sometimes you just have to go with it. So we'd go with it. The first dog we chose was a handsome four-year-old.

'Is he still available?' we asked nervously.

'Yes, but he's deaf, poor thing. Of course, you can learn canine sign language if you're keen.'

Sign language? We barely knew how to attach a collar and lead! Instead, we chose another dog with what seemed like a good CV and waited outside. In a peculiar kind of blind date, he was brought out to us to walk round a patch of grass. There on the end of the lead, with his nose glued to the turf as if in pursuit of an invisible radio-controlled car, was a dog which could be ours. Even better, we'd been told we could take him away that very day. A classic Border collie: a working dog and a working man's dog. He pulled; we pulled… and sometimes even in the same direction. Halfway round, he stopped to cock his leg and unsheathed what could only be described as a prize salami. Sarah stared open-mouthed and then burst out laughing. I just stared, aghast. Five minutes later, we returned him and meekly declined the offer of adoption. I'd lost my nerve. He was too big, too strong, *too* male.

Truth be told, I was starting to get sick of looking. Sick of looking and not finding. The whole experience had been a flop. I felt like crying.

Next evening, after a full day at my freelance desk, I walked downstairs to meet Sarah at the conservatory door.

'I've got something for you,' she said.

'Yeah? What's that?'

She wheeled her bike into the garden shed before coming into the house. In her hand was a folded piece of paper.

'This was on the noticeboard at work – see what you think,' she said with a coy smile. 'I know I shouldn't have taken the whole thing, but I wanted you to have first refusal.'

It was a small poster, handwritten in thick black pen. At the top, in a mixture of upper and lower case letters, was the question: 'CAn you Please GiVE Me a Home?' It continued in the first person, an open-hearted doggy address to the world: 'My name is Beautiful Energy. I was racing at Oxford Greyhound Stadium. Now, because of injury, I'm not able to race any more... I'm sure I would make a great pet.' It went on to specify age ('3½'), sex ('bitch'), colour ('black with a white chest'), weight ('25 kilos') and temperament ('very friendly'). Interested parties were asked to contact Peter, one of the security guards, who also had photos. Dodgy spelling and punctuation only served to make the plea feel all the more authentic and desperate. I got the kind of tingle you get when destiny calls. This greyhound had come out of nowhere – a small black female with a fine line in self-promotion. Admittedly, I'd set my heart on getting a male dog, but could I handle a bitch instead? I tried to think of any famous female dogs I'd read about in books or seen in films or on TV. Not a single one came to mind. Did that mean they weren't any fun? Perhaps they just did the doggy equivalent of lying around and painting their nails. Only one way to find out. There was a mobile number at the bottom of the poster and I decided to phone it straight after dinner.

The phone rang twice, three times, four...

''Ello?'

'Hello,' I said confidently. 'My name's Andrew. My girlfriend saw the notice at work. About the dog. I'm ringing about the dog.'

'She's a bitch,' came the reply, in a strong Oxford accent.

'OK. Right. No problem,' I said, getting into my stride. 'So it's, er, *she's* a greyhound.'

'Yep. Lovely little thing... quite a runner. But she got injured, pulled a muscle – one of them big 'uns on the back leg, you know. Lost a few seconds of pace, she did, and never as quick out the trap after. She can run, but she can't race no more.'

'Ah, got you. So... can I see her?' I asked.

'I've got photos,' Peter replied. 'She's kennelled at the trainer's for now. You can see the photos.'

I said I'd like to see the photos very much. I had to ring Ron, the trainer, to ask him to bring the dog to Oxford Greyhound Stadium. In the interim, Peter would visit us at home to see if it was suitable for the dog – *his* dog, it transpired, since he was the owner of Beautiful Energy.

Whenever I referred to the 'dog' he methodically corrected me: 'Bitch. She's a bitch.' By the end of the conversation I had it down pat, sounding like a regular gangster rapper. Sarah was stifling her laughter in the corner of the lounge. I fixed a time for Peter to visit and whooped triumphantly.

Now to ring Ron. Greyhound folk, I learnt, can be pretty direct. They live and breathe 'The Dogs' in a way no casual pet owner can quite appreciate. Ron, it turned out, was very obliging. Yes, he could bring the bitch to the stadium on Wednesday next week. He was due to go there anyway and one extra in the van wasn't an issue. We needed to meet him and Peter before the race. The bitch wouldn't race but could be kennelled trackside with the others, no problem. We could look her over and see what we thought. No bother at all. So that was it – we finally had our date with 'Dash'. I hugged and kissed Sarah in excitement and gratitude. I probably would've done the same to Peter and Ron if they'd been there.

Two evenings later, Peter *was* there. A shortish man in his fifties, he was bald with a broad white moustache which gave him a permanent smile. He declined tea, coffee, beer, wine or even water and perched on the sofa, keen to show us a couple of photos he'd brought. He said he was up at the stadium every Wednesday and Saturday when not on nights, either to help Ron or just follow the races. Beautiful Energy had done him proud and more than earned her keep. If he couldn't find a good home for her, he'd pay her board at Ron's kennels till she breathed her last. I nodded earnestly and studied the photos. Both were of the winner's podium at the track – smiling faces, trophies, floodlights and a greyhound in the centre sporting a gold-fringed coat.

'Bitch of the Year,' Peter said proudly. 'I've got the silver plate at home, I should've brought it.'

So, she was a real champ. She looked it too – standing foursquare and leaning into the lead as if ready for another lap. She was jet black – so much so it was hard to pick out her eyes – but there was a stripe on her chest like the freshly whitewashed line of a football pitch. It was as if she'd dipped her toes in it too, and the white tip of her tail blazed like a lit fuse. She was certainly smaller than the long-faced loners – males I now realised – that I'd seen at the rescue home.

Peter broke in: 'My daughter gave her the name. This is her.' He showed another picture of a girl of eight or nine with her arm around the dog.

'Beautiful Energy, eh? That's some name,' I said. 'Very distinguished,' wondering just how ridiculous I'd feel shouting it at the top of my voice in the park. Then, with a clap of his hands, Peter announced it was time to check out the greyhound's potential new home. We walked him through the kitchen and into the conservatory.

'I was thinking this would be the best place for her to bed down,' I said, pointing to the corner next to the radiator.

This seemed to meet with approval. Next the garden. We strode round and Peter paused by the fence.

'It's fine over that side but this is a bit low.' He indicated the waist-high wire fence which was all that stood between our garden and one of the neighbours. 'Greyhounds can jump up to six feet,' he added.

'Surely not without a good run-up,' I said, trying to avoid turning the garden into a prison yard.

'And you'll need something 'ere,' he said, pointing to the end of the fence which opened onto a short path between the two houses.

'A gate, you mean?' I asked, hoping that was all he meant.

'Yep, just so she don't take to wandering off into other folks' gardens. Has either one of the neighbours got a cat?'

I said I didn't think so but agreed we probably needed a gate there. Apart from that, no other modifications were deemed necessary. When we next saw Peter, it would be trackside with the dog... or rather, the bitch.

Oxford Greyhound Stadium is plum in the heart of Cowley. South-east of the historic centre, this sprawling quarter has seen the roller-coaster rise and fall of the motor car industry, the building of science and retail parks, and has long been home to a mix of residents. Grubby students and lefty academics, kebab van owners, boy racers – all the seedier sides of life were there. On the Wednesday in question, we drove through the stadium gate reserved for staff and VIPs. Peter was waiting at the corner of the car park with the same moustachioed smile. He led us round the outside of the track – it was the first time either of us had actually seen one – and over to an open patch of ground opposite the grandstand where a dozen vans were parked. It was time to meet Ron and Beautiful Energy.

Ron was a gent. On the squat side with a bit of a shuffle, he'd been round the block if not the track. His voice had a croak that made him seem like a genial spiv. Did *he* wonder why we wanted a greyhound? Why wouldn't we? According to Ron, they were athletic beasts and would run till their hearts gave out. They were obedient, neat and remarkably clean. They paid his wages. Beautiful Energy was, 'An A1 bitch, a bloody good racer'. He pulled back the side door of a black van and invited us to look inside. The interior had been customised and stacked with travel cages from floor to roof. Each cage had just enough room for a dog to lie down in, if it rested on its haunches like a sphinx.

'There she is,' he croaked, and pointed to a cage on the bottom row. A black greyhound looked up then pricked up her ears. Her nose poked between the bars and snuffled the air. Two dark eyes stared into mine, as if comprehending. Then Ron undid the small wire door and, in one easy motion, buckled a wide leather collar round her neck.

When she jumped down from the van, we could see that Beautiful Energy was much longer than either Sarah or I had guessed from the photos. As if to show she could do 'tall' too, she promptly rose up on her hind legs and rested her front paws on my chest. Quite a greeting – and one that we'd have to wean her off if we were to adopt her. If she tried it with someone shorter, she'd knock them over like a skittle.

'Walk her round a bit to get the feel of 'er,' Peter suggested.

She pulled hard with her head upright and moved in a swift and businesslike way, obviously excited to be back on familiar turf. Should we be looking for something significant – signs of lameness due to her pulled muscle? Or were we after a certain rapport? There were nicks and small scars on her flanks, but her muscles flexed with remarkable ease.

DASH

When the sun hit her fur, it shone peaty-black. She seemed in the peak of health.

'She's *strong*,' whispered Sarah as she took the lead. 'She's really pulling.'

'Maybe she can smell the hare,' I joked, surprised at how a dog just a third of our weight almost made us break into a trot.

'What do you think?' I asked.

'She's certainly pretty… but will the house be big enough?'

'If she fits into that travel cage, she'll fit into the house,' I replied confidently. 'Well then, madam. Are you our Dash?' Her smile widened into a grin and her brown eyes blazed. She nudged her nose into my hand and licked it delicately as if licking a stamp. When we got back to the van, Ron and Peter were chatting with other trainers who were out exercising their own dogs: white, white with brown patches, fawn, striped, even grey.

'Well?' said Peter hopefully. 'She's friendly, ain't she?'

We agreed. Friendly and fit, a good size… gorgeous.

'You don't have to say yes right now,' he added. 'Think it over and call me tomorrow.'

OK, we'd think it over. I wanted to ask how much she'd cost, but couldn't quite get the question out. Instead, we talked about the races scheduled for that evening, what time Ron and his dogs would finish and how long the drive back to the kennels would take. Realising there was plenty of work to be done, we thanked them both, gave Beautiful Energy a farewell stroke and went back to the car.

Decision time. And best taken on a full stomach. We headed down the Cowley Road to Oxford Thai. It was our favourite restaurant for a number of reasons: it was cheap; it was tasty; Sarah had lived and worked in Thailand as a teacher. It was also where we'd had our first date. Two years earlier, we'd sat at a window table. Sarah had looked stunning, smiled the whole evening and ordered in Thai. I was smitten. We'd spent that autumn cycling to and from work together, going to the movies, cooking, sleeping over, falling in love and having a fabulous free-and-easy time. That was then. Now we had another choice to make: to welcome a hound into this cosy twosome, to kiss goodbye to long lie-ins and last-minute weekends away... and to say hello to a world of something altogether different.

'So... is she the one?' Sarah asked after we'd ordered.

I paused thoughtfully. 'Hmm, I don't know. She's not exactly a "he".'

Sarah's face fell.

'And a greyhound – even a small one – isn't exactly a whippet.'

Sarah's face fell further.

I paused again. 'And *I'm* the one who'd be looking after it all day.'

'But *you're* the one who's always wanted a dog!' Sarah exclaimed.

I carried on as if thinking out loud. 'Well, I suppose she *was* quite pretty.'

'And a champion,' Sarah added enthusiastically.

'Bitch of the Year, no less.'

'Bitch of the Year,' repeated Sarah.

I paused for a final time, then grinned slyly. 'Hey, let's go for it. How hard can it be?'

Sarah beamed and reached across the table for my hand.

'You'd already made up your mind at the stadium, hadn't you?'

'Sort of,' I said. 'Well, it took a good minute or so.'

So that was it. I'd ring Peter first thing in the morning to say yes, we'd like to take the champion greyhound off his hands. Her racing days were over; the adventure had begun.

After lunch on a Wednesday in mid-September, I picked Dash up from the stadium. Quick off the mark, I'd made a visit beforehand to a pet shop where I'd bought two dog bowls (one for food; one for water) and a little bone-shaped tag engraved with her new name and my phone number. I'd also been given a cast-off dog bed by a friend and filled it with an old duvet. Ron could furnish me with the rest: a lead, collar and black plastic muzzle in case she got frisky in the park. Amazingly, he didn't expect any payment. And neither did Peter – it was enough that he'd found her a good home. They both liked Dash's new name and were sure the bitch would too. Personally, I'd had some second thoughts about whether it was perhaps a bit macho for a girl, but, from what I'd seen on our first encounter, she was feisty enough to merit it.

It was only when I got Dash back to the car that I realised I had no idea where to put her. So much for me being super-organised. The car itself was far from enormous – a Ford Ka I'd bought off my mum as a runabout. Should Dash sit in the front seat, belted up with the window down? I'd seen cars and vans with dogs' heads sticking out many a time, but wasn't sure this was advisable on a maiden trip. Or what about in the boot and let her wedge herself against the sides? It seemed a bit hard and she didn't have much natural padding. In the end, I thought she'd be comfiest lying on the back seat. I spread out an old car blanket and opened one of the side windows. Dash paused at the car door and looked in. Then she looked at me.

'Go on. Hup! Up you get.'

She didn't budge. Perhaps she needed some gentle encouragement? I pushed her rear end but she actually pushed backwards. How about the other end instead? Picking up her front paws, I plonked them in the footwell behind the driver's seat. This seemed to do the trick. She tentatively hauled herself up onto the seat and stood there – her head touching the roof.

'Sit!' (No response.) 'Lie down!' (Blank look.)

She's bound to settle down once we're under way, I thought. I got into the car, started the engine and pulled out, eyeing her in the rear-view mirror as she swayed against the seat. The first left turn and I saw her slide over to the right like a coffee table on its way to the tip. After a series of little prancing movements, she regained her footing. We stopped at the lights and I felt a paw on my shoulder. She was panting and her tongue lolled out. Was this her way of telling me to slow down... or to speed up? I reached round and encouraged her to lie down, patting the seat vigorously. Green – we drew away again and she tottered backwards. The rest of the journey continued in the same haphazard fashion as I monitored her progress in the mirror like an anxious parent watching their kid on a bouncy castle. Thankfully, it wasn't long before we reached our destination and her new home.

The first thing Dash did was pee in the garden. Slap bang in the middle of the lawn. Still, at least it wasn't in the house. Peter had recommended we take her out at regular intervals 'to empty' until she found her natural rhythm. She gave the rest of the garden the once-over, sniffing in the vegetable patch and along the borders of the path. Then it was time to go inside. I opened the conservatory door and she followed me in, nose still stuck to the floor like a magnet on a trail of iron filings.

'Well, Dash. This is it. Make yourself at home.'

She roved round the conservatory, ignored the bed and then trotted through the kitchen into the lounge. I was determined not to let her lay claim to the sofa or chairs but anywhere else, in other words the floor, was fair game. I'd put work on hold for the afternoon, so we set about getting acquainted. I tried using her new name as much as possible, calling her to me every few minutes and rewarding her with little pieces of cooked chicken. I needn't have worried – it was like having a canine shadow. If I made a cup of tea, she stood and watched; if I went into the lounge and sat down, she followed and then thrust her nose against my hand. I kept expecting her to sit down or even lie down, but no. She was fine standing, thank you very much. Perhaps if I showed her the bed again – was she tired from the ordeal of adoption? I walked into the conservatory and pointed to the bed.

'Bed.' I patted it. 'Bed.'

We both looked at the bed like schoolkids staring at the Rosetta Stone. Well, if she was determined to copy me, I'd catch her out. I crouched down and curled up in the bed, or at least half in the bed with my legs hanging out and my head over the side. Dash gave an enormous yawn, as if wanting to know what on earth I was doing. I asked myself the same question. It was going to be a long afternoon.

When Sarah finally returned from work, we were out in the garden again. I was parading Dash round on her lead, the same one with the wide collar that we'd used at the stadium. Apparently, this kind of collar stopped her reversing out of it if she got startled.

'They've got tiny heads, greyhounds. Do it up tight like this, to the last hole,' Peter had advised us.

It was true, Dash did have a tiny head – it looked like a racing bike saddle with ears. When she saw Sarah, Dash rose up on her hind legs. The old paws-on-the-chest greeting. Sarah laughed and gently pushed her down.

'So, here she is – we've finally got ourselves a dog, our very own Dash!'

I recounted my afternoon of basic training and all three of us went inside to start on some dinner. As part of the essentials, we'd also been given a fortnight's supply of dog food. It was the same stuff Dash had eaten when she was racing – protein-rich biscuits that you soaked in water for an hour till they turned spongy. Over the next couple of weeks, we had to mix in another brand until she was weaned off the high energy stuff altogether. I poured a beaker of the dry biscuit into her bowl and Dash immediately stuck her nose in it. After adding water, I decided the safest place to let it soak was in the microwave. Here, it would be both beyond reach and her obviously keen sense of smell.

Sarah and I started to make dinner and Dash insisted on joining in. She stood on her hind legs with her front paws resting on the worktop nosing the ingredients and hoovering up scraps that dropped to the floor. I didn't mind the scraps so much – it saved us cleaning up, after all – but every time she tried to surf the worktop, we said 'No!' loudly and wagged a finger at her. Hadn't they fed her properly at the kennels? While one of us chopped the veg, the other was on 'dog watch'. When it actually came to sitting down and eating, it was obvious we'd be fighting a losing battle. Dash wouldn't rest and rushed from one end of the table to other, whining. In the end Sarah and I ate standing up, wedged in a corner of the kitchen with our backs turned. Once Dash realised we were impregnable, she sat on her haunches with her head resting glumly on her paws.

After the requisite hour's soaking, her food was finally ready. At the sound of the microwave door, her ears pricked up and the rest of her followed. No sooner had I set off for the spot we'd designated as her feeding station than she was dancing on her hind legs again. She even let out an excited yelp, the first bark since she'd arrived. Bowl down; nose in; food gone... in less than a minute. She ate with rapid, grabbing mouthfuls, swallowing the spongy mixture whole and then taking a long slug of water. Licking her lips and nose, in fact her entire snout, she then wandered back into the kitchen like a drunk returning to the bar. She paused and gave a low belch. This bitch definitely had to learn some manners.

Not wanting to fuss over her, after dinner we tried to act normally and watch a bit of TV. Dash stood directly in front, with her ears pricked up and her eyes glued to the screen. At one point when channel-hopping, we came across a nature documentary on wolves. As her distant cousins growled and howled, Dash charged round behind the TV set in the hope of tracking them down. The call of the wild was obviously still strong in this particular ex-racer. With the autumn evenings getting shorter, I rounded off the entertainment by taking Dash out 'to empty' in the garden. She duly obliged. Now for the real test – lights out and bedded down, her first night alone in her new home. How would she fare? How would *we* fare?

The whining was intense. A high-pitched note on an endless loop. I'd had earplugs in for an hour and it made no difference. At first, we'd shut Dash in the conservatory.

'She's got to learn, she's got to tough it out,' I said as we went upstairs to bed.

Dash continued whining and then started scratching at the door as if she wanted to claw her way out. Sarah went downstairs to reassure her. And then came back up, shaking her head severely.

'She's really not happy – she's got these crazy eyes.'

Another sleepless hour and Sarah whispered: 'Look, we've got to go down before… before she hurts herself.'

It was two in the morning. We dragged ourselves out of bed and went downstairs again. The conservatory was devastated. Anything free-standing had been pulled over; anything fixed had been attacked. There, in the middle of the scene, the queen of chaos herself was standing on top of the table with rolling eyes and a tongue twice its normal length. I had to admit I was scared – scared of not knowing what to do, of never having another night's uninterrupted sleep... and not just a little scared of her. She'd destroyed the conservatory – was she now about to set on us? Perhaps her madly wagging tail was just a bluff to lure us in? She wouldn't bite the hand that fed her (admittedly only once to date), would she?

I made a shushing sound and stepped forward. Dash's white front paws did an excited tap dance on the table. I stroked her chest and then slowly lifted her onto the floor. The teeth marks on the furniture were certainly impressive. A low table on which we kept a winter-flowering orchid had come off worst, with bites taken out of it, like toast. Apart from the casual carnage of the broken plant pot and dirt strewn everywhere, she'd also taken the time to sever an electric flex and crack a thick plastic box where we kept the recycling. I was at a loss. We cleaned up the dirt at least, before it turned the room into a mudbath. Dash watched and continued to wag her tail. So what to do? I had to sleep. We all had to sleep.

In the end, Sarah did what I couldn't, or wouldn't. She fetched the spare duvet and went downstairs to sleep on the sofa. Dash's basket was placed next to her on the floor; the lounge door was left open for Dash to come and go as she pleased. Feeling selfish and a failure, I trudged back upstairs and closed the bedroom door. No sound came from downstairs – no whining, no scratching, nothing. I turned out the light and climbed into the cold bed.

Dash, it transpired, had slept like a baby. The presence of Sarah on the sofa had reassured her and she'd settled down within half an hour. In the bathroom next morning, we discussed our options.

'I don't think we're up to it... or at least *I'm* not,' I said crossly to Sarah. 'You can't spend all night on the sofa either. I tell you, if it's the same story tonight, she's going back tomorrow. She's eaten half the furniture!'

'You've got to be patient,' said Sarah. 'It's all so new and different for her. Imagine – up to now Dash has lived her whole life in a kennel with other greyhounds. When she wasn't at the kennel, she was at the track. Suddenly that's gone. This house must seem like a different planet... and god knows what she makes of us. Give her a chance – if you're like this with a poor dog, how would you cope if we ever had kids?'

The whole dog idea had been mine in the first place and here was Sarah pleading Dash's case. But she did have a point. I agreed to give Dash till the weekend at least.

After breakfasting in the corner of the kitchen with our backs turned – the only protection against Dash's attempts to nose the cereal bowls out of our hands – Sarah left for work. I was on my own again with the beast. Trying to play it casual, I went upstairs to the office. Dash stood at the foot of the stairs like someone watching the last train leave without them, then turned tail and settled down for a snooze. A small triumph, but one which didn't stop me feeling sick and anxious about the whole thing. There had to be some help out there – a newsgroup, or forum, or website for people who'd rescued a rabid greyhound by mistake.

The search results for 'retired greyhound' ran into hundreds of thousands. There was even a Retired Greyhound Trust, offering support, advice and equipment, as well as trying to find homes for the dogs themselves. Rescuing retired racers had long been popular in the States, I discovered. I hadn't even known there *was* greyhound racing in the States. In terms of what to do about destructive nocturnal behaviour, the advice was unanimous and hinged on one magic word: 'crate'. Essentially, a large collapsible cage. The dog had enough room to stand up and turn round, but not much more. Far from exacerbating feelings of claustrophobia, it provided a safe place to retreat to and mimicked the kennel environment. So, we had to put our new dog behind bars. If she was lucky, she'd get time off for good behaviour. I quickly searched for a supplier of crates. One large enough for a greyhound, even a small greyhound, wasn't cheap. Nor were they readily available. The quickest they could deliver was Monday. It was now Thursday. Other suppliers couldn't do any better – it seemed there'd been a run on large crates recently. Don't tell me, I thought, it's 'Rescue-a-Greyhound Week'. Four more sleepless nights on the sofa seemed a distinct possibility.

In the end, Sarah and I embraced it – and each other – and spent a full week on the sofa. The crate finally arrived two days later than advertised. It was huge and heavy, but by folding out the four walls, it snapped up into place. There were even two little doors – centre stage and stage left – for Dash to make her entrances and exits. Both of them had sturdy locks, I noticed. For her first few nights 'inside', we would leave one of the little doors open. After that, once she was comfortable, we would lock her in overnight. We put in her duvet, a couple of battered cushions and made it even snugger by folding an old curtain over the top. This we planned to pull down at night like the drape over a parrot. The transformation was immediate and astonishing. Dash loved it. We may have had a crate the size of a small car taking up most of the conservatory, but at least our dog didn't spend the small hours wreaking havoc on all she surveyed.

The frustrating thing about dogs is that they can't just *tell* you what the problem is. The even more frustrating thing is that *you* can't tell them what it is either. 'I'm just nipping out to the shops', can get the same reaction as 'I'm abandoning you forever.' Separation anxiety can be worse with rescue dogs. As soon as the house keys jingle or you put on your coat, they whine, they run in circles or bar the way to the door. No amount of reassurance will help, in fact, it often makes things worse. If you're nice to them, they'll miss you even more. Howling, panic attacks, peeing on furniture, loss of appetite, self-mutilation, vomiting, even jumping through open windows are common among dogs left alone. I'd read stories online about owners becoming practically housebound for fear of putting their dogs through such distress. With this in mind, we'd been building up to leaving Dash in an empty house by doing it in stages. Five minutes at first, then ten, then twenty. On the last Sunday evening in September, Sarah and I were ready to leave her alone for a full hour. Our destination was the local pub. But at the last minute, I bottled.

'Perhaps we should wait... you know, get one of those baby walkie-talkies or something?' I said to Sarah.

'What, so we can *hear* her chew the furniture?' said Sarah, looking at me with a frown. 'She'll be fine. It's just for an hour. Besides, the conservatory's been dog-proofed.'

It was true – we'd removed everything breakable and the corners and edges of what little furniture was left had been covered in thick gaffer tape for protection. The only other things that remained were our slippers and spare shoes, which Dash had shown absolutely no interest in.

Nonchalantly and without looking back, we closed and locked the conservatory door. We figured this was better than leaving by the front. At least this way she'd see that we'd gone rather than thinking we were hiding out in the lounge. As hours in the pub go, it was unspectacular. For a start, the pub was almost empty. Not that we minded. The important thing was that there was no dog, no black shadow constantly at our heels. We supped our pints and chatted and were a couple again. I looked into Sarah's eyes and felt thankful she'd convinced me to give Dash a second chance. Both of us knew what the other was thinking. We'd opened up our home and hearts to something new. It wasn't what we'd thought it would be, but perhaps these things seldom are. Could any dog take the burden of all that hope? Could she – would she – live up to expectation?

After an hour we walked back home hand-in-hand, but as we got nearer my palms were getting clammy. What if Dash had gone berserk and hurled herself against the glass? What if she was unconscious… or worse? The key turned in the lock and we nudged open the door. Dash was lying in her crate and cocked an ear as if she'd been disturbed from a deep and peaceful slumber. Every last one of our spare shoes was in a pile next to her. She sprang up and wagged her tail frantically. The Bitch of the Year was pleased to see us.

October

Owning a greyhound does have its advantages. For a start, most people know the breed. Most people also know something about it – usually that it goes like sleet off a shovel and is second only to the cheetah in the four-legged sprint. I can still remember an illustration from a children's encyclopedia showing the relative speeds of various land mammals. The cheetah was way out in front, with the greyhound in pursuit at about 40 mph, then the horse, the hare, the lumbering giraffe and right on down the carnival line till the world's fastest man, who came in at a leisurely 25 mph or so. Away from the world of picture books – and according to the latest online statistics – the greyhound would actually be outpaced by a wildebeest, lion and a couple of species of antelope and gazelle. Even the Mongolian Wild Ass would pip it to the post. That said, I'd like to see a wild ass catch a hare. The thing most people don't know about the breed is the single most important factor that shaped the following weeks and months for Dash and me. Unless you're lucky, an ex-racing greyhound can never be let off the lead with total confidence. If you're out walking it, you're pretty much stuck with it.

Dash stood at the conservatory door, staring out through the glass. During the first few days, dog walks had consisted of sorties round the block. This morning would be her first real outing as a pet rather than a champion racer. Our destination was the local park. Sarah had already left for work, but not before giving me an encouraging hug and wishing me luck.

'Enjoy it! You'll be fine.'

More than a little nervous, I said: 'I hope so.'

I donned my 'new' dog walking kit of a ripped jacket, trousers I'd previously used for decorating and a pair of scuffed, dirty trainers. Over my shoulder was a small grey satchel containing poo bags and dog treats. The muzzle we'd been given by Ron was a kind of black, gridded nosebag, which fastened behind Dash's ears. I buckled it on and stood back to get a full picture. There was obviously plenty of room for her to breathe and even pant. That wasn't the problem. The problem was that it made Dash look like the canine version of Hannibal Lecter. Suddenly, she was the kind of dog you'd cross the street to avoid; the kind of dog you wouldn't let your children approach. Still, the advice had been clear and I didn't have the confidence to disregard it. We should keep her muzzled and firmly on the lead until we'd got a good idea of how high her 'prey drive' was. In other words, until we knew whether she'd take to trotting alongside us peaceably... or sprint off in pursuit of everything from cats to stray plastic bags.

The ten-minute walk from the house to the park gate was a battle. Dash pulled forward with all her strength; I pulled back with mine. If I hadn't physically stopped her at each road junction, she would've waltzed under a car quite happily. Why the rush? I soon discovered when she squatted on the first patch of grass. Unlike male dogs that cock their legs against the nearest lamp post or tree, bitches do it differently. Crouched down with her back legs splayed like a cricket wicketkeeper, she released a long stream of golden pee and took in the scene.

Florence Park in east Oxford is, by any standards, a pretty park. Well-kept grass and flower beds, a trio of tennis courts, a bowling green, a bandstand and children's play area. Local dog owners take the air there up to four times a day, every day – their lives and that of their dogs regulated by the opening and closing times which change with the seasons. The 'regulars' are on first-name terms, as well as being acquainted with the names, ages, temperaments and toilet habits of most of the dogs they come across. As a freelancer who didn't get out of the house much, gatecrashing this club was going to be a godsend.

I decided we'd do a quick lap and see how it went – a reasonable objective considering this was the first time I'd really walked a dog of any kind, let alone a retired greyhound. One thing which struck me immediately was how much smelling and sniffing Dash did, in spite of the muzzle. Her nose barely left the ground. What was she after? Surely there weren't *that* many odours to sample? I tugged the lead to keep her moving; she braced herself against it in an effort to stay put. A minute later, she started to walk on bandy legs and circle in a way that I'd seen her do in the garden. I got a poo bag ready and checked my watch. Eight thirty-five. Must write that on the calendar in the kitchen, I thought. The idea was to build up a record of her motions and thereby avoid any accidents at home. 'Anal' was the word, in every sense. As it turned out, a ladle would have been more useful than a poo bag. We'd also been warned that greyhounds have delicate digestion and it may take some time to find a new food which didn't turn her guts to soup. This was certainly proving the case. With her offering bagged up and binned, both of us felt better. We were ready to meet and greet.

The first dog we came across was Casper, an Old English sheepdog and a good head taller than Dash. His fur was matted and clumps of mud hung from it like dirty brown berries from a bush. For her part, Dash seemed diffident – she sniffed at Casper through her muzzle and then looked away. Casper promptly trotted around to shove his nose up Dash's rear. Pity he hadn't tried it two minutes earlier.

'Cas, stop that! Come away.' A man in his fifties produced a choke chain from his pocket and shook it at Casper. Casper continued his inspection. 'He's a bugger, he really is.'

Tony, Casper's owner, was a classic case of a man who resembled his dog. With ragged sideburns, wiry eyebrows and a flat cap that came over his eyes, he wore a donkey jacket which looked like it'd been dragged through a hedge backwards more than once. Mind you, I looked little better myself, and soon learnt that most of the dog walkers didn't exactly dress for the catwalk, as it were.

'New, is she?' Tony asked.

'Yes,' I said. 'A matter of days.'

'Oh, right,' he said. 'Handful, I bet. I was thinking, I ain't seen 'er in the park before.'

'Ex-racer,' I said – a phrase I was to use repeatedly that first month of walks as both a description and an apology.

Tony sucked thoughtfully on the stub of a hand-rolled cigarette.

'Hmm. There's a couple of ex-racers in the park of a morning. You seen 'em yet?' I shook my head.

'One of 'em's a big 'un. Up 'ere,' he said, indicating his waist. Bigger 'n Casper, he is.' He paused for another puff. 'What's with the muzzle?'

I gave him the spiel about 'high prey drive'.

'Oh, right,' he said again, not quite convinced. 'Anyway, expect we'll be seein' you.' He nodded and we went in opposite directions. Casper withdrew his nose and jogged off in search of the next dog's rear.

'Good girl,' I cooed to Dash, wondering if that was the calibre of conversation we were to expect in the morning.

In fact, the next encounter was to prove far more typical. A little white terrier appeared around the corner of the bowling green, caught sight of Dash and stopped dead. Dash lowered her head and stalked forward slowly. Her body language was unmistakeable – from the plains of Africa to the forests of India, the same scene is played out morning and night: the hunter and the hunted. The terrier turned quickly and toddled off; Dash pulled in pursuit. As we got closer, I was pulling back so hard to restrain Dash that her front paws paddled in mid-air. Then she started to bark. Prior to that, I'd never heard her bark more than once in succession – a high-pitched yelp at dinner time. Now she wouldn't shut up. Shouting 'No' didn't seem to have any effect. If anything, it made her more agitated and she spun round and tried to shake herself free of the lead. The terrier and its owner, a chubby woman who scowled, gave us a wide berth. I didn't blame them. Imagine a bigger-than-average mostly black dog with a muzzle, barking incessantly, and a man in ripped, dirty clothes looking like he couldn't control it.

'Sorry!' I called out and flashed the woman my friendliest smile. She waved me away and speeded up. Welcome to the life of a dog-walking pariah.

The thing is, racing greyhounds *are* a special breed. They can't sit down conventionally, don't fetch sticks and, contrary to the show Dash had just put on, seldom bark. For an ex-racer, the local park is another world entirely. Accustomed to life in a kennel, the only dogs they see – the only dogs they've *ever* seen – are other greyhounds. They're walked first thing in the morning and late in the afternoon by the kennel-hands, often in packs of six at a time. At lunch, if lucky, they get turned out for a romp in the paddock. The trainer will work on developing an individual greyhound's prey drive using a basic lure (often a white cloth or something fluorescent for high visibility), and then progress onto timed sprints over a measured stretch. From there, if the dog shows promise, it'll be trialled on a proper track. A racing greyhound gets used to being handled and groomed but not petted. The owner himself may drop in at the kennels from time to time to see how his charge is shaping up, but neither he nor the trainer would ever think of teaching the dog commands such as 'Sit' and 'Heel', which are as much use as the Highway Code to a racing car driver. Of course, I knew none of this on my first walk and was shocked and thoroughly disappointed in Dash.

On the way back, she insisted on nosing up every single driveway and dancing on tiptoe to look over garden walls. If a gate or door happened to open, she stood there in anticipation – maybe she thought they were all 'home'? I soon discovered she knew exactly which one *was* home when she pawed excitedly at the large wooden gate at the side of our house. How did she do it – some kind of canine satnav perhaps?

In that first week of October, a pattern to our walks soon emerged. It started with Dash pulling me along the pavement like a husky over pack ice. Whenever she stopped pulling, I praised her with a 'Good girl' in my most encouraging voice. She did her business by the park gate and then bustled off in search of new smells or friends. If the dogs were her size or bigger, there was a civilised encounter and I could chat to the owner. The topic of conversation was almost exclusively about the dogs or the weather (and the effect it had on dog walking). If the dogs were smaller than her, she went into her 'attack mode'. Occasionally, we'd get close enough for the dogs to actually have a sniff at each other before Dash would lunge at them – barking and snapping behind her muzzle. Puppies were the most enticing since they wriggled and squirmed away from her. Depending on how weary I felt, I usually avoided smaller dogs altogether, taking a detour down a different path rather than face the humiliation of appearing to own an aggressive dog.

It was depressing. What had happened to my dream of running through the fields if I could barely make it round the park? I was at a loss and, worse, felt responsible – Dash was in my care and I couldn't seem to help. The funny thing was, despite her behaviour, I just knew she wasn't a dangerous dog. Very, very few greyhounds are. The *All-Colour Book of Dogs* describes them as 'good-natured' and 'supremely laid-back'. At home, she'd already settled into a routine where she would doze all morning, stretch and then go back to sleep for the afternoon. In the evening, she crashed out in the lounge on a padded mat and watched TV. As the book said, a '40-mph couch potato'. Dash was also a real love sponge, quite happy to soak up affection for hours on end. This wasn't restricted to affection from Sarah and me. Anyone would do. It became clear that she just loved meeting people. She never missed an opportunity to wander up to complete strangers: shoppers, builders, even drunks, and nudge them with her muzzle or lean against them. It was up to me to bring out her good side and suppress the bad. Could I go against thousands of years of breeding that had turned her into a four-legged heat-seeking missile? Well, I could only try.

The idea is that once a dog knows its name, you can tell it what to do. One of the first commands to teach is recall. Sarah and I started Dash's obedience training in a 'highly controlled environment free of external distractions' or, as we liked to call it, the garden. Standing just outside the conservatory door, we watched as Dash browsed in the flower bed. Every minute or so, in a deep voice (deep equals authority), one of us called her: 'Dash, come!' It has to be said, she was surprisingly responsive. The fact that each time she came back she was rewarded with a small piece of cooked chicken may have had something to do with it. She was even able to distinguish which one of us had called her and return to that particular person. Admittedly, this wasn't the hardest trick to master, but we were inclined to go over the top with our praise rather than stint on it. Could we increase the level of difficulty by getting her to come back into the house itself? This would be useful if we wanted to train her to toilet on her own instead of being taken out on the lead as currently happened. Wedging the door of the conservatory open, we stood inside and called her: 'Dash, come!' She charged down the garden, bounded through the doorway and into our outstretched arms. One piece of cooked chicken later, we were ready to repeat the drill. Again, she performed perfectly.

'Doesn't she need to slow down a bit?' asked Sarah after the second time. 'If she trips, she's going to do herself an injury.'

'I'm not sure she *can* do slow when it comes to running,' I said.

Not wanting to overdo it on the first session, we left Dash outside and went in to prepare dinner, closing the conservatory door behind us. After a few minutes, I went to check she wasn't up to mischief and stood and watched through the door. Dash caught sight of me and – thinking the game was still on – charged back down the garden. There was a loud thud like the sound of a knee cracked on a table leg. This was Dash's head making contact with the closed conservatory door, at 20 miles an hour. She rocked backwards and rolled her eyes. Was she seeing the doggy equivalent of songbirds circling her sore head? Bunnies chasing each other's fluffy tails? If I hadn't been so concerned, I would've laughed out loud. Instead, I opened the door quickly and caught hold of her.

Sarah rushed out of the kitchen looking alarmed. 'Maybe we should check for concussion?'

I wasn't sure how to do that with a dog. How many pieces of chicken am I holding up? Dash promptly ate the two I offered and seemed fine, if a bit stunned.

'Obviously a tough nut,' said Sarah.

'Not tough so much as thick,' I replied, shaking my head at Dash.

This episode confirmed something I'd suspected about the breed as a whole, that is, greyhounds aren't exactly top of the class when it comes to IQ. Show Dash an electric hare and she'd burst from the trap and negotiate four bends at high speed, but show her a double-glazed door and she'd run slap bang into it when closed. To prevent a repeat performance, I made a poster and stuck it on the door at Dash's eyeline. It featured the head of a greyhound wearing a pair of shades. 'COOL IT!' the slogan read, and then in small print at the bottom I'd typed the simple statement: 'Glass hurts'.

Greyhound, beagle, Border terrier – every dog in possession of four legs (and even some with only three) will want to chase a squirrel. Florence Park, where I walked Dash every morning, was Squirrel Central. They scurried across the grass, up and down tree trunks and along fences like moving targets in a video game. It was as if all of Dash's race days had come at once. The squirrels even had their own bushy flags to wave behind them and attract her attention. Invariably, Dash saw them long before I did, but I soon became attuned to the stages in the process. Stage one was when she sighted the squirrel and froze. Stage two was location refinement via radar – pricking up both ears. The third and final stages were locking on and launching. The difficulty was that all of these stages happened in a split-second. Once she set off, nothing, not a path, stream, cyclist or line of school kids hand in hand, was going to get in her way.

Somehow, I had to disrupt this process. With a conventional short lead this wasn't a problem, Dash wasn't going anywhere. In order to dissuade her from pulling however, we'd started to use a chest harness and retractable flexi-lead instead. This meant that Dash had a head start of 5 metres before the lead ran out. Greyhounds can accelerate to 30 mph in 5 metres, which is enough to give your arm an almighty wrench. Getting jerked to an abrupt stop wouldn't do Dash any good either. The 'deterrent' I found was an empty tin of chilli powder, which I filled with half a dozen dice. The next time Dash sighted a squirrel, I shook the tin behind her, rattling the dice loudly. She jumped round in fright. When she looked back the squirrel had disappeared, leaving nothing but an unpleasant and shocking association. The squirrels sometimes hung around as if to tease us, but it certainly made Dash think twice before taking off in pursuit.

Here's where I confess that I wouldn't have been too distressed if Dash had actually caught a squirrel. Throughout my childhood, I'd helped my dad wage war against a generation of them that lived in a Scots pine in our garden. The squirrels certainly proved an implacable foe – skittering down the trunk each morning to raid the bird table and swinging from the feeders like circus acrobats. At first, Dad rattled the bolts of the back door to scare them off. When this proved ineffective, he rushed outside making a strangled sound like a giant squirrel caught by the throat. We even tried surrounding the bird table with cat-shaped cut-outs made of stiff card but the squirrels only used them as convenient perches to scoff their pilfered nuts. Never one to throw in the towel – and in this respect, my dad and I were similar – he eventually resorted to trapping the squirrels in cages and driving 10 miles to local woodland to turn them loose. 'I'd like to see them find their way back to the bird table from there,' he declared triumphantly.

At the age of eighteen, I surprised myself by getting a place to study English at Oxford. And it was a genuine surprise – I'd gone to a decidedly average comprehensive school in the Midlands and always preferred Art to English. My social skills weren't exactly honed and I wasn't what you'd call worldly-wise. In freshers' week, gaffes included diluting a splash of orange with half a pint of vodka as if it was cordial, and thinking taramasalata was something they spoke in Turkey. After three years' hard study and socialising, I was slightly less naive but still not fluent in taramasalata. So I took a teaching qualification and set off to see the world, only to find myself returning to the same city fifteen years later to start a new career as an editor.

Sarah had also moved to Oxford after teaching abroad to work in publishing. Since she'd originally gone to university in Leeds, she found the fact that I'd gone to somewhere as highbrow as Oxford slightly amusing. The image of me being brainy didn't quite square with my initial lack of success as a dog walker.

'When am I going to get a *proper* tour of Oxford?' she complained one day.

'What do you mean? You've lived here for three years.'

'Yes, but you've never actually shown me the sights. You're the one who studied here. Why don't you take me to a few places which meant something special to you?'

So it was, on a Saturday morning in mid-October, that Sarah, Dash and I were standing in Radcliffe Square in the centre of Oxford. I was about to give my ladies a guided tour.

In a way, modern Oxford must seem like quite a strange place. Thirty-eight colleges are crammed into a couple of square miles. Each year, students swell the population by thousands; tourists visit in their millions. Aerial photos show dozens of gardens, quadrangles, cloisters and even a deer park, but, at street level, everything is behind solid doors which are firmly shut or, if they do actually open up to the public, it's for half an hour every third leap year.

'Ahem. So that's the Radcliffe Camera, part of the world-famous Bodleian Library.' I pointed at the imposing, bell-like building in the centre of the square.

'No-o-o,' said Sarah, 'not the obvious stuff. Tell me some things you got up to when you were a teenager here.'

'Oh, right! You mean student stuff, scrapes, that sort of thing?'

For the next hour, we walked and I talked. I told Sarah how I'd once padded down Broad Street at dawn in my socks, my shoes slung over my shoulder after a night of dancing; how I'd altered the sign of the Oxford Tuck Shop, changing the 'T' for an 'F' in protest at its rip-off prices; how I'd 'borrowed' the key to the rooftop observatory of Edmund Halley (he of the comet) and filled it full of duvets for my twentieth birthday party. I pointed out the bedroom windows of students I'd known: one whose only piece of furniture was a step ladder on which he hung his clothes; another whose collection of vinyl records outnumbered his books by a hundred-to-one; another who went on to become a famous actress. We passed the Bridge of Sighs, under which I cycled on my way to lectures; the Turf Tavern pub, where I knocked myself out on its low-beamed ceiling; the Sheldonian Theatre, where I eventually graduated. At one point, I even felt myself getting misty-eyed. It was hard to connect the green student of twenty years ago with the grown man I'd become. I was changed, undoubtedly. Sarah and I were now living together, I had a fledgling career as a freelancer and was the owner, at last, of a dog.

I was proud to show Sarah my student haunts, and we were both proud to show off our Bitch of the Year. It was fair to say that Dash herself followed the tour inattentively. With few other dogs to distract her, she regularly pulled up to sniff at lamp posts or stepped off the kerb to explore the gutter. The steady flow of students and tourists meant she dodged from side to side on the pavement. I still hadn't taught her to walk to heel, and more than once she wrapped the lead round passers-by and almost brought them down at the knees. Most took it in good humour, and I apologised cheerily with phrases like: 'Sorry, she's a girl-racer', or 'She's a trailblazer', or simply with 'She's a greyhound'.

As we passed a newsagent Sarah nipped in for a paper and I sat on a bench outside. Dash leaned against my legs and panted. She was wearing the harness we'd bought to stop her pulling – black nylon with a fluorescent yellow trim. A burst of autumn sun came out so I put on my shades and sat there smiling absent-mindedly.

'Now there's a lovely dog,' a woman's voice said suddenly.

Two grey-haired, doddery women wearing golf visors and matching T-shirts had stopped in front of us and were looking at Dash. Since I assumed one was addressing the other, I didn't reply but continued to smile.

'Isn't it just,' the other woman said loudly. 'Do a wonderful job, you know, those types of dogs... I said they do a wonderful job.'

Were the old dears a couple of dog-racing enthusiasts? I'd never have described pursuing an electric hare as a 'job' but there you go. I continued to smile benignly and patted Dash.

'Come on, Daphne,' the first woman said after a pause. 'He can't see us – poor man must be deaf as well.'

It took a while for the penny to drop; there I was wearing dark glasses in October and, standing in her fluorescent harness, I suppose Dash must have looked like a skinny guide dog, though why a guide dog would be wearing a muzzle is anyone's guess.

Our route home took us down New College Lane. It had long been a favourite of mine and, with its narrow twists and turns, belonged to a part of Oxford which had probably changed little in a hundred years. As a student, I'd walked down it one evening only to stumble onto a film set. The double yellow lines had been covered in horse manure; the electric lamps replaced with gaslight which glowed through a fog of dry ice and a man in handcuffs was being escorted by two bobbies towards the dark, heavy door of New College as if it was Newgate Prison.

I was especially fond of the street because New College was the one I'd attended.

'Roughly how "new" is "New" then?' asked Sarah.

'About fourteen hundred or something. Hang on, we might even get a peek inside.'

A student a few paces ahead of us was approaching the door and taking his keys out. If we were quick, we could follow him into the college for a look round. Dash, sensing some kind of chase was suddenly under way, speeded up and nimbly skipped through the doorway behind the student. This threw me and, as the door swung to, I pulled back instead of carrying on. It clicked shut, trapping the flexi-lead. Dash was now on the inside but we were stuck out in the street.

I looked at Sarah. She put both hands to her mouth and gasped. For a moment, it was comical. It looked like I was taking the whole building for a walk.

'Is it locked?' Sarah asked.

I pushed hard but the solid wooden door didn't shift. I knocked and stepped back. No answer. I banged on the door and shouted loudly: 'Hello! Anyone there? Open up!'

Then I heard the high-pitched whine which Dash had used to such good effect on her first night in her new home. The keyhole of the door wasn't even big enough to squint through to see what she was up to. She must have thought we'd abandoned her.

'Don't worry, Dash. We're still here!' I yelled.

After a few more bangs from me and whines from Dash, the door suddenly swung open and the head of a fierce-looking man in a bowler hat appeared. A college porter. The hairs of his moustache curled upwards in indignation.

'Sorry,' I said hurriedly. 'Can we have our dog back, please?'

By mid-October, Dash was getting more into the swing of domestic life, and I was getting more used to being 'owned by' a greyhound. I say 'owned by' rather than 'owning' since with all the training, feeding and grooming it felt more like I was there for her benefit and amusement rather than vice versa. In exchange, however, I was rewarded with a playful bow each time I came downstairs from my office – her front legs flat to the ground and her rear in the air – and a wag of the tail so vigorous it could have powered a kettle.

Our walks together were still chaotic and nervy, but in the second half of October we had what turned out to be a very significant encounter indeed. Dash was trotting beside me as we passed the bandstand in Florence Park when she suddenly stopped in her tracks. If she'd been a pointer, she would've raised a paw and straightened her tail. Suddenly, there, not six feet ahead of us was a greyhound – *another* greyhound. It was black and sleek, unmuzzled and off the lead! A collar hung loosely round its neck. Dash was transfixed. After a moment, the other greyhound pranced towards us with its ears upright and tail held high. I relaxed Dash's lead cautiously and they stood nose to nose like mirror images. Their tales flicked from side to side, then they danced round to sniff each other's rear. Unlike the clumsiness of Casper the sheepdog, this was done delicately, gracefully. No doubt about it, the new greyhound was a real beauty. Slightly bigger and bulkier than Dash, she (a bitch, too) was pure black, from the tip of her tail to her toenails. Her coat was short and so well groomed it looked like sealskin. She had poise, balance and, above all, confidence.

'Jess! Je-ess!' A short woman with a shock of silver hair was striding towards us. Like her dog, she was dressed mostly in black.

She beamed and observed: 'They seem to be getting on fine.'

'Yeah,' I said (as if it happened all the time), then added, 'mine's new. I've only had her a month.'

'Ri-i-ight,' the woman said, drawing out the word and raising an eyebrow, either in interest or sympathy, I couldn't work out which. 'She's lovely. Ex-racer?'

'Yes, yours too?'

'Yes.'

We introduced ourselves and the dogs and stood there sharing what felt like a special connection. Much to my surprise, Dash stood calmly alongside Jess. They resembled two horses waiting to be hitched to a cart. Jess the greyhound, it transpired, was more than four years Dash's senior at eight years old. The woman, whose name was Sally, had had her for eighteen months. That made her a greyhound pro in my eyes. I could have clung to her with relief and had a hundred questions to ask. Perhaps best to stick to the basics if I didn't want to come across as inept or desperate.

'What was Jess like at the start, you know, when you first got her?'

Sally rolled her eyes. 'Awful, in a word. I couldn't leave her on her own. Or if I did, I'd come back to find she'd run amok in the house. It was a nightmare.'

I frowned at the news, but couldn't have been more pleased. At least I wasn't the only novice who'd had trouble with a new greyhound.

'And how long did it take till she got better?' I wasn't quite sure whether I wanted to hear the answer to this one.

'Funny you should ask that. Only yesterday, she had a little accident and peed in the kitchen.'

Now it was my turn to draw out my words: 'Oh-h-h.'

'Mmm,' she continued. 'That's why I'm thinking of getting another one, you know, another greyhound to keep her company.'

Two greyhounds at once? Sally was mad, surely. Although, when I looked over at Dash and Jess, they were now roving round – one on the flexi-lead, one running free, but still side by side – sniffing at the same patches of grass. Since I probably had one question left before coming across as hopeless, it had to be a good one.

'When did you start letting her off the lead?'

'Right from the start, really,' she said. My heart sank. 'But she's got arthritis in one of her front paws. She doesn't run that much any more and never strays too far.' My heart rose again. Perhaps there was still hope for Dash, even if I couldn't imagine letting her off the lead any time soon.

Sally had a question for me before we went our separate ways.

'Have you met Kate and Arnie yet?

I said I hadn't.

'Oh, you'll like Arnie. Gentle giant of a dog.'

I guessed this must be the greyhound that Tony had claimed came up to his waist. After Sally and I had said our goodbyes, my step was a little lighter and more relaxed. Here was someone who'd gone through what I was going through and had come out the other side. I'd also witnessed Dash in a different state – calmly engaged rather than creating mayhem.

A couple of days later, Dash and I were walking home across an open field by the river. In the opposite corner, a white shape was moving along the hedge like a piece of pale sky fallen to Earth. Its loping stride was regular and easy and its flanks were massive. So this was Arnie. Behind him at a distance of 50 metres or so was a slim woman with straight shoulder-length blonde hair, a smart waterproof jacket and wellies so tall they could have doubled as umbrella stands.

'You must be Kate,' I said, smiling.

'And you're Andrew and Dash,' she laughed. 'I heard from Sally that there's a new greyhound in town.'

Owners of the same breed of dog, like owners of the same make of car, have a particular bond. They also share certain character traits. As I would soon learn, in the case of ex-racing greyhound owners this is usually a stubborn persistence and indulgence. They go easy on their dogs because they know what they've been through. Only a tiny number of racing greyhounds are truly successful; the majority retire in their third or fourth year after loss of form and a run of failure. The owners also know a good proportion of retired greyhounds are still cast aside by the racing industry – dumped in rescue homes or simply put down. Like the legacy of a conflict, this is the shadow behind everything that makes the modern greyhound what it is. They're bred for a sport which loves them only when they rule the track. A quick flick through the greyhound's history, from its origins on the plains of the Middle East in 6,000 BC, reveals the same thing. It's prized for its scorching speed. Add to this its phenomenally keen eyesight (the name 'greyhound' is actually thought to be a corruption of 'gazehound' rather than anything to do with the colour 'grey') and the result is a dog supremely well adapted for pursuit of all manner of fleet-footed game. Among the greyhound's fans are pharaohs, emperors, kings and nobles. Without wanting to boast, it's also the only breed of dog that gets a namecheck in the Bible.

I stared at Arnie. He was a hell of a specimen; it was clear why he shared the first name of Schwarzenegger.

'Forty kilos,' said Kate in a murmur which suggested even she couldn't quite believe how big he was. His head alone was the size of a bowling ball. Dash patrolled round him as if inspecting a monument.

'Does she bite then?' asked Kate, indicating Dash's muzzle.

'Not exactly,' I said. 'She just behaves like she will. Anything smaller than her and she'll charge up to it as if she wants to rip its head off.'

'Oh, Arnie seems to ignore anything beneath him, as it were. I ended up taking the muzzle off after a week.'

I looked at Arnie again. He was so docile he could have been drugged.

'I still don't feel that confident about Dash after a month.'

Kate nodded. 'Well, you might just have to feel your way. It's probably a question of managing the problem.'

I wondered what she meant by 'managing'. It sounded a bit like 'living with it' to me. That said, it was encouraging to talk with another greyhound owner. Kate definitely knew her stuff, but confessed that Arnie was so easy-going that he'd never really given her much trouble.

'He just gets on with things himself. I wanted a greyhound for beginners,' she said, 'and this great big hunk of love is what I got.'

One weekday morning when I picked up the post, there was something unusual among the assortment of bills: a booklet of white card. On the front cover, just underneath a silhouette of a greyhound, were the words *Official Identity Card – Greyhound Stud Book*. The name, handwritten on a dotted line, showed it belonged to 'Beautiful Energy'. Peter must have dropped it off on his way to work. I left the bills unopened on the table and scrutinised the booklet over a cup of coffee. Besides Dash's name on the cover, there was also her 'earmark'. I'd already noticed the blurred, blue-green tattoo in Dash's right ear and wondered what it meant. It turned out that every single greyhound bred to race in the UK and Ireland has one. Racing greyhounds, like racing cars, need a unique registration number.

Inside the front cover of the booklet was a table which recorded Dash's trial races. There was the date, distance, her racing weight and finishing time as well as technical stuff about the condition of the track, or 'going'. The next page was even more interesting. It gave Dash's date of birth and breeding details. Her birthday was the nineteenth of November, just nine days after mine. She was a Scorpio too, so we had the same star sign after all! Another surprise was that she was Scottish, born at a breeder's in Ayrshire. Her parents were listed as 'Droopys Woods' (the father, or 'sire') and 'True Swallow' (the mother, or 'dam').

I turned over to see a double-page spread of what could only be described as Dash's vital statistics. Outline drawings showing a greyhound from the front, back, left and right were marked to show the colour pattern of her fur – even down to the white tip on her tail. There were measurements of her height to the shoulder (26 inches), girth (27 inches) and length of tail (17 inches). Her eyes were recorded simply as 'brown', which I didn't think did justice to the teardrops of dark chocolate she gazed at us with. Finally, there were neat little diagrams of her 'fore' and 'hind' paws, including the colour of every one of her sixteen toes and eighteen toenails (including 'dew claws', the vestigial claws which a greyhound, in common with most other dog breeds, retains on its front legs).

But why all the detail? Then it struck me – this must be the canine version of fingerprinting. I was well aware of stories of people getting siblings to sit exams for them, or even to take driving tests or attend job interviews on their behalf. Did similar practices take place in greyhound racing? Were there trainers who'd substitute a hopeless outsider for a spitting-image winner? Was there really that much at stake? I guessed there must be.

Little by little, Dash's character came to the fore. Working at home all day, I saw (and heard) the oddities of her behaviour. Some were charming, most were unorthodox and a couple were downright peculiar. Once, coming downstairs to make tea, I was shocked to see Dash stretched out on her mat with all four legs sticking up in the air. I gasped. Had she suddenly expired? No, her eyes flicked open and her head revolved like a security camera, tracking my movements as I walked around her. She was obviously in a state of being supremely laid-back. I later found out that this position of complete abandonment is known as 'the cockroach' or 'roaching'. The only thing that saved it from being totally brazen was Dash's habit of curling her tail back over her private parts. She was a lady, after all.

Another endearing routine was what Sarah and I called Dash's 'comedy run'. When excited, often before mealtimes, Dash would tuck her powerful back legs under her and lurch forward for two or three strides with her front legs in mid-air. This was often accompanied by her tongue lolling out of the side of her mouth. A toddler learning to ride a tricycle has a similar expression.

A whole catalogue of impressive tics happened when Dash was asleep, ranging from shivery flicks of her feet to mini-barks, yaps, yips, snorts, sneezes, huffs and almost human sighs. I'd also read online that some greyhounds even howl or 'roo' at night, and that there was something terrifyingly nicknamed the 'Greyhound Scream of Death'. Fortunately, Dash never treated us (or the neighbours) to this werewolf cry.

When out and about, Dash was definitely on the prim side, skipping over puddles and mud rather than getting wet or dirty. She'd rather die than plunge into a river after a ball. If having a good bath was to be such an infrequent occurrence, Sarah and I thought we may as well get Dash's first one out of the way early on. Who knows, it might also help with the bonding process. We ran a little lukewarm water and I carried Dash into the bathroom cautiously, like a removal man with a work of art. She looked round her with an expression of mild enquiry. As I lowered Dash gently into the tub, Sarah moved in with an old sponge to squeeze water over her. It was all we could do to stop laughing. Once wet, Dash seemed to slim down to half her size. She'd become a sopping black weasel with big brown eyes! We squirted shampoo on her back and massaged it into her fur, Sarah taking the rear end, me the front. I sculpted silly shapes with the foam, giving Dash a pair of Halloween horns and white mousse for a beard. We laughed out loud now. It was even funnier since Dash stood there so stoically. Suddenly, as we were rinsing her off, I felt Dash's legs give way. The warmth of the water combined with the shampooing had softened her muscles and she collapsed.

'Whoa, Dash. I've got you.'

She was fine. I'd got her, but my shirt front was now soaked through. I lifted her out of the tub onto the bath mat. Quick! If we weren't fast enough with the towel, Dash would shake herself dry – that loose-limbed full-body shake, which all dogs do. We weren't fast enough... Dash had the last laugh. That evening she had a bath; Sarah and I got a shower.

For all the trouble Dash caused us in her first six weeks, she also brought an enormous amount of pleasure. After a full day stuck at a desk, there was nothing better than a long dog walk. When I went alone, it gave me chance to switch off, to get some headspace and perspective on things. It also began to connect me to nature and the neighbourhood in a way I'd not previously appreciated. As I trailed Dash for mile after mile through parks, fields and woods, I marvelled at my surroundings – the changing autumn colours, the sheer variety of plants and wildlife to be found, even in urban areas. I also discovered how little I'd known about the area where I lived. The walks revealed a dozen new footpaths and shortcuts. I wandered down streets that I'd barely noticed before and paused in front of buildings I hadn't even known existed.

When Sarah joined me on the walks, we cherished the time in each other's company. We talked more; we listened more. We passed Dash's lead between us comfortably and without comment. Dash had become the symbol of what we wanted to build and share – something new and exciting, something rewarding. With each passing day, I became even more convinced that Sarah was the woman I wanted to marry. My concerns were hers; her hopes and dreams I wanted to come true.

On the last Friday afternoon in October, we went on one of our favourite walks. South Park is closer to the centre of Oxford than Florence Park where we usually walked Dash, but it's also larger and hillier. There are no pretty paths, no genteel bandstand or bowling green but what it does have is bags of space and the most sublime and romantic view over the city. With the working week at an end, Sarah and I were relaxed and relieved. We walked hand-in-hand, chatting and filling our lungs with fresh air. Dash zigzagged happily on the end of her 5 metre lead. After twenty minutes, we stopped at the crest of the hill to sit on a solitary bench.

The beautiful scene was spread out before us: a postcard view of the dreaming city. Spires and steeples, turrets and towers all ranged in the distance like pots of pens on a gigantic desk. The weather was close and the sky both light and dark at once, making it feel as if something dramatic was about to happen. I felt inspired. Maybe this is it, I thought. The hairs on the back of my neck prickled. Maybe this is the perfect time to propose to Sarah. We were happier now than we'd ever been. She was the one, I was sure of it. Then it struck me with the force of a slap – I didn't have a ring. What could I do? I'd never worn any rings myself, so couldn't use one of my own. Could I improvise instead? The closest thing to a ring was the name tag on Dash's collar. Could I slip it off and use that?

I looked at Sarah and softly said her name. She turned to look at me.

Just then, a large drop of rain landed on the bench between us. Then another, swiftly followed by a thunderclap. Dash – happily leaning against Sarah's leg till that moment – suddenly bolted. Sarah was jerked to her feet by the lead. As the heavens opened, Dash took off in the direction of the trees, forcing Sarah to sprint to keep up with her... leaving me stunned and alone on the bench.

November

WHEEEEEE-BA-BANG! Dash jumped to her feet and started to tremble. Bonfire Night. Although barely dark, the sky had already begun to echo with the screech of rockets and thuds of bangers. Before getting a dog, I'd always loved it... suddenly it was purgatory. Somehow, if Dash wasn't to relieve herself indoors, I had to get her outside for an evening walk.

Dash had been jittery for a whole day after we'd been caught by the thunderstorm in South Park. So had I, for that matter, after missing my chance to propose to Sarah when Dash had galloped off with her in tow. Once I'd recovered from the shock, I got up from the bench and caught up with them sheltering under the trees. We'd stood there for fifteen minutes till the shower subsided, sopping wet and me silently cursing both Dash and my bad luck. But this was silly, I'd told myself later, there'd be another opportunity soon. I'd go shopping for a proper engagement ring this very month.

Dash paced the lounge nervously and lay back down on her mat, only to spring up again a minute later at the sound of another firework. Rather than mollycoddle her and make it worse by seeming to reward her fear, I tried to ignore her. She stared at me in silent appeal and her skinny legs shook so much she could barely stand. We'd better go now, I thought, or we'll never get out at all. I stamped into my trainers and quickly buckled Dash into her harness. Outside, it was cool and breezy but we got no more than a few metres from the house before Dash froze.

'Come on, Dash. Good girl.' She looked away warily.

I gave the lead a quick tug. She stood her ground. I wandered back to her and held a treat in front of her nose: the carrot approach. Nothing.

'Right,' I declared loudly, meaning business. I gave the lead a firmer tug and she took a step or two forward before leaning back with all her strength. She wouldn't budge. Then another banger went off and she did an immediate U-turn and stood at the side gate to the house. That's it, she seemed to be saying, that's all you're getting out of me tonight.

I'd had Dash just six weeks and figured it was time to assert my authority as 'pack leader'.

'Dash, listen up. We're going for a walk.' I held my index finger in front of her nose – something I'd noticed had worked before when it came to correcting bad behaviour. She went slightly cross-eyed as she stared at it. I turned round and jerked her forwards roughly. The harness almost pulled off over her head but at least she was moving. We managed as far as the first road junction and then she braced herself again. Thus far and no further. Incensed, I strode back to her and showed her the finger again. She looked away. Determined not to be dictated to, I picked her up – all 25 kg – and carried her across the road, plonking her down on the pavement. A rocket screamed overhead, launched from someone's back garden. Dash promptly turned and ran back into the road. Luckily, no cars were passing but the lead was now stretched taut between us like the rope in a tug-of-war. That was it. If she wanted a battle of wills, I was ready. I marched back, picked her up again and crossed the road for a second time. She was not a happy dog. Her tail curled beneath her body so far it almost touched her belly. We were going to finish the walk; she was going to go to the toilet. I put her down and dragged her forward with all my strength. A couple walked past and gave me a black look. I didn't care; I was too far gone. Five minutes later, Dash managed a single poo the size of a cocktail sausage. As soon as it hit the pavement, she turned for home and this time I let her go.

When Sarah came back from work, I was still fuming. Dash was hiding deep in her crate with her head buried in a fold of the duvet.

'What's the matter?' Sarah asked when she saw me.

I gave her the abridged version of the walking fiasco.

She bit her bottom lip, wary of taking Dash's side with me in my current state. 'You took her out with all these fireworks going off?'

'They've been going off since mid-afternoon and they'll carry on till after midnight. Then it'll be the same for a week. What am I supposed to do? She's got to go to the toilet! I'm the poor bastard who'll have to scrape her poo off the carpet.' If Sarah wanted an argument, I'd take her on, too.

She didn't. Instead she retreated into the conservatory to check on Dash. Typical – trust the girls to stick together.

Later that evening, with Sarah acting as intermediary, Dash crept back into the lounge and curled up on her mat. Every so often, she shot a furtive glance in my direction, as if attempting to gauge my mood, and with each glance I felt my anger and frustration subside.

The next day, a little gizmo like a plug-in air freshener sat on the table courtesy of Sarah. 'Dog Appeasing Pheromone', or DAP. According to the leaflet, this would 'ensure calmness by providing a feeling of comfort, safety and reassurance at times of high stress'. We'd give it a go. Maybe I should try inhaling it myself? By now, of course, I felt sick with guilt for how I'd behaved. I replayed the events in my mind – my shouts, Dash's confusion and abject fear, even the desperate scrabbling of her claws on the pavement as she'd tried to scurry for home. How could I have been such a bully? Dash, thankfully, seemed to have forgiven me. Later that same evening, she'd sauntered over to lean against my leg and nuzzle my hand. Greyhounds, I'd learnt, have long memories but bear precious few grudges.

One evening in the second week of November, in torrential rain, we received a surprise visit. Peter called in on the way to start his night shift.

'Evenin'. Sorry to disturb,' he said when I opened the front door. 'I've got something for you.'

He ducked inside and there was promptly a bout of whining and scratching from behind the closed door to the kitchen. Dash had recognised his voice.

'How's the bitch?' he asked, looking as if he expected the worst and was somehow to blame.

'See for yourself,' I replied and jerked the kitchen door open.

Dash let out a yelp of joy and flew round the corner.

'Remember me, old girl?' said Peter warmly and bent to stroke her, dripping rain off his coat.

Dash remembered him. She *definitely* remembered him. I'd never seen her more animated. Wheeling in circles around him, she did her 'comedy run' with her tongue lolling out. She sniffed his shoes and licked his hands. When she stood up and put her paws on his chest, Peter laughed and beamed.

'You've not cured her of doin' her special greetin', then.'

I raised my eyebrows and smiled helplessly, wondering if Dash would ever put on such a welcome show for me. Sarah came into the lounge to witness the scene.

'Look at her!' she said. 'She's gone ballistic.'

As usual, Peter declined any drinks and said he wouldn't stop long. Instead, he rummaged in the lining of his jacket.

'I've got this for you. Well, it's hers really.' He nodded down at Dash, who was now leaning against his leg as if she'd been superglued there.

He pulled out a slim, square box and placed it ceremoniously on the coffee table. It was covered in black velvet and had a couple of metal catches. I looked at him blankly.

'Go on! Open it,' he said.

I crouched down and flicked open the catches.

'The trophy!' I exclaimed, looking up at Peter, who was now grinning.

Sarah peered over my shoulder.

The silver trophy was the size of a dinner plate, but had a heavily bevelled edge and gleamed like polished mirror. I read out the inscription: *Oxford Owners' Association – Beautiful Energy – Bitch of the Year*. In the centre was a slightly comic engraving of a greyhound in full flight. It was wearing a racing jacket that looked like a bikini shrunk in the wash.

'It's no use to me at home now,' said Peter, sniffing. 'Reckon she earned it.'

'Peter, are you sure?' I said, lifting the plate carefully out of its box and showing Dash. 'What do you think, Dash? Shall we keep your "bling"?'

Dash looked at the trophy then up at Peter adoringly.

'You really won't stay for a drink?' I asked.

'No, thanks. I'm due at work. This weather will only slow me up.'

We thanked him again and showed him out, restraining Dash from following him into the rain. Just before the door closed, he popped his head back round.

'Oh, you should check out her races. You know, on the computer. I'll jot the website thingy down and post it through the door.'

When I came back into the lounge, Sarah was examining the trophy.

'Hmm,' she mused.

'Nice, isn't it?' I chirped enthusiastically. 'So where do you think we should put it?'

'Not in here!' she said, laughing.

'Why not?'

'Just look at it. "Bling" is the word all right. If you want it anywhere, you can put it in your office. Or we could melt it down – it'd make a decent-sized necklace.'

'Oh, it's like that is it?' I pouted and held the trophy behind my back in a playful show of protectiveness. 'We're not melting anything down! That's her heritage, that is.'

Sarah rolled her eyes and went back into the kitchen. I put the trophy carefully back in its box. Should I leave it on the coffee table for now? No, that would be the perfect nose-height for Dash. The mantelpiece would be too conspicuous for Sarah's liking and the top of the dresser too dusty. In the end, I slid it under the sofa cushions, out of sight of both Dash and Sarah. For a moment, Dash stared at the front door through which Peter had left. She then whimpered and trotted quickly after me as I followed Sarah into the kitchen.

On a scrap of paper in blue biro was a website address: www.greyhound-data.com. In the two months that we'd had Dash, I'd never even thought to check if she was out there online. I'd never actually been to the 'The Dogs' before and had only a vague idea about what went on – a bunch of greyhounds belting round a track after an electric hare, with the winner being the first past the post, I thought. The website, however, was a gateway into a foreign world – a vast library of doggy data. There were tabs labelled 'Active sires', 'Test-mating' and 'Tattoo'. If I was so inclined, I could find the results of a particular race on a particular track, anywhere in the world. Greyhounds, it turned out, were not only bred and raced in the UK, Ireland and the States (which I knew about) but also in Australia, New Zealand, Germany, Sweden, Denmark and Finland! I decided the tab labelled 'Dog search' was the most likely way of tracking Dash down and duly typed in the name 'Beautiful Energy'. I waited while the website trawled through an astonishing 1,547,892 records. Would Dash be among them? I felt like a nervous parent on exam day. Then suddenly there she was – a photo of her at her racing peak, at the head of a pedigree which went back five generations. I was amazed by the detail. All thirty-two of her great-great-great grandparents were listed, with some born back in the nineteen seventies. This was information of a different order than I'd been able to get from the stud book which Peter had given us. It also showed her racing statistics, or 'form'. Out of a total of fifty-seven career races, she'd won fourteen of them and come runner-up in thirteen. That meant first or second place in almost half. I flushed with pride. As well as the result, it listed the box or trap number she'd started from, the distance of the race in metres and the finishing time down to a hundredth of a second. I couldn't even make sense of some of the information – there seemed to be a kind of grading system for the races and the column headed 'Comment' was full of baffling abbreviations like 'QAw' and 'LedNrLn'. What was this secret language I'd stumbled on? In fact, what was this secret world?

I showed Sarah. 'What do you think of that?' I said, gesturing at the screenful of data. 'More than you'd get on a second-hand motor.'

'Wow,' she said, suitably impressed. 'Who records all this stuff? It's like an MI5 dossier or something. What do these funny abbreviations mean?'

She scrolled down and stopped at the bottom of the page, pointing with the cursor to a two-line table. 'What's this?'

I leaned over her shoulder. We both read the information but Sarah shrieked first.

'Dash is a twin! She's got a brother!'

It was true. There were two greyhounds listed in the same litter – one bitch and one dog. The male's name was 'True Joe'. Sarah clicked on his name and the photo of a striped or 'brindle' greyhound appeared. I searched True Joe's face for a likeness of Dash. Something about the shape of the head perhaps, or the line of the nose? Were they her pert, little ears and quick grin? Her chocolate-coloured eyes?

'How many did he win?' asked Sarah excitedly. 'Or is he still racing?'

I checked the form. 'None', I said, surprised, and read out a footnote: 'Never made the grade at Walthamstow. Gone flapping in Scotland'.

Sarah and I looked at each other. 'Flapping?'

Whatever it was, it sounded like second best. Dash had obviously been the star twin. On the strength of our findings, we went downstairs and showered her with praise as she lay on her mat. She looked puzzled but soaked up the affection. I tweaked her nose.

'You're a champ, Dash! A real winner. And you've got a twin brother. Why didn't you tell us?'

Over the next few days, I became addicted to the website. I'd never had that much interest in my own genealogy but this was fascinating stuff. I asked Sally and Kate, the other two greyhound owners from Florence Park, for the kennel names of their charges. Jess or 'Sheilbaggan Jess' – the black bitch Dash had met first – had won only one race out of twenty-eight starts. Arnie – aka 'Avid Gunner', the huge white male – had run more races than Dash but not won as many. That made Dash queen of the heap, at least locally. It probably also accounted for why she was unstoppable. Her 'prey drive' was sky high. She was used to being out in front and going flat out. Judging from the records, Dash raced over two distances: 450 and 595 metres. Her fastest times occurred within three weeks of each other one December, with her time for the longer distance being 37.44 seconds – a hair-raising 16 metres per second. Put another way, it meant she could cover 100 metres in just over six seconds. This bitch was lightning fast.

I soon discovered that it was possible to 'read' the narrative of each race from the form guide, making it come alive as if I'd been there. For that particular race over 595 metres, Dash had begun as the favourite. She was in box two because she was small and a quick starter. This meant she could avoid the crowding which often took place at the first bend. There'd been five other runners – four bitches and just one dog. According to the 'posts' – markers positioned at quarterly intervals round the track – Dash had burst from the trap in second place behind another black bitch by the name of Solid Funky. Amazingly, the two bitches shared the same father, making them half-sisters and thereby (I like to imagine) giving the race an extra bit of needle. Solid Funky had led until the first post – 150 metres or so – and then

Dash had drawn level. There was crowding further back in the field with another bitch, Mustang Yank, taking a tumble. At the halfway post, Solid Funky was still on Dash's shoulder but Dash put on a burst and edged ahead. By the time they rounded the final bend and came into the straight, Dash was in the clear – her ears back and her teeth bared. The crowd roared. 'Go on, girl! Go on, my beauty!' Could she hold off the challengers? The one dog – Deenside Lord, a 31-kg hound from Ireland – was making up ground. Fandango Dawn, another bitch that had started wide, was coming from nowhere. The finishing post was metres away – there were four dogs in it. Sand from the track flicked off their paws. It was neck-and-neck, nose-and-nose. The crowd roared louder, on the edge of their seats. Dash was flying. Peter and Ron – they would've been there, surely – urged her on. Then it was over. Dash had won! The crowd cheered. Peter jumped up and down, all smiles, and shook Ron's hand. Dash's tongue lolled out, flecked with spit, and her eyes shone. Her breath came in quick, sharp pants.

'Don't you think you're getting a bit obsessed with that website?' Sarah said at breakfast. 'In fact, don't you think you're getting a bit obsessed with Dash generally?

She had a point. I'd talked about little else recently. At the house of a couple of friends for dinner, I'd bored them rigid with details of Dash's track history, and then her diet: 'At first she seemed to prefer pigs' ears to dry tripe, but now I'm not so sure.' The friends in question were staunch vegetarians and, sensing their discomfort, Sarah had had to kick me under the table.

I'd also got into 'accessorising'. Due to their lack of body fat and thin fur, greyhounds are one of the few dog breeds that justify wearing a coat when it's cold. I'd noticed that Dash had started to shiver towards the end of our walks, so it seemed only natural to buy her an extra layer. A racing green coat with faux-sheepskin lining arrived in the post and fitted her perfectly. It was waterproof on the outside and snug on the inside. I then thought Dash might be getting cold in the conservatory at night once the heating had gone off. Another coat, this time of red fleecy material with blue trim, promptly arrived in the post. If an overnight frost was likely, I swaddled Dash in her coat before putting her to bed and closing the crate door.

'Just mind you don't start singing her lullabies or getting *too* soppy,' Sarah remarked pointedly one evening as she went upstairs to bed. So she wasn't in the mood for my rendition of 'Twinkle, twinkle, little Dash'? I sat and thought about it, however. Maybe I had gone too far. Was all this dog stuff just a big distraction, even from my own girlfriend? Sarah was the woman I wanted to share my life with. So what was I waiting for? I'd redress the balance by finally buying *her* something – an engagement ring.

Sarah loved surprises. I was pretty certain that she'd want both the proposal and the ring to come out of the blue. I'd given her jewellery before – a multicoloured bracelet for Christmas and a square, silver pendant last Valentine's Day – but a bracelet is something worn occasionally, and

I'd cheated in choosing the pendant by enlisting the help of one of Sarah's friends. There was a lot more riding on getting an engagement ring right. How would I handle the array of choices I now faced if I wanted to go solo and get the ring myself?

An online search revealed an infinite selection of stones, metals and styles. Would Sarah expect diamonds? Or would she prefer something more contemporary, perhaps with rubies, pearls or semi-precious stones? If it was indeed diamonds, then did I want to make an impact and choose a single solitaire or deploy more subtlety with a few smaller ones? Had I then considered 'The four Cs': carat, clarity, colour and cut? Of course, I was well aware there was a very big fifth 'C' to consider: cost. In terms of metals, all I knew beforehand was a sort of Olympic medals rating – silver is cheapest; gold is more expensive. If you're feeling really flush, then platinum is the king of the rings. But what about 'white gold' or 'rose gold' and, if gold was the metal of choice, was she a nine-, eighteen- or twenty-four-carat kind of girl? Or perhaps she'd fancy a more industrial piece in titanium? Or something original in carbon-fibre or granite even?

I studied the rings in her jewellery box when she was out. The few she wore regularly were silver and reasonably plain. So would she want something understated after all? They also seemed to be marginally different sizes. Which one would fit her ring finger? My head began to spin. I realised I actually needed to get out there and see something for myself.

As I toured the high street jewellery shops of Oxford over the following week, I was beginning to wish I had some company after all. I wanted the proposal to be a surprise – not only for Sarah but for our families and friends at large. This meant I couldn't ask anyone else for help. I couldn't even take Dash along for moral support since she wouldn't have been allowed to set foot in the shops and would have fretted and whined if left outside. As I seemed to do so often, I'd made it hard for myself. The shop assistants were attentive, but a little less so once I revealed my budget.

'Five hundred pounds?' Pause. 'Oh, right. We have some lovely looking rings back here. Just one moment...'

Was I being too tight? Five hundred pounds seemed a lot of money to me. Since going freelance, I'd been saving a little each month but would have the taxman breathing down my neck before long. Five hundred was all I felt I could afford, particularly if we were to have the expense of the wedding itself soon after. As I contemplated my reflection in a shop window, I realised I'd felt this inadequate only a few months before – when I was first looking for (and not finding) a dog. That time Sarah had come to the rescue by bringing home the poster about Dash. I needed Sarah's help now but to ask her would feel like failure.

People say, rightly, that owning a dog is therapeutic. If you're bad at your job or feel like a wreck, a dog will love you just the same. You're never a failure in your dog's eyes. Life on the end of a lead is all it aspires to as long as its owner is holding the other end. I was out walking Dash one afternoon when I had an idea so obvious I couldn't believe I'd not thought of it before. I would just buy the loveliest ring I could find for fifty quid. The stone, metal and style – all that stuff was irrelevant. I'd propose with this ring and, hoping Sarah said yes, we could choose her 'real' engagement ring together at our leisure.

'Good girl,' I shouted out loud to Dash, and spanked her on the rear as if she'd come up with the idea herself. She jumped and looked round at me accusingly, then trotted on with her nose held high.

Down a side street in central Oxford there was a little boutique shop that sold one-off jewellery and custom-made clothes. The ring I had in my hand was only the second one I'd looked at. It was silver and, strangely, more square than circular, with a line of sparkling orange stones studded along one edge. Orange was Sarah's favourite colour. I slipped it onto the ring finger of my left hand. It slid easily over the knuckle. Sarah's fingers were certainly no fatter than mine.

'Excuse me, what kind of stones are these?' I asked the man at the counter.

He smiled and scratched one of his sideburns. 'Well,' he said with genuine honesty, 'I'm not exactly sure.'

'I'll take it,' I said, without hesitation.

He laughed, surprised, and looked for a box. Slightly giddy with the speed of my purchase, I let him in on the secret.

'Wonderful,' he said. 'A sort of "holding ring" till the real thing? Good for you – I like your style.'

Back home, I let Dash smell the dainty little box. The man in the shop had dressed it with a dark pink ribbon and bow. 'What do you reckon, Dash? Will Sarah like it?'

The only problem now was where to hide it. Somewhere Sarah wouldn't find it by mistake. So not in the lounge, the kitchen or the bathroom. I couldn't risk the conservatory. Dash would find it or, worse, chew the box and swallow the ring. The bedroom? Having been bald since my late twenties, I often wear a variety of hats – woolly ones for winter, caps and jauntier stuff in summer. On a shelf in the bedroom wardrobe, I kept all the hats stacked in a tall pile. That was it, the perfect place. I'd do what anyone would do with an important secret. I'd keep it under my hats.

Having only just discovered Dash's bloodline, we were now going to snuff it out. One of the first things we'd been advised to do after adopting her was to get her spayed. A bitch from a dogs' home has usually already had the op, but Dash came straight from the owner and could still have puppies. We weren't planning on opening a kennel, however, and I'd been horrified to learn that the number of greyhounds being 'euthanised' each year was still well into the tens of thousands. Not all of them were as lucky as Dash in finding a home when they retired, and it wasn't right to add to the number. At least that was the theory. When it came down to it, I found the decision troublesome. There was just something about spaying a bitch that seemed more awful than neutering a male dog. The feminist in Sarah agreed.

'What's the downside of not doing it?' she asked, wrinkling her nose thoughtfully.

'Well, twice a year when she comes into season, she'll drip blood on the floors and the carpets,' I replied.

'OK – we can clean that up.'

'We won't be able to take her for a walk without being pestered by male dogs.'

'We can shoo them away.'

'She certainly wouldn't be able to go off the lead.'

'She's doesn't go off the lead now!'

I paused. 'We might wake up one morning to find the doggy population of the house has gone from one to... nine... or even ten.'

'*Ten?*'

Sarah phoned the vet herself and booked Dash in for the end of the month.

In the last week with Dash's anatomy intact, we planned a trip for her. It was also her birthday – she was four years old. We were all going to spend the weekend with my mum who still lived in the family home in Stafford where I grew up. This would be Dash's first night away from home since her adoption just two months ago. Getting ready on the Saturday morning was a Herculean task. While Sarah walked Dash, I packed the car. The Ford Ka is hardly capacious, but I was determined to make everything fit. First of all, I put the back seats down, then collapsed the crate and heaved it in through the boot. On top of this I piled the curtain we used to cover the crate at night, Dash's duvet and her mat. Wedged in at the side were two bags containing her food bowls, a toy, her leather lead, her flexi-lead and harness, her green coat and, of course, a box of her food. Once we'd loaded up our own bags, there was barely room to squeeze in Dash herself. One notable thing about greyhounds, however, is that despite their size they can make themselves quite compact. Kate, the owner of Arnie the greyhound, had joked that like stuff from IKEA, greyhounds can 'flat-pack'.

We set off and Dash immediately wriggled forward from her perch on top of the piled-up stuff. As I sat at the wheel, her paw rested limply on my shoulder like a kid's hand over the side of a bunk bed. For the next journey, we'd definitely have to sort out a different arrangement. Apart from anything else, it was clearly unsafe. Sarah and I had seatbelts, but braking suddenly would mean Dash flying straight through the windscreen. I shuddered at the thought. Perhaps we could put the collapsed crate on the roof to make more room for her inside? Or how about strapping Dash into a customised sidecar to ride alongside us in the slow lane?!

Stafford in the Midlands is the kind of town you grow up in and move away from. The only reason I still went back there was to visit my parents, or rather just my mum since Dad had died the year before. Mum had soldiered on. She grieved; she missed Dad; she tried to keep busy. Nevertheless, the house felt too big. She loved company and was particularly pleased by the idea of a doggy visitor. When Mum answered the door, I held Dash back in case she barged straight in. At only five foot tall with silver hair and doll-sized feet, my mum was hardly a match for a speed freak like Dash. What Mum lacked in stature however, she made up for in tenacity. Although now a pensioner, she'd previously been the deputy headteacher of a large school and had enforced discipline on students and teachers alike.

'Oh, yes,' said Mum as she looked Dash up and down. 'She's adorable. Very athletic.'

'You'd be surprised by what a slouch she is in reality. She's retired, like you!' I laughed.

'Well, she'll fit in just fine here then,' said Mum. 'Up at half nine, breakfast by eleven, I've become a real lady of leisure!' Leisure was just what Sarah and I were after. The rest of the day was measured out in cups of tea, homemade cakes and handsome doses of dog talk.

In one respect, some dogs are exactly like kids. They fear change. The slightest deviation from routine can send them into a wild panic. That evening, I took special care to make sure the set-up of Dash's crate was exactly the same as in Oxford. I crawled in myself to plump up the cushions; I folded the curtain precisely and draped it over, leaving a corner uncovered for her to peek out. I'd even brought a nightlight and put the kitchen radio on low. Once Dash was settled inside, I quietly slid the bolt on the crate door and tiptoed away. No luck. She started whining as soon as I left the room. In bed, even a duvet, pillow and earplugs were no protection against the noise – it was like her very first night all over again. This time I was prepared, however. I'd read that – as cruel as it sounds – squirting a jet of water at a dog's nose will often act as a deterrent. The dog connects the unpleasant sensation with its 'bad' behaviour and stops. So that night, when Dash's whining reached fever pitch, I came downstairs and shot her in the nose with a water pistol. Time to toughen up, I told myself by way of an excuse. After the third 'showdown' with the pistol, Dash fell silent and then fell asleep.

Another reason I'd been keen for Dash to join us on a weekend away was that I was going to let her off the lead for the first time. A ten-minute walk from my mum's house is Rowley Park – a large green space free of obstructions. If I could get there early enough, it would probably be free of distractions too, in the form of other dogs. I planned to leave her muzzle on in case there were squirrels about, but it would be an ideal opportunity to give us both a taste of freedom. Sarah had agreed it was the next logical step but was worried about Dash's recall.

'You know what Dash is like – she's sometimes got selective hearing.'

On the Sunday morning, I woke up early, left Sarah slumbering and crept downstairs. After the whining and antics of the night before, Dash was ecstatic to see me. She pawed at the gate of the crate and then sprang out, dodging around me in case I was about to lock her up again. It was clear and crisp outside. I began to wish I'd worn a woolly hat but was too excited to go back. The walk to Rowley Park was pleasant, through streets of large Georgian-style houses. Since I'd had a newspaper round there as a school kid, I knew the area well. I'd even daydreamed about buying one of the houses when I was older, wondering just how I'd fit the full-size snooker table (which I was also going to buy) through the front door.

We reached the park entrance and I scanned the scene. I was right – no other dog walkers and no dogs in sight. After checking one last time, I unclipped the lead from Dash's harness and casually walked off round the perimeter fence. She padded after me with her head bobbing up and down. So far, so good. Every now and then, she paused to sniff in the long grass and when she caught up with me, she got a treat. Starting to relax a little, I picked up the pace. She followed and broke into a trot. This was easy – perhaps I could even train her to run alongside me if I went out jogging? I took my eye off her for a second to look round. An empty football pitch, an empty running track, leafless trees and bushes... and still no other dogs to be seen. Time to assess whether Dash could handle something a little more complex than just tagging along behind me. I stood in front of her and held my hand out like a policeman stopping traffic.

'Stay!' She duly stopped. I then took a dozen strides backwards with my hand in the same position. Amazingly, she stayed put. Without breaking eye contact, I reached in my bag for a treat and shouted 'Come!' Dash sprang forward, covering half the distance in a split second... and then continued straight past me at full speed. My first reaction was pure panic. She streaked across the grass, running in a large loop. What on Earth was she doing? Then I realised. It was the shape of a greyhound track, an invisible greyhound track. I'd never seen a dog run so fast or so fluidly. At full stretch, her belly almost touched the floor. How did she stay on her feet at that speed? It even looked as if all four legs were off the ground at one point. Was this what the *All-Colour Book of Dogs* had termed 'the double suspension rotary gallop'? One thing was certain, this was what she'd been born to do – her ears pinned back and her back legs like jet engines blasting her into space. After a couple of imaginary laps, she made a beeline for me, but showed no sign of slowing up. If I wasn't quick, there'd be a collision. Which way to jump? Left or right could end in disaster.

I leapt straight up into the air just in time to watch Dash veer away at the last minute and career off on another lap. Was there no stopping her? In fact, there was – this time her footing wasn't so sure. As she rounded a bend into what must have been the home straight, she slipped in the mud. Her front end hit the ground and she flipped over like a Formula One car spinning off the race track. I ran towards her. Apparently unharmed, she righted herself and shook the mud from her coat. Behind her muzzle, her mouth was gaping in a wide greyhound grin and her tail wagging with joy. Relieved, I gave her a mild reprimand.

'Very impressive, madam! But you'd better take it easy, you're going to hurt yourself if you carry on like that.' I clipped the lead back on and we continued the walk where we'd left off. It took a good ten minutes before her breathing returned to normal.

By now we were approaching the corner of the park and confident Dash couldn't get too far ahead of me I'd slowed to an amble and let her off the lead again. It was then that I saw a gap in the fence. It'd obviously been made as a sneaky shortcut into and out of the park. Dash saw it too.

'No!' I shouted loudly. Whether it was the shout that startled her or she was making a genuine break for freedom, Dash suddenly charged off in the direction of the gap. At a time like this, the advice to any dog owner is to run the other way. As counter-intuitive as it seems, the idea is that the dog will stop in its tracks for fear of being left behind and chase after its owner. I turned and ran in the opposite direction, calling Dash's name and looking over my shoulder as I did so. Oblivious, she carried on in the direction of the gap.

Another tried-and-tested ploy is for the dog owner to fall to the ground and make a noise in the hope that the dog is curious and returns to investigate. By now, Dash was almost at the gap. I threw myself on the ground as if a bomb had gone off, shrieking loudly. By the time I looked up, she was nowhere to be seen. For a second, I was stunned. How could she have just run off and left me? I was her master, her *world*. Then I jumped up and started to run. Not the civilised jog of a man in his late thirties, but the adrenalin-fuelled sprint of a man possessed. I tore across the park and burst through the gap, coming out between two trees onto a narrow path.

Dash was 50 metres down the path, and just about to turn the corner and disappear. At that distance, she looked impossibly thin and vulnerable. I knew from my old paper round that the path continued before coming out at a road. And even on a quiet Sunday morning, a road meant cars. I charged headlong after her, calling her name in between gasps of air. Would she stop in time?

I turned the corner to see Dash crossing the road at the same time as two cars approached from opposite directions. I put my hands to my head in horror. The cars drew level; Dash swerved slightly in front of the first and carried on. The cars passed. There was no screech of brakes, no horns. The drivers probably hadn't even seen her. I stood rooted to the spot until the view was clear. There, scurrying off down the path which continued on the other side, her busy little head still bobbing up and down, was Dash. The Bitch of the Year had just had the luck of the decade.

All I had to do now was stop her. I sprinted off again and charged across the road. Then I had a brainwave. A week or so earlier I'd dropped the plastic squeaker from a toy Dash had destroyed into one of the pockets of the dog walking bag. Perhaps I could use it like a dog whistle? I took it out and blew a single high-pitched squeak. Dash stopped and turned round – her ears pricked up like table napkins at a fancy restaurant. I blew it again, twice, three times and she galloped towards me. 'Good girl!' I shouted out, overjoyed. 'There's a good girl!' I repeated, encouraging her to speed up. Dash arrived with her tongue lolling out and her eyes wide. I promptly caught hold of her collar. Then, despite knowing it was unfair and wrong, I administered an almighty telling-off which had her cowering away from me with her tail between her legs.

On the walk back, I was so angry with Dash I barely looked at her. To tell the truth, I was angry and hurt. Her swift exit from the park had felt like a personal affront. Where had I gone wrong? Where would she find a more committed and doting owner? I was also a little worried about whether Sarah would be angry with me when I told her what had happened. Perhaps I'd better give her the alternative version of the story – the one without the gap in the fence.

Mr Barker the vet had come highly recommended by Peter. As well as having a practice of his own, Mr Barker was the vet at Oxford Greyhound Stadium and obviously very well acquainted with the breed's physiology. There was something of the university professor about him. Over six-feet tall in his socks and sandals, Mr Barker was balding with a tufty beard and silver-rimmed glasses. He spoke crisply and didn't repeat himself. If he had a sense of humour, it would probably take an X-ray to find it.

When I'd taken Dash for an initial check-up back in October, he'd remarked that she was a 'fine animal' and that he'd seen her race. I'd puffed my chest out proudly and fondled her ears. He'd also issued me with verbal instructions to keep her weight at 'twenty-five and a half kilos' and 'certainly no more than twenty-eight'.

When I dropped her off to be spayed, she was bang on twenty-five and a half. After she'd been weighed, I was told to take her round the back of the practice to a door in the basement. This made the whole thing feel a little sordid and I felt twice as bad about putting Dash through it. Ever-trusting, Dash followed me down a ramp to an unmarked door. On cue, it opened and the vet's assistant appeared.

'We'll phone at two this afternoon then,' she said.

I smiled weakly and handed her the lead as if it was the cut rope of a mountaineer. Dash trotted in happily without a backward glance. The door closed behind them.

The clock above my desk ticked loudly. I couldn't concentrate. I could barely bring myself to look at Dash's trophy, which I'd lovingly polished the week before and put on the wall of my office. I emailed Sarah at work to ask what she was doing.

'Trying not to worry about Dash,' came the reply.

When I went downstairs, the kitchen felt cold and empty. I shook out Dash's duvet – partly because it was scruffy, but also because it still held her shape from the night before. What had gotten into me? It wasn't as if she was a child or a relative going under the knife – she wasn't even human! I should buck my ideas up and be more detached about the whole thing. She'd be fine. If she wasn't fine, then no big deal. Greyhound, guinea pig, stick insect – at the end of the day, they were all pets, plain and simple. Life was brutish and short, no question. Especially for animals. Dash had had a good run, literally, and at four years old, she was already in her late thirties in human years. But it was no good; I couldn't kid myself into not caring. Undergoing general anaesthetic was a risk for any patient, particularly one with as little insulating body fat and fur as Dash. Feeling decidedly worse, I trudged back upstairs and sat at my desk again. There was nothing to do but work… and wait… and try to think of something else.

At just after two o'clock, the phone rang. I picked up the handset and clamped it to my ear.

'Hello, yes?' I said, trying to hide the anxiousness in my voice.

'Hello, Mr Dilger? It's the vet's here. Dash is fine. You can come and pick her up in an hour.'

'Fine,' I said, echoing the key word. 'I'll be there at three.' I put the phone down, puffed out my cheeks and let the air out in a long sigh of relief. Our champion greyhound and new companion would live to see another day.

The vet's assistant in reception explained that the operation had gone well. However, when checking Dash's teeth as part of a once-over, the vet had seen they were in terrible condition. He'd had to remove six of them.

'S-s-six?' I stammered, wondering how many Dash had left.

'She won't really miss them,' she said.

I knew *I*'d sure as hell miss six teeth if I'd had them taken out!

'Right,' I said grimly, trying to concentrate as I was given instructions for Dash's convalescence. I was also given a bottle of medicine and box of tablets. I felt like taking them myself when I saw the bill – it was almost £300.

'Ah, yes, that'll be the number of teeth she had out,' the receptionist mused, reading from the computer screen in front of her as if from a script.

I studied the printout of the bill. She was right – each extraction had cost twenty quid plus VAT.

'Greyhounds do have notoriously bad teeth,' she added. She wasn't kidding.

When I met Mr Barker himself at the basement door, he passed me the lead almost apologetically. Dash was on the end of it, looking very sorry for herself. Her nose and mouth were red where blood had stained the fur. She managed a faint wag of the tail and stumbled forward. While the anaesthetic was wearing off, it was quite obvious she didn't have much idea where she was or what she was doing. I drove back in third gear, avoiding bumps and potholes and checking she was still on the seat whenever I stopped.

Outside the house, the kids from the local school were making their way home – shouting, swearing, dropping litter. I lifted Dash slowly from the car and she stood trembling on the pavement, sniffing the air. The kids streamed past her and gawped vacantly. Just let them so much as touch her or say anything, I thought, just one word. But they said nothing, or nothing audible, and I led Dash safely through the side gate and into the conservatory. Her eyes had a glazed look, and when she lay down on her side with her legs sticking out, she looked as if she'd been stuffed. The scar on her belly was four inches long and puckered like the edge of a Cornish pasty. Fine stitches of blue thread stuck out at odd angles and the surrounding area had been shaved so short the hair was barely visible. I spread her night coat over her and filled a hot-water bottle. Her slow breaths condensed in droplets on the floor tiles and she stared into the distance.

I called Sarah at work. 'Hey, it's me,' I whispered over the phone. 'Dash is home.'

'How is she?' Sarah asked, whispering as if she was there in the kitchen with us.

'Groggy and hurting but OK, I think.'

'Poor thing. I'll get back when I can. Look after her in the meantime, won't you.'

I said I would. That afternoon, I never left Dash's side.

December

December is a time for toys. The first of several that the convalescent Dash received was a pink rabbit. Made of fluffy fabric, it flopped about and squeaked when she chewed it. When I took it off her, she prostrated herself with both front paws stretched out and looked up, half in awe of its mysterious power and half ready to tear it to pieces. One of the biggest hits was 'Sausage', a furry Dachshund, which had the advantage of having *two* squeaks – one high-pitched at the head end and the other a low growl in its belly.

Most plastic toys had a lifespan of about an hour, but one that outlasted them all was a red, rubber chicken that we christened 'Pullet'. Each evening before getting fed, Dash had half an hour of 'Pullet time'. Its soft rubber mollified Dash's toothless gums and just before dinner was also when she was at her most bothersome. Without something to distract from her hunger pangs, she'd crouch on her mat like an athlete in the starting blocks. The slightest move we made in the direction of her bowl of soaking food and Dash would whine and prance round the kitchen. So Pullet fulfilled the role of soother, dummy and all-round panacea.

For a week after her operation, Dash was on soft food and a course of antibiotics. These were to be administered whole through the tricky process of placing them on her tongue, holding her mouth shut and then blowing on her nose till she swallowed. Getting her mouth open wasn't easy at the best of times, let alone when she'd had six teeth removed. Almost the whole of her front, bottom row had gone. Just two canines remained, giving her the peculiar look of an upside-down vampire. She took her medicine bravely. In addition, the wound on her belly had to be dabbed with clear liquid from a bottle labelled 'No Lick'. It got its name from the harsh, bitter taste and was designed to stop Dash pulling out the stitches until they were ready to be removed a fortnight later. Sarah and I took turns to apply it with cotton wool as Dash obligingly lay on her side, cocking a leg in the air. She sniffed and probed the wound with her nose, but kept her tongue firmly out of sight.

December was also the month for the 'holding' engagement ring which I'd bought Sarah. Barring any Dash-related disasters, I was finally going to propose. The chosen date would be the nineteenth of December, Sarah's birthday. The nineteenth was proving an auspicious date – we'd had our first date on the nineteenth of September two years previously and we'd welcomed Dash into our lives on that same date just three months before.

When it comes to a proposal of marriage, there's a certain amount of pressure to 'get it right'. Male friends of mine had whisked their brides-to-be off to Paris or Prague or Florence. All bona fide romantic locations, but perhaps not that unexpected. This was the element I was after – surprise and novelty. I also wanted the place itself to be meaningful, to be important to *us*, not just because lovers loved it. Having less money than imagination at my disposal, I also fancied the idea of somewhere local. I'd always wondered why families got so attached to where they lived. Since getting out and about with Dash, the newest member of our family, Sarah and I had likewise become more involved in our community. Where we now lived mattered more to us, and this made it a fitter place to propose than any far-flung destination.

Harcourt Arboretum is 6 miles south of Oxford. Before Sarah and I visited it, I hadn't even been that sure what an 'arboretum' was. The idea of a garden where trees and bushes rather than flowers are the main attraction was appealing, however. I had been vaguely aware it was 'twinned' with the more famous Botanic Garden in the city centre, so supposed it would be similar. Not in the slightest. There are no walls, glasshouses or perfect plots at the arboretum and, unlike at its twin, an array of colours and species are on show throughout the year. We'd first gone there one summer when it was ablaze with azaleas and rhododendrons. At the side of the arboretum was a massive meadow full of wild flowers and waving grasses. A path had been mown straight across and we'd wandered down it in bare feet – a green pathway into the heart of nature.

So it was on the eighteenth of December, the day before Sarah's birthday, that I arrived at the arboretum an hour before closing time. The car park was empty except for two cars; a lone gardener trundled past with a half-empty wheelbarrow. With me in my trusty Ford Ka were my accomplice, Dash, and a plastic spade. I'd brought Dash along for the ride, as well as needing to talk to someone – or some*thing* – to calm my nerves. I had the ring as well, of course, but its little box was now inside a second plastic one which I'd filled with white rose petals. The symbol of Yorkshire, Sarah's home county. Since even dogs on leads were officially banned from the arboretum, I gave Dash a pat and left her in the car with instructions.

'If anyone comes, just yelp – nice and loud.'

She looked at me with wide eyes and flicked out the tip of her tongue, a habit she'd developed since losing her bottom row of teeth.

It's hard to walk nonchalantly while hiding a plastic spade down your trousers. Having started off like a lopsided war veteran, I gradually developed a rolling gait which wasn't too conspicuous. The grasses had died away in winter, but the mown path across the meadow was still clearly visible. What I was looking for was a suitable marker – a large bush or tree. In the end, there were no bushes and only one tree close to the path. The soil round its base was hard and cold, and covered in a kind of tussocky grass. I leaned on the trunk and looked round. If I were a smoker, it would have been the perfect moment for a cigarette. Perhaps pretending to make a phone call would look *too* casual? There was a couple way off in the distance, but too far to see anything clearly. Besides, they looked like they were walking in the opposite direction towards the car park. I quickly unbuckled my belt and pulled out the spade. Doing my belt back up and looking down at the turf, I suddenly felt self-conscious. What if someone did see me? What if they called the police? I was behaving more than a little suspiciously, after all. Too late now, I thought, and tried to put the idea to the back of my mind.

The best way to bury the ring without leaving a telltale heap of earth, I guessed, was to chop a neat square out and then replace it afterwards. I forced the plastic spade down with my foot, only for it to crack in half just below the handle. Great – now I had something about as much use as a kitchen spatula. After three more careful incisions however, I levered out a large clod and held it up as if for inspection. I looked up furtively. Still no one to be seen, so I quickly scooped out an extra handful of soil, put the plastic box in the hole and replaced the clod. You could hardly tell the difference. Just in case, I left a white rose, pristine and intact on its stem, to mark the spot. Delighted at the completion of part one of the plan, I wiped my hands on the grass and stashed the spade (now in two bits) down my trousers again. When I got back to the car, Dash the guard dog was fast asleep.

'Well, Dash', I said, waking her up as I opened the car door, 'that's it. No going back now...'

Next morning, I woke Sarah with breakfast in bed. My head full of thoughts and plans, I'd got up early and made bagels with smoked salmon and cream cheese. I also gave her, with much ceremony, the first of her two birthday presents. It was a garden trowel. Its smooth wooden handle had real heft and sat snugly in the palm; the blade itself was bright as silver. Sarah was pleased, but also a little underwhelmed.

'You'll be needing that for later for the second present,' I said cryptically. 'Make sure you bring it with you when we go out this afternoon.' I bit my lip to avoid breaking into a broad smile. Nevertheless, Sarah studied me curiously. Did she suspect something or was I just getting paranoid?

She'd arranged to take half a day off, and when she went to work after breakfast, I swung into action and picked up a picnic lunch. Pink champagne and plastic glasses, deli-style sandwiches, pork pies, olives, pears, blue cheese and two potted chocolate desserts (with built-in spoons). I stowed it all in the car boot under a blanket. Since there was no way Dash could join us on this particular adventure, I'd asked Kate, the owner of Arnie the greyhound, to walk and feed her that evening. I'd also left her a sheet of info about Dash's bad habits ('The Quick Guide to Dash') in case she played up. Just after noon, I set off to pick Sarah up from work.

'Have you got your trowel?' I checked as Sarah got into the car.

She smiled and patted her handbag. 'Are we going gardening then?'

I still hadn't told her where we were headed and teased her by taking an unusual route out of town. After a while, she thought she'd guessed it.

'Oh, great!' she said. 'We're going to The Mole! Are we going to The Mole?'

The Mole was a gastropub in the village next to the arboretum. It served fabulous food on huge plates. The décor was lovely; the lights always dim. We'd cycled there on my last day as an employee to toast the start of my freelance career. As we reached a T-junction I pretended to confirm her guess by signalling left. Instead, I turned right. The Mole could wait an hour or so.

Despite being just a week before Christmas, the weather that day was mild. The arboretum was bright and quiet. We parked and I opened the boot to reveal the first surprise.

'Da-dah – behold our winter birthday picnic!'

Sarah was thrilled. We took the blanket and a bag of food and found a bench in one of the pine groves. Amazingly, the sun came out – here we were in mid-December and it was suddenly almost warm. We ate, laughed and chatted and I soaked up some Dutch courage with a full glass of pink champagne. Would the rose still be there, I wondered in between gulps? It'd been cold overnight and perhaps the ground frost had finished it off. And the ring? Would the ring still be there? Or maybe a dreaded squirrel had turfed it up and made off with it?

The champagne went to my head and I suddenly sat bold upright. What if the rose and the ring were there, but Sarah said NO? Although we'd alluded to the idea of getting married, we'd never actually discussed it seriously. We were in our mid to late thirties, after all. If we hadn't succeeded in getting hitched before now, then who was to suppose it would ever happen? True, in our twenties we'd both travelled a lot and lived abroad. Things had been more transient than expected. Speaking for myself, if I stopped to think – I mean *really* think – I'd always imagined I would get married some day. Call me a diehard romantic. But Sarah? Could I be absolutely sure what was in her heart or mind? Well, there was only one way to find out.

After the picnic, I suggested a wander round the arboretum: 'We may as well, since we're here.'

It barely felt like winter – the trees and bushes were jostled by a light breeze and most still seemed to have their leaves. Twenty minutes later we rounded the path and reached the highest point, looking down on the meadow.

'Let's go this way,' I said. 'Do you remember when we walked through here last summer?'

We held hands again, as we had that first time. Halfway down the path we drew level with the tree. My heart was racing.

'What's that?' I whispered, 'Over there, under that tree?'

Sarah squinted then shrugged. I led her off the path to investigate.

'A rose. It's a white rose,' she said, looking down at it and then at me.

She bent to pick it up. The frost had chilled the petals so they looked like crystal. I smiled coyly. She looked confused.

'Get your trowel out of your bag,' I whispered.

'What, now?' she said.

'Yes, start digging. Your second present's under this tree!'

'You're joking!' she burst out.

I held my breath and she laughed – her high loud laugh which I loved so much. We both got down on our knees.

'Here?' she said, and I nodded, helping her by moving a few loose stones and clumps of grass.

Every now and again, she looked at me, as if to check it wasn't all an elaborate prank. After a minute or so, the soil started to come apart in chunks and her trowel hit something solid. She used her hands to scoop away the last of the earth and pulled out the plastic box. The smaller box with the ring in it was visible inside, nestling on its bed of white rose petals. Her face suddenly lit up. She unfastened the first box and took out the second, setting it on her palm. It still had the dark pink ribbon round it, with a perfect bow. When she opened the lid, the orange jewels in the ring sparkled fiercely.

As we were both already on our knees, I would have felt silly scrambling into the traditional proposal pose. Instead I cupped her hands. 'Let's get married. Will you marry me? Will you?'

Tears rolled down Sarah's cheeks and she beamed.

'Yes... yes!' she said, and we kissed and hugged each other like lottery winners.

Now there was so much to talk about. Not just the last twenty-four hours or the surprise of how an engagement ring came to be buried beneath a tree, but the next few months, the future and forever. This time, we did go to The Mole. We sat side by side on a leather sofa, sipped our drinks and talked as if we were the first and last two people in the place. Sarah was full of questions.

'How long had you been waiting to propose? Where did you get the ring? When did you bury it? When shall we tell our families? What about the wedding?'

Likewise, I was desperate to hear her side of the story – whether she'd guessed, how she felt, if it was easy to say yes, and the big question: 'Where to from here?' It felt very serene but also surreal. This was one of the few things in life worth shouting about, but it felt almost too precious to share. To do so would risk bursting the bubble, the incredible intoxicating bubble in which we alone existed.

The final surprise that day was the restaurant booking I'd made for dinner. Just a few miles from The Mole an altogether more exotic creature awaited us: The Crazy Bear. It was expensive, chic and served the best Thai food around. It didn't disappoint. We floated from one course to the next, transported by flavours and tastes so authentic they made you want to jump on the next plane to Bangkok. But we were enjoying ourselves too much to want to go anywhere. We had five courses, dessert, coffee, mints... and it was only when we remembered Dash on her own in a dark house that we asked for the bill. She would be the first to hear our news. When we finally got home, her tail was wagging so hard it was going full circle. A scribbled note on the sheet of info I'd left Kate, our dog walker, read: 'Didn't get very far with Dash – think she missed you!' Dash licked our fingers and smelt our clothes, trying to work out where we'd been without her.

'Sarah and I are going to get married,' I announced proudly. 'From now on, it's the three of us all the way.'

Sarah and I planned to travel up to my mum's place for Christmas. One of my two elder brothers would meet us there. As we drove up in the car – the crate packed and Dash stowed safely between bags of clothes and gifts – we summarised how far we'd got with our wedding plans.

We'd established straight away that we both wanted some kind of ceremony... and thirty minutes at a registry office wasn't it. Received wisdom suggests it's either best to go big or stay small – spend a fortune and do it properly or opt out of the whole shebang altogether. Obstinately, we wanted something in between. Sarah thought about sixty guests seemed reasonable. I agreed but, as yet, we had absolutely no idea about a location.

Then there was the question of religion. I wasn't what you'd call a believer; Sarah felt similarly despite a Methodist upbringing. With this in mind, a humanist ceremony appealed. I didn't know much about the movement, but the fact that it promoted the values of human rights, gender equality and social justice seemed just about right. My dad's funeral the year before had been humanist and was a more tender, more humane occasion than any church service that I could remember.

So what about the month? Certainly, the past two summers had been total washouts. September, we felt, would be more reliable. I'd long known who I would ask to be my best man, or rather my best *men*. My ex-college friends, Ben and Mark, would do the honours. Along with members of our immediate families, I'd phoned them the day after the proposal to break the news. Ben and Mark had agreed straight away. It also had a nice symmetry to it since Mark and I had been joint best men at Ben's wedding a few years earlier. Sarah's two sisters would be her bridesmaids or matrons of honour. One thing we didn't actually discuss was what would happen to Dash on the day. For once, it was all about Sarah and me.

When we arrived in Stafford, Mum stroked Dash affectionately and listened to our plans, saying 'Great' and 'Sounds lovely' with real enthusiasm. She then delighted us by pledging a little money to help in lieu of a wedding gift. Sarah and I both had some savings but any contributions to the pot would be gratefully received. We'd done a spot of preliminary research and discovered that the average amount spent on a wedding in the UK that year was over £18,000. This seemed like a staggering amount for what was, in effect, a day's entertainment. With a limited budget, we aimed to bring ours in at ten grand or less.

One of my elder brothers, Mike, was still to arrive, so we agreed to save the wedding talk for later and set about helping Mum finish off the Christmas decorations. Since becoming a widow, she hadn't felt like decking out the house in the way she used to. The long multicoloured streamers which had always been hung in every downstairs room were replaced by just a few chandelier-like flourishes. The centrepiece was still the tree – a real pine from a local woodland which filled the hall and completely blocked the front door. Underneath, there was a stocking for every member of the immediate family. Made from old curtain fabric and finished with a capital letter in felt, these were my mum's speciality. There was one for each of her three sons: Paul, Mike and Andrew. The eldest son, Paul, his wife and their two kids were staying Ireland this year but their stockings were all under the tree just the same. This year, there was also a brand new addition – a stocking with a bright yellow 'S'.

'Wonderful! Thank you,' Sarah exclaimed when she saw it. I hugged Mum and beamed. It was a warm welcome into the family.

Dash didn't have a stocking, but I did have a favour to ask Mum. Could she possibly sew a double 'D' onto Dash's winter coat? A silly indulgence, but just the kind of fun she liked to be involved in. I asked for a double 'D' because every dog deserves a first and a family name. If done in red ribbon, it would also reference the logo of blind comic superhero 'Daredevil'. Lightning fast… but with a bit of a handicap. Enough said. It described Dash perfectly.

It was after dinner when Mike's car finally turned into the drive. I met him at the back door with Dash.

'Hey, Andrew,' he said. 'Congrats again on the engagement!' He reached out his hand but Dash beat me to it and plonked her nose in his palm.

'Sorry,' I said. 'It's Dash's first Christmas outside of a kennel. She's just glad to be here.'

'Me too,' Mike said. He stroked Dash and hoisted a massive bag off his equally massive shoulders. If people can be described in terms of their similarity to dog breeds, Mike is definitely a boxer – thickset and muscly, with a shaved head and broad, flat features. He also has a bluff charisma, is always busy and usually late. As brothers, we're the closest in age and had shared a bedroom until well into our teens.

We spent the rest of the evening catching up. Dash dozed flat out in front of the television. Every now and again she stretched and raked score marks in the thick carpet. On her November visit to my mum's, Dash had whined all night until her showdown with the water pistol. Mindful of this, Sarah made a suggestion before we assembled the crate.

'Why don't we forget the crate this once and try her at the foot of the stairs? She can sleep on her mat.'

I looked at Sarah sceptically. Was she out of her mind? This is the dog that had destroyed our conservatory.

'Let's give it a go, come on,' she insisted.

We gave it a go. Dash spent the entire night dutifully curled up on her mat and just like that, after serving a three-month sentence inside, she never needed the crate again.

Every family has its Christmas Day rituals: things it does or doesn't do, in a certain order. The first rule at home had always been that you couldn't open any gifts until you were fully dressed, had been for a walk and had breakfast. This was to stop us three brothers tumbling out of bed in pyjamas and feasting on chocolate all day. We no longer wore pyjamas or had a sweet tooth, but the rule still stood. With Dash in tow, an early walk suited us fine. The second rule was that no one could start opening the gifts until every stocking had been handed out. The signal to start was a tall rubbish bin being placed in the middle of the room. Once unwrapping was under way, it became a crazy spectacle – whoops and cheers as the gifts were held aloft in glory; groans as screwed-up balls of paper bounced off the rim of the bin or missed altogether. The third and final rule was one of our own making. Each one of the brothers tried to make his pile of gifts seem the smallest and most pathetic. All spare packaging was discarded and any books, CDs or DVDs were then used to create a firm base. New clothes were folded flat and laid on top with socks or gloves, chocolate coins or the obligatory tangerine hidden inside other presents to take up less space. Quite why we did this no one knew, perhaps out of some warped sense of wanting more. Obviously, if you'd asked for something big that year – a jumbo jigsaw or spacehopper, say – you really had your work cut out to 'shrink' the pile.

This year, the ritual and rules had a new element: Dash. The first breach of Christmas protocol was that she had only one gift, so was sure to win the smallest pile. Sarah and I had wondered about getting a 'little something for the dog' but decided against it since we didn't want to spoil her. Mum wouldn't hear of Dash being left out however, and had bought her a toy. She'd even wrapped it in cheap paper. As soon as Mum gave Dash her present, Dash attacked it. She bit it. She flung it round the room and then pounced on it triumphantly. She shook it from side to side. Finally, with one paw holding it down, she dragged the toy sideways out of the paper. So much for waiting till everyone else had their stockings! Her reward was a plastic bone, which survived till Boxing Day.

The second and most embarrassing breach of protocol occurred just before lunch. I was helping Mum in the kitchen when I heard a shout in the hall. It was Mike.

'Andrew, Sarah! Come here... quick!'

I rounded the corner to see Dash squatting in front of the Christmas tree with Mike standing over her helplessly. Too late. She was part way through what looked like an extremely long and satisfying pee. Her eyes had a wistful faraway look.

'I didn't see her… and then I couldn't stop her!' Mike said, not sure whether to laugh or look appalled.

Dash wandered off, leaking the last few droplets like a beer tap.

'At least she didn't fuse the fairy lights,' I said, wagging a finger at Dash as she skulked into the lounge.

Mum arrived with an old towel and took the assault on her carpet in good spirit. To be fair, it was our fault. With all the gift opening and preparations for lunch, we'd entirely lost track of time. It was way past when we normally let Dash out to toilet. A creature of habit and routine, schooled to relieve herself on the dot and on the spot – what was she to do? Well, how about whining or standing at the door? I made a mental note to add that to the long list of tricks she still had to learn.

On Boxing Day, we had chance to resume the chat about wedding plans. What was becoming disturbingly apparent was just how many choices there were to make and how much to do.

'That's why there are professional wedding planners,' Mike mused.

One thing was certain – we wouldn't be going down that route. Sarah and I didn't want someone else planning *our* wedding. Some men may have been happy to outsource the whole thing, or let their future wives take care of it, but not me. I was freelance after all. Surely I could take on the bulk of the organisation myself between jobs? Sarah was delighted by the idea. She'd seen female friends who'd recently got married become increasingly frazzled as the wedding planning intensified. So that was it. We agreed Sarah would pitch in at weekends, but I would take on the task of being project manager, administrator and dogsbody. If I'd made a half-decent start in rehabilitating a retired greyhound, then I could certainly organise a wedding... couldn't I?

The thirty-first of December and the three of us were heading south. My good friend Charles had invited us to see in the New Year at Camber on the coast. Dash was going to the beach for the first time in her life.

En route, we stopped off to see a friend of Sarah's, Soraya. They'd met while living in Thailand and they'd remained firm friends. Soraya was energetic and opinionated but extremely endearing. She was also a plain clothes police officer and the proud owner of no less than four English toy terriers. The *All-Colour Book of Dogs* gives the breed's nickname as 'The Rat-Killer', but at just over 3.5 kg and 25 cm in height, I expect one would have its work cut out if it ran into a king-sized rat. Dash was almost twice as heavy as all four of them put together.

Soraya suggested we introduce Dash to her pack on neutral territory, so we phoned ahead and met them near her house for a walk. Given Dash's behaviour to date towards small, snappy dogs, Sarah and I were extremely nervous. How would she fare with four of them at once? This could be make-or-break. We reassured ourselves with the thought that at least they weren't white. In the long list of things Dash loved to chase, small white dogs were right at the top, just behind squirrels. (God help an albino squirrel if it ever strayed into the park.)

When we pulled up, Soraya was waiting with two terriers under each arm like a farmer holding piglets. But there the similarity ended – Soraya was half-Iranian, with thick black hair and bright eyes. Far from looking like pest exterminators, the dogs were adorable, with sleek black-and-tan coats and white teeth that put Dash's miserable, yellow pegs to shame. The only things that seemed disproportionate were their large gremlin-like ears. After a round of kisses and congratulations at the news of our engagement, we opened the boot to let the hound out.

'Aww, she's tiny,' Soraya cooed. 'I expected a great big greyhound.'

I looked at the terriers that were busying themselves round the wheels of the car and barely reached the hubcaps.

'Well, she is a bitch,' I observed as I clipped the lead on, 'and she certainly curls up small.'

Dash jumped out and nosed the grass by the kerb. Four little tails wagged and the terriers toddled up as if they ran on batteries. We held our breath and I relaxed the lead. Don't let me down, Dash, I thought. Soraya didn't have any kids – in fact, it wouldn't be unfair to say the terriers *were* her kids. If Dash had a go at them, there'd be hell to pay. The little delegation sniffed both ends of Dash and back again. Dash's tail swung steadily from side to side. She lowered her head to sniff each one in turn. Was this just a prelude to deciding which one she'd devour whole? Not yet, at least. Formalities over, it was time to step out together – our destination was the local sports field. On the way, people smiled and nodded. Village life, I thought, but it wasn't till a passing woman whispered to her daughter 'Look at the mummy dog with all her babies' that I realised why. There was a funny similarity. The Terriers were mostly black; Dash was mostly black. Also, they all had the same cocked ears. The picture was completed by the fact that Dash was strutting out in front as usual, with the four miniatures following on behind like kids on the way to school.

Once we reached the field, Soraya let her dogs off the lead. All four immediately ran off in different directions, frisking and chasing imaginary rats. Thinking it might send out the wrong signal, we'd left Dash's muzzle in the car so she had to stay put rather than pursue her 'offspring'. After watching this charming scene for a few minutes, Soraya produced a tennis ball and threw it for one of the Terriers to chase. They all ran after it but Millie, her favourite, got there first. She picked it up and trotted back like a waitress with the bill. Soraya threw the tennis ball again and it duly came back in the mouth of another dog. Whenever I'd thrown a ball for Dash, she caught up with it in a few strides, careered past it and lost interest. Disappointed, I always ended up trudging after the ball myself.

Back at Soraya's, we greeted Sam, her husband and fellow dog lover. The terriers had the run of the place downstairs. The sofas in the lounge had covers, there was a large dog bed in the kitchen and toys everywhere. There was even a cat flap (or 'rat flap', perhaps) in the back door so they could nip out into the garden whenever they fancied. I wondered how big the flap would have to be at our house so Dash could do the same. About big enough for a burglar or two. We all sat down for coffee but Sam surprised us with champagne.

'This is for you two… or three… from all of us. For your engagement – fantastic news!'

He popped the cork and Sarah gave an abridged version of the proposal story. I listened and smiled at her lovingly as the story made her voice quaver with emotion. Meanwhile, Dash picked up one of the terriers' toys and commandeered their bed. They buzzed round her and then chased each other back and forth between the table legs. Dash looked on, slightly perplexed. At home, they were distinctly noisier than they had been out on the walk. They yapped hysterically. Every now and again, one would pause and rise up on its hind legs like a circus dog, resting a paw on my knee. With the squeaks from the toy and yaps from the toy dogs growing in volume, it wasn't long before we made our excuses. The coast was still an hour or so away.

There are no fond goodbyes between dogs, no waves or shouts of 'Have a great New Year!' or 'Thanks again. Hope to see you soon!' Instead, Dash dropped the pilfered toy and made her way to the car without so much as a backward glance. Personally, I was just relieved that there were still as many terriers as when we'd arrived. Dash had passed the test. Her reward was that we were on the road again, beach-bound.

Camber Sands is a special stretch of beach. On the border between Sussex and Kent, it's also a well-kept secret. The approach is unpromising – a B road zigzags through flat scrubland; the square cliff of Dungeness Nuclear Power Station looms in the distance. The road eventually runs parallel to a high bank of dunes. If you park, get out and take the short walk over the top, you behold an unbroken curve of breathtaking beach. Seven miles of it. Admittedly, the weather isn't always that kind – the wind can give you a workout – but the beach is flooded with light even in winter and has a kind of crisp majesty and is seldom crowded. It's also a dog walker's paradise. There's the fun of the dunes – banks of sand with grains as fine as in an hourglass and hillocks of stiff grass harbouring every sort of smell. Then there's a band of deeper sand at the start of the beach proper, solid enough to leave paw prints in. This hardens up as you move in the direction of the sea, becoming a sort of flat strip perfect for windswept ball games, kite-flying and any attempts to break the canine land-speed record. From there, the sea starts to leak in, darkening the sand to mud which oozes between toes and splashes your belly if you're as low to the ground as the average dog. Dash was going to love it. She'd have to be patient however, since by the time we arrived it was getting dark and our host and his family were waiting for us.

My friend Charles had bought a house in Camber a few years before: a square two-story number with high windows facing the sea. To look at, it was like a huge beach hut.

For the last few miles of the journey, we'd opened a back window to let Dash get a whiff of sea air. Every now and again, she held up her nose and took quicker sniffs. As soon as we turned into the driveway, she stood up and bobbed her head. Whether she picked up on the relaxation of the driver or just responded to the car's change of speed was hard to tell – but either way, she always knew we'd arrived somewhere just before we actually arrived there. We were all excited and relieved. It had been a long year filled with hard work and we were ready for the new one. For her part, Dash jumped out of the boot and immediately marked the corner of the lawn with a lengthy pee. Business as usual.

By now, Charles was standing in the doorway. He was a big man with a bigger grin. We'd first met at college – despite seeming incredibly laid-back, he'd sailed through his medical studies and played sax in a student band. We ran into each other at a gig and just got along. Looking back, the differences between us were comical. He was born in Nigeria and public-school educated. But the thing we both shared was a desire to take each other seriously. One summer while still at college, we'd spent a fortnight in Portugal together. He'd taught me how to play chess and rescued me from drowning in the undertow of a beach; I'd bored him with the *Collected Poems* of T. S. Eliot.

'Hey – what took you? The New Year won't wait, you know,' he called out.

We hugged and I introduced Sarah and Dash, in that order. Close behind him was his wife, Julie, and their two knockabout boys, Oliver and Daniel. Oliver was six years old and Daniel just four, the same age as Dash. Both were bursting to see the dog and forced themselves between their dad's legs to get a look.

'You can stroke her,' I told them, 'Just take it easy... and don't pull her ears or tail!' Dash stood there nobly as they laid on hands.

'I hear you got engaged,' Charles teased us as he helped us in with our bags. 'About time!'

We smiled and promised to give him the full story that evening.

The centrepiece of the house was the open-plan lounge and kitchen which fronted the first floor. It contained a sofa that wouldn't have looked out of place in a sultan's reception room. Choice items of sculpture and pottery and lamps were scattered about on the floor and low tables. All very chic and relaxing, but not very dog friendly. It hadn't occurred to me to ask if there would be any problems about having Dash in the house. 'Love me, love my dog,' and all that. But this wasn't exactly the kind of place where a greyhound could be allowed to run amok and we all knew it. As much as the kids moaned and Dash herself whined, she would have to stay downstairs for the night. The ground floor had a large, dog-friendly hallway which could be sealed off from an assortment of other guest rooms. While we were upstairs having dinner and toasting the arrival of the New Year, Dash curled up in the hallway at the bottom step like an old fox fur. Feeling terrible, Sarah and I made regular trips to reassure her or sent the kids to check.

'It can't hurt – she's got to learn,' I told Sarah, realising I'd said exactly the same thing just a few months earlier on Dash's first night. But her life had changed a lot since then. Dash now knew she belonged. Home was wherever Sarah and I were and we weren't going to abandon her. Besides, tomorrow we were going to the beach. It was also the year that Sarah and I were going to get married... and 'tomorrow' was already 'today'.

January

'Can you get sunglasses for dogs?' I asked Sarah in bed.

No answer. I nudged her with my foot and snuggled closer.

'Do you think you can get sunglasses for dogs?'

Sarah groaned and then rolled over, squinting at me in the sunshine that angled through the blind.

'Uh?'

'Happy New Year,' I said and planted a kiss on her nose.

New year, new start. Dash was going to the beach without sunglasses but, more importantly, without her *muzzle* either. She would still be firmly on the lead but we didn't want to deprive her of the full range of smell sensations once we hit the sand.

Charles's two sons, Oliver and Daniel, were dressed in quilted jackets and each wore dark woollen hats with long ear flaps that made them look like a pair of bassett hounds. No sooner had we come down the dunes and onto the flat sand than Oliver had a question for Charles.

'Daddy, can I hold Dash's lead?'

Charles, ever the diplomat, told Oliver to check with me. An awkward one. While Dash had always been friendly with children, walking her was a different proposition. The flexi-lead was difficult to handle, and since it was Dash's first time at the beach *and* her first time out without a muzzle, we weren't quite sure how she'd react. The open expanse must have looked extremely tempting and already we could see other dogs and their owners dotted in the distance. Oliver was certainly strong for his age, but Dash was likely to be stronger.

'Er... OK... why not?' I said, glancing at Sarah for reassurance. I showed Oliver how to work the lead and warned him to keep it short when other dogs were near. If he looked like he was having difficulty, Sarah or I would step in and take over.

'Invigorating' was the word for it. A blustery wind and strips of cloud like torn cloth made for a dramatic seascape. The waves lapped in low frills at our feet. Thankfully, Dash was calmer than expected. She padded alongside Oliver, who obligingly stopped when she found something salty worth a sniff. Chuffed with his new status as 'chief dog walker', he looked back at his parents or brother as if he walked a dog every day of the week. I fell behind to walk alongside Charles.

'So, big stuff then,' he said after a few paces.

'What, Dash? Oh, she's no trouble really.'

He smiled. 'No, the *wedding*, I mean. What have you got planned?'

'We're looking for a venue with an outdoor element, if possible. Ideally, in or near Oxford. About sixty guests, so not too lavish.'

'Great – when?'

'September – *this* September!'

'And the stag party… you are having one, aren't you?' he asked, concerned.

'Of course,' I replied then added mischievously: 'Do you want to come?'

In truth, I'd already given the stag some thought. I'd even had the idea it would be great to bring a group of friends down to Camber. It had everything we'd need – the beach, the sea, a couple of decent pubs and, not too far away, the bracing wasteland of Dungeness. Charles must have read my mind.

'Why don't you come here?' he suggested. 'We can all stay in the house. I'll check with Julie first but I'm sure it'd be fine.'

The nice thing about getting married is that friends – *real* friends – are only too glad to help. You can call in the favours without compunction. Charles and I walked a few paces more in silence.

'Is Dash going?' he asked.

'Where?'

'To the wedding.'

'God, no,' I said after a moment's hesitation. Sarah and I hadn't even considered the option. It would be a logistical nightmare anyway.

'Probably best,' agreed Charles. 'Never work with children and animals, and all that… speaking of which, where's Oliver got to?'

By now, Dash, Oliver and his younger brother, Daniel, were 100 metres ahead of us. The two boys were both holding onto the lead as Dash tugged them towards a young couple... and their dog, a little Westie! I shouted to Sarah who'd been chatting with Julie to catch the kids up. I needn't have worried. A textbook doggy greeting took place. Front, sniff, wag; rear, sniff, wag. Maybe Dash had decided to mend her ways after all. I congratulated myself for the decision to get rid of the muzzle – the pesky thing had probably invited trouble from the start.

Further up the beach, we all stopped for coffee and milkshakes at a small café. Since dogs weren't allowed inside, we braved the wind and sat in a row on the edge of the decking. Dash stretched out in the sand at our feet. Having a dog really is fun, I thought. Oliver was making sucking sounds through the straw of his milkshake; Daniel was sitting on Sarah's lap and laughing as she jogged him up and down. Having kids of our own one day would be fun, too. I was happy. I was in love with Sarah and we were engaged to be married.

We couldn't have been more than a minute from Charles's house when it happened. Oliver had confidently walked Dash all the way back. Suddenly a woman, her young daughter and their puppy – a Cavalier King Charles Spaniel – turned the corner and bumped right into them. Dash barked and pounced on the puppy, pulling Oliver clean off his feet. The daughter screamed and fell off her bike. The adults converged in a scrum. Dash had the puppy pinned to the floor with her front paws and was just about to see if it squeaked when I caught hold of the lead and yanked her backwards. The woman was furious.

'That was an unprovoked attack! A vicious dog like that needs a muzzle. It could have bitten my daughter if she'd been in the way.'

All three children were crying now. I apologised and said Dash had been startled. I was genuinely shocked. The woman gave me another piece of her mind. I could tell it was coming from a very indignant place – the kind of place that calls a lawyer or writes letters to the newspaper; the kind of place that lets other people know *their* place in no uncertain terms. I decided to walk away before I got angry myself. Dash, for her part, was bounding and wagging her tail as if she'd just saved the nation from a rabid wolf. I apologised to Charles and his family, who I could see were a little shaken. Oliver didn't want to walk Dash any more. So much for a 'muzzle-free' start to the year.

How long does it actually take to plan a wedding? Back in Oxford, this was the question I was now asking myself. I figured a full-on formal affair with hordes of guests, a six-course meal, entertainers, themed decorations and transportation to and from the venue, would probably need twelve months minimum. Similarly, a shotgun wedding at a registry office could be done in around a fortnight. Sarah and I had eight months. I say 'Sarah and I' because it made me feel better. To all intents and purposes, however, I was about to set myself up as a one-man wedding planner. Or a one-man-and-his-dog wedding planner. I just hoped I wasn't making a colossal mistake.

My first act was to visit the local newsagent and buy up every wedding magazine I could find. Quite quickly, I gathered I didn't exactly fit the profile of the target reader. Features and articles on hairstyles, make-up, the dress, flowers, decorations, catering and photography were all written as if men didn't exist, let alone would be present at the wedding. Unfortunately, it seemed most grooms-to-be were hopeless cases, passive blockheads who were more likely to make a woman wonder why she'd chosen to marry them at all rather than share the highs – and lows – of planning a wedding. In an effort to keep it simple, the number one piece of advice could be summarised thus: 'Just tell him what he needs to do.' Poor man. Nevertheless, I did learn something useful from flicking through the stack of magazines. There was a certain way to plan a wedding, and this meant doing the right things in the right order.

The number one booking to make is the wedding venue. This determines everything from the number of guests and catering and accommodation options to the 'look and feel' of the big day itself. Sarah and I had already decided on a humanist ceremony rather than something in a church or registry office, so this gave us a little more latitude. I started off by looking at hotels and restaurants. As far as I could tell, the main advantage of a hotel was that wedding guests with full stomachs and light heads had only to stagger upstairs at the end of the evening. Although alcohol would obviously play a part in our wedding, guests were more likely to want to dance all night than prop up the bar.

There was also something uncomfortably 'corporate' about getting married in a hotel. The blandness of the furnishings; the glacé smiles of the waiting staff; the smooth machinery whirring away behind the scenes as it had done a hundred times before. Could I imagine taking the lift downstairs to meet my bride? No, I could not.

What about a restaurant? Were there any with outside dining areas or set in an impossibly scenic location? Oxford certainly had a number of attractive riverside restaurants and pubs, the most suitable being an old boathouse. If the weather was fine, guests could stand and chat outside on a sloping terrace. The bride could even arrive by punt, which would certainly turn a few heads. The only problem was the 'M' word: 'marquee'. British weather being as unreliable as it is – even in summer – almost every venue with open-air facilities opted to cover them up. At that point, why not go for the warmth of a hotel over what was essentially a 'big top'? The boathouse's marquee looked better than most but we wanted to get married, not go to the circus.

A theatre, on the other hand, now that was a different proposition. Having crossed hotels and restaurants off the list, could we entertain the idea of a theatre as a possible wedding venue? The summer before, Sarah had gone to see a play in the market town of Abingdon, near Oxford, and been enchanted by the location.

'It was a lovely, little place – really unusual. I don't know how many seats it had but I'd say at least sixty or so. What do you think? Shall we check it out online… you know, just in case?'

Just in case, we looked online and fell in love with it. The Unicorn Theatre was originally part of Abingdon Abbey next door and both buildings, we discovered, could be hired out for 'events', including wedding parties. I rang the caretaker and made an appointment to look round the following Saturday morning.

Abingdon is 7 miles south of Oxford. No need for a map but for good luck, Sarah and I took our mascot, Dash. The theatre and abbey nestle in the centre of the town, down a network of narrow roads which ends in a small, quiet square. Even in mid-January, it was very picturesque. The ancient stone of the abbey buildings was the colour of root ginger; trees and shrubs seemed to defy the winter weather, poking over walls and round corners to get in on the scene. A hardy thrush sang on a branch. We leant on the car and enjoyed the serenity; Dash dozed off in the back. Ten minutes later, an elderly woman jangling a large bunch of keys came through an archway.

'I'm sorry to keep you waiting,' she said. 'I hadn't forgotten, don't worry.' She gave a little smile by way of apology and then, as an afterthought, added, 'I'm Jenny, the caretaker.'

Jenny was a small, neatly dressed woman in her sixties, with a kind face and lively eyes.

'Now do remind me,' she said. 'It's for a wedding, isn't it?'

Sarah and I nodded and smiled at each other fondly.

'Well, I have to say straight away that we don't do very many. To be honest, couples are usually looking for somewhere a little… well, a little more formal. Anyway, I'll show you the theatre first.'

As we walked past the car, Dash's head popped up at the side window like a glove puppet, her ears sticking up enquiringly.

'Oh, is that your dog?' Jenny asked.

'Yes… ,' I replied, hesitating slightly in case Jenny wasn't a fan.

'She's lovely,' she said, guessing the gender. 'Greyhound?'

'Yes, ex-racer. Her name's Dash.'

'A very apt name, no doubt. And will Dash be playing her part in the wedding ceremony?'

That question again.

'Er…' I paused. Was Jenny testing us? We hadn't yet seen the theatre but would be surprised if animals were allowed inside. 'We'll give it some thought,' I said diplomatically.

'You'd want her in the photos, at least. Very pretty indeed.'

As if to acknowledge Jenny's comment, one of Dash's ears flopped down like a salute. Sarah and I couldn't help smiling. Trust Dash to get the meeting off to a good start. I put my hand to the window as we passed and whispered: 'Clever girl.'

On one side of the square and down a small flight of steps was the Unicorn Theatre. There were no signs or notices outside and a plain wooden door seemed to do everything it could *not* to advertise the theatre's presence. Inside, however, it was exquisite. At one end was a small Elizabethan-style stage, complete with a painted façade and a balcony. The walls of the theatre were rough stone and topped with an open roof space of timber beams. Light streamed in through two large windows flanked by heavy velvet curtains. Opposite the stage, the bank of seats rose sharply, so that someone sitting on the back row would be twice as high up as someone on the front. The whole thing felt like it had been designed by children – slightly tatty, whimsical, but completely charming. Sarah and I stood and looked on wide-eyed with delight.

'Wonderful,' I said at last.

Jenny smiled demurely.

'Perfect,' breathed Sarah.

'Yes,' said Jenny, 'it's an intimate space… atmospheric, you might say.'

In a niche on one of the walls was a little model of a unicorn. It was rearing up on its hind legs and reminded me of Dash's comedy run. We walked up a narrow flight of steps to the lighting gantry and looked down at the stage. Was this where it would happen then? I tried to imagine the theatre full of family and friends in their wedding best; the buzz of excited chatter. Where would I be standing and how would I feel? I looked at Sarah and guessed she was thinking the same. We linked fingers.

The abbey itself was a revelation. Adjoining the theatre, it was a low two-storey building. The top floor, the long gallery, must have been 50 metres in length, with dusty wooden floorboards and the same timbered roof space as the theatre. One side of the room was open to the elements except for a row of upright beams and green blinds. It looked like it could comfortably seat a hundred people for dinner, let alone sixty.

'Sorry about that,' said Jenny, pointing to a line of pigeon droppings along the floor. 'You can imagine a building this old has a few holes for them to get in.' She added quickly: 'Of course, I'd get it cleaned up if you decided to hire the abbey as well.'

Downstairs, the lower hall was equally spacious. Russet-coloured tiles covered the floor and the stone walls were cold to the touch.

'I don't know quite what you'd do down here,' said Jenny, 'but I'm afraid I can't allow amplified music, you know, a discotheque. We've had complaints from the neighbours, you see.'

'What about live music?' Sarah asked. 'A dance band or something.'

'That's fine,' nodded Jenny. 'But one of the conditions of hire is that everything must finish at midnight.'

'Out by the witching hour,' I said to Sarah. 'We can handle that, can't we? Midnight's late enough if we start early.'

We followed Jenny outside for the final surprise. Through a walkway was a large, rambling garden and the river. Of course, we'd forgotten! The theatre and abbey were so central that they backed directly onto it. If the weather was fine, the guests could quaff bubbly next to their very own stretch of the Thames.

'There's no fence between the garden and the river,' said Jenny. 'So you'd have to warn any guests with children.'

A sign reading 'DANGER – DEEP WATER' was sticking, half-obscured, out of the shrubbery.

'What about catering facilities?' Sarah asked, as if she'd only just remembered that there were other things to consider besides the look of the place.

'Ahh,' said Jenny. 'We don't really have any. There's a room next to the long gallery and people tend to use that as a makeshift kitchen. You can warm food up... but you can't really cook it.'

Warm food up? Would sixty wedding guests be happy with a tepid buffet?

Sarah tried not to look concerned but I read her expression as plainly as a poster. Jenny explained that the wiring of the abbey was too fragile to handle anything other than a couple of small ovens. One final restriction was – 'under no circumstances with absolutely no exceptions' – were we allowed to use any naked flames.

'All it takes is one dropped candle and the whole place will go up like a bale of hay.'

On the drive back to Oxford, Sarah and I did our best to weigh up the pros and cons.

'So... apart from the death-trap garden, the pigeon mess, the dust, the damp, the lack of windows in the long gallery and the complete absence of a kitchen – what's wrong with it?'

By nature, we were both idealistic, but choosing the theatre and abbey as our wedding venue would be quite a risk, and we knew it.

'I don't know,' said Sarah. 'I feel guilty now because I suggested it. Don't get me wrong – it's an amazing place, really special, but it'd mean a lot of work. Are you sure we're up to it? Are you sure *you're* up to it?'

Blinded by the romanticism and sheer quirkiness of the place, I was convinced we had what it took.

'It's a one-off,' I said. 'Think how unique it would be to get married in a theatre. We could have the reception outside in the garden and the meal in the long gallery. We could turn the lower hall into a dance hall. It's just a matter of organisation – I'll put a file together.'

'A file? It'll take a bit more than that,' said Sarah breezily and laughed.

'Well, it's not as if I'm going to do it *totally* single-handedly. You said you can help after work or at weekends and then... and then...' I was floundering.

'You'll be telling me Dash can help out next.'

'Don't be daft,' I said, slightly wounded. 'But I tell you what, she'd love that riverside garden. You'd love it, wouldn't you, Dash?' I said, looking in the rear-view mirror to where she lay in the back. Dash flicked an ear as if bothered by an invisible fly. She'd been flat out for the entire morning. This wedding stuff was obviously hard work.

Future in-laws: a blessing or curse? In mid-January, Sarah's mum and dad came to stay for the weekend. In truth, we'd got on famously ever since we'd first met. I was particularly fond of Sarah's dad, Harry – partly because I'd lost my own dad, but mainly because of his affable good humour and Yorkshire common sense. A tall man of sixty, he led from the front, spoke his mind and had the kind of rangy strength you'd expect from an ex-builder. When the construction work ran out, he went on to invent a fibre-glass manhole cover – 'the bestseller in the field... or forecourt'. Eventually selling the company to free himself and his wife for a slice of the good life, they retired to southern Spain. Sarah's mum,

Lesley, was a beautiful woman with rarely an ash-blonde hair out of place. She spoke in a benign, slightly dreamy way, liked her home comforts and was always happy to visit the UK as she missed her grandchildren. Sarah's two sisters and one brother had already given her a total of six to dote on.

'Well, I think it's a lovely idea,' said Lesley. 'Fancy that – getting married in a theatre!'

'Just as long as it doesn't turn into a bloody farce,' Harry chipped in.

'And when did you say the date was?' asked Lesley.

'We were offered two dates in September,' I said. 'But plumped for Friday the nineteenth. It'll be our third anniversary of being together… and the first anniversary of adopting Dash.'

'Ooh, yes,' said Lesley, seeing the significance. 'It's got good associations then.'

All four of us were sitting in the lounge, with Dash dodging from one person to the next for strokes. Harry and Lesley had a dog of their own in Spain, so were used to dividing their attention (and the conversation) between humans and canines.

'You know, Dash is probably a bit smaller than Fizz, less stocky… but she's definitely longer,' said Lesley. Fizz was a stray they'd taken in after she'd been found on a mountainside. He was part podenco – a continental breed of hunting dog – and slept outside in a kennel that Harry had built for her.

Then came the same question again: 'Will Dash be going to the wedding?'

'Just don't dress her up if she does,' said Harry. 'She'll look like a right clown.'

'Oh, I don't know,' said Lesley. 'You could always get her a pretty outfit.'

'I'm sure we could, but we've got plenty of other wedding stuff to worry about first,' said Sarah, 'like finding accommodation for everybody.'

'You want a hotel close to the abbey,' advised Harry. 'You can't expect folk to kip overnight on the floor.'

'They won't be able to anyway,' I remarked. We've only got the abbey till midnight.'

'What? Out by midnight, like a vanload of bloody pumpkins? I don't know.' Harry shook his head in mock exasperation.

'The idea is to start the ceremony about three,' said Sarah. 'That would last about forty-five minutes and then we'd all go into the riverside garden for champagne and canapés, followed by photos. Then up to the first floor, the long gallery, for dinner and speeches, finishing in the lower hall with dancing.'

'Ooh, lovely,' said Lesley. 'What kind of dancing – ballroom, like on TV?'

I caught Sarah's eye and smiled. We'd already wondered how possible it would be to hold onto what *we* really wanted, rather than get swayed by other people's ideas.

'Probably not,' I cut in diplomatically. 'We were thinking of something a bit less formal – maybe a cèilidh.'

'Ooh, yes! A cèilidh. That'll get everyone moving.'

'What about a bar?' asked Harry. 'If you're gunna ask folk to dance, they'll need some fuel.'

'The abbey does have a licence to serve alcohol,' I said.

'You want to set up a couple of tables in the corner of the dance hall then.' Harry made a broad sweep with his hands as if carving out a counter with himself behind as barman. This *was* a good idea and one we'd take up with the caterer, just as soon as we found one.

That evening there was talk of little else but the wedding. In the way my mum had pledged to make a financial contribution, Harry and Lesley did the same. I thought about making a poster of a large thermometer like charities use, with the red mercury rising to indicate how close we were to our target of ten grand – but in the end I settled for a spreadsheet, nicknaming it 'The Love Budget'.

On the Sunday afternoon, just before Sarah's parents were due to leave, we had another very welcome visitor. My eldest brother, Paul, was over from Ireland on business and called in to say hello. If he were a breed of dog, the cheeky younger brother in me would say he was a chihuahua or Mexican hairless... but neither breed is really solid enough. Although only five feet five and bald, Paul is reasonably stocky. He'd lived for a number of years in the States before finally settling down in Galway with his Irish wife and two kids. Perhaps influenced by the American-Irish connection, I'd have to say he is most like a Boston terrier. Short; compact; extremely good-natured. He certainly made a good impression on Sarah's parents, which I was grateful for. Funnily enough, one thing he is not is a dog lover. Not that he is a dog hater either – just one of those people who find dogs a little mystifying. If I wanted something to take care of and keep me housebound on a Saturday night, then why didn't I just have kids?

'So what do you think of Dash?' I said. This was the first time he'd met her since she raced into our lives the autumn before.

'Yeah, great,' he said, standing with his arms folded and looking at her quizzically. 'Doesn't she sit down then?'

I explained the closest we'd get was her sphinx-like squat. Most of the time, if unsure what to do when visitors came, Dash stood round panting mildly before stretching out and dozing off. This was invariably at my feet or Sarah's. Occasionally, if the guests were family or close friends, I'd take my socks off and let Dash lick my toes. Paul, naturally, thought this was a bit much. Particularly since Dash's breath wasn't always at its freshest.

'Wait till you see us clean her teeth,' I said.

'You have to clean her teeth?' he echoed, disbelieving.

'Every Sunday and Wednesday night.' This was the regime we'd introduced ever since Dash had lost six teeth. At first, we brushed her teeth with a baby's toothbrush with soft bristles. We'd finally settled on using a ladies' popsock stretched over one finger, together with a cocktail stick for getting between Dash's front teeth.

After Sarah's parents had left, we gave Paul a demo.

'I'll watch if I have to,' he said. 'But don't think I'm having a go.'

The first thing was to get Dash comfortable and captive. She'd slowly got used to having her teeth brushed, but that didn't mean she particularly enjoyed the experience. Sarah and I divided the task between us. It just seemed more natural that way – rough with the smooth; in sickness and in health. With Dash lying on her mat, Sarah blocked her in by kneeling next to her and then started on her front teeth with the cocktail stick. Since Dash's diet was composed exclusively of soft food to help digestion rather than dry, crunchy stuff, the food had a nasty habit of sticking between her teeth. As Sarah poked out the bits that had been there for a few days, Paul looked away and held his nose.

'Yeeuch! What a stink!'

'Come off it,' I said, taking it as a personal affront, 'you've got two kids. You had to change nappies for years.'

'That's different – kids are your own flesh and blood, your *family*.'

'Dash is part of the family now,' I countered, surprising even myself.

With Sarah's half of the job done, I stretched the popsock over one hand and squeezed a slug of turkey-flavoured toothpaste onto it.

'What a palaver,' said Paul, and sighed. Dash flicked out her tongue in anticipation.

'Check these out,' I said to Paul and prised opened Dash's jaws to reveal two rows of cream-coloured daggers. Her canines were almost an inch long. Paul pulled another face. I then proceeded to scrub vigorously – trying to get as much of the paste onto Dash's teeth before she licked it off. The whole procedure ended with Dash receiving a treat for her patience. For his part, Paul needed a drink. As we sipped a glass of wine, I had a question for him.

'Listen… I was wondering… would you be my chief usher at the wedding?'

'Chief usher? But I thought you had two best men already lined up?'

'Yeah, I do… but there's so much stuff to sort out… and I need all the help I can get. Besides, you're *family*.' I gave him a wink.

'Touché! I'd be delighted,' he laughed, then paused. 'You're not thinking of taking Dash to the wedding. Are you…?'

I grinned broadly. Paul clapped a hand to his forehead in despair.

Dogs, like people, can have bad days, too. In the second half of January, Dash had a bad fortnight. She tugged her way to the park and back, harassed every dog she came across and fouled the pavements or people's driveways. She also started snaffling food on our walks – dropped crisps, bits of bread, even vomit – and was sick herself as a result. Admittedly, it wasn't helped by the fact that nature had shut up shop. It was cold and dark and wet – the worst kind of dog-walking weather. Getting ready to go out in the morning seemed to take forever. First, there was Dash's green coat to put on, and then the harness over that. I'd actually managed to teach her to stand with a front paw in each of the loops of the harness on the floor. From there, I pulled it up and buckled it behind her like a bra – a sort of erotic fumble in reverse. I then climbed into my waterproof trousers, winter coat with a hood and wellies. Most mornings, we looked like we were off for a spell on a North Sea trawler.

The only command that I seemed to give Dash that fortnight was 'No!' and praise sounded hollow. Prohibition became the name of the game – and like anyone who has to lay down the law full-time, I got bored by it. Dash became tiresome, moody and a burden. As much as you can ever claim to know an animal, I suddenly felt I didn't know Dash at all. She was a drain on my energy... and our finances. What did Sarah and I actually get in return? Any signs of affection Dash gave seemed to consist of her leaning against us or pawing to be stroked. She wagged her tail madly when fed, but this was just greed. Even the knowledge that we'd rescued a retired greyhound from an uncertain fate was no consolation during those dark days. Peter had told us at the very start that he would have subsidised a lifelong stay in kennels, no question. Maybe it was New Year blues. Maybe I needed more help.

There was only so much Sarah could do – she worked office hours and in winter, at least, wasn't home until well after dark. Ever since Bonfire Night, Dash had become reluctant to walk at night. On the few occasions we were forced to go out late, she'd loiter on the pavement and take the first opportunity to head for home. Sarah, too, hated the short days. After living in Thailand for years and then Morocco, she found the British winter interminable. She adored the sun and had the kind of complexion that tanned in an afternoon.

'I'm fed up,' she said to me one evening after cycling home in the pouring rain. 'The weather's rubbish; we never go out any more; Dash is a complete pain.'

I felt ashamed not to have noticed she was at such a low ebb.

'But... but there's the wedding to look forward to,' I stammered.

'That's months away,' she said. 'It's January; I feel fat. I can't even think about stuff like the wedding right now.'

Sensing a wobble was imminent, I slid next to Sarah on the sofa and put my arm around her shoulders. Dash, thinking she might be missing out on some affection, jumped up from her mat and joined us with all the delicacy of a wrecking ball. She shoved her nose into Sarah's hands.

'Don't worry. We'll think of something,' I said.

Perhaps starting some dog-obedience classes at the weekends would help us all? Sarah and I discussed it. Dash would be a disaster, we knew it. She was a greyhound who'd been trained to do only one thing, and that was race round a track at breakneck speed. Besides, we'd never seen Jess or Arnie – the other more malleable ex-racers in the park – able to do anything other than please themselves. They didn't sit, heel, lie down or roll over. They didn't even come back regularly! What hope was there for Dash? Should we finally give in and approach an animal psychologist? I had visions of an overpriced consultation where we would discover that it was *us*, not Dash, that was really the problem. The psychologist would look at us over his or her glasses (these people always wear glasses) and say something like: 'Well, you need to start by modifying your own behaviour. A dog is only a mirror of the way you are in the world.'

They'd probably be right, but we just didn't want to hear it. Faced with these choices, Sarah and I did what most people do when it all gets too much. We decided to go on holiday.

February

It would be the longest Dash had been apart from us for five months. After her troublesome behaviour in January, I was thoroughly looking forward to it. Sarah and I were off to Egypt for a week of sun worship.

We'd successfully found a wedding venue, so finding a kennel for Dash while we were away should be a breeze. I'd narrowed the choice down to two and, coincidentally, both were south of Oxford, in the direction of the venue itself. I phoned the first one and a man answered briskly. He said he had a group of owners coming for a 'tour' the following morning. Could I make ten twenty-five? A little amused at the preciseness of the appointment, I said I could. The woman at the second kennel told me to drop round anytime before lunch.

Next morning, I got off to a slow start. Dash had been in a particularly obstructive mood after breakfast, dancing away from me round the garden before I could put her harness on. It was gone ten thirty by the time we arrived at the first kennel – a long barn-like building – so I hurried through the double doors, half-tripping over Dash in the process. More like a hotel lobby than the reception of a kennel, there were a few comfy-looking chairs, potted plants and a desk behind which sat a man with greying temples. Also in reception were four women, smartly dressed. One woman was busy on her mobile, telling someone called 'Greg, darling' just what she thought. Another stood and stared into space like a high-class shop dummy. I went up to the reception desk. The man was on the phone while typing at a computer. Up close, his face was so smooth that it looked like it might be razored twice daily and buffed to a sheen by a team of barbers. Dash raised her nose like a periscope and sniffed at his eau de cologne over the edge of the desk.

'Please leave your dog in the car,' the man said, putting his hand over the phone receiver but not looking up. I glanced round, not quite sure who he was addressing. None of the women had dogs with them.

'No dogs on the tour, I'm afraid,' he said, and looked at me sternly.

'Oh... oh, right.' I said, surprised and slightly irritated. 'Come on,' I said to Dash, 'let's pop you back in the car for ten minutes.'

When I returned minus Dash, the tour had already begun and the man was standing at the entrance to the kennels with the women round him in a small group. He looked like he was about to open a new supermarket.

'Do come this way,' he said with a flourish.

The group shuffled forwards to stand at the head of a long corridor. On either side, at regular intervals, were metal-framed doors of thick glass giving on to individual kennels. The strains of classical music came from speakers overhead.

The floor was tiled, the lighting soft and everything spotless. For a busy kennel, it was also remarkably quiet – none of the yaps, woofs and whines you'd associate with twenty plus dogs in close proximity. The smooth-faced man cleared his clean-shaven throat.

'Welcome to the kennels... and thank you for being so punctual.' He shot another stern glance in my direction. 'As I'm sure you all know, we pride ourselves on the high standard of care and attention we give to your pet dog when he... or she,' (smile and slight incline of the head) 'comes to lodge with us.'

I craned forward to hear – did he say 'lodge', did he actually use the word 'lodge'?

'Our kennels are designed to maximise comfort. The sleeping zones all have soundproofing and embedded radiators...'

By now, he was walking backwards down the corridor. He made an odd little gesture with both hands for the group to follow him, as if he was pulling on a bed sheet while we held the other end. We stopped outside one of the glass doors. I leaned against the wall and then, as if back at school, jerked up straight again. A clipboard on the wall showed the name of the dog ('Rameses'), special dietary requirements and a cleaning record like that of an airport toilet. In the kennel itself, there was a raised canvas bed in the corner. A big, pale Retriever lay curled up on it, pretending not to notice us.

'You'll see there are very few bars. This isn't a prison, after all... more like a holiday camp.' One of the women nodded solidly as if she was in a business meeting.

I couldn't help noticing the man paid no attention to the retriever at all. Perhaps it was time to break his flow.

Crouching down next to the glass door, I asked: 'Do the dogs get out much then?'

He smiled at me like a magician would at a volunteer from the audience.

'All the guests are exercised daily on sixty acres of stunning farmland. That includes a solo walk of fifteen minutes before breakfast and bedtime, and a walk on a long lead in the morning and afternoon.' More nods of approval. The man smiled again and turned briskly on his heel.

'Guests?' 'Stunning farmland?' I was beginning to wonder if Sarah and I shouldn't cancel the week in Egypt and check into a cubicle alongside Dash.

We walked through a pair of double doors at the far end and out into a yard and paddock. The February wind whipped round the corner of the building.

'Breezy,' I remarked to one of the women on the tour.

She smiled fleetingly but didn't break her vow of silence.

As the man began again, I scanned the view. The paddock opened onto a few brown fields. In the distance, one of the kennel hands was being hauled along a hedgerow by a collie on a lead.

'... routine and respect – this is what we offer our guests. Of course, your part of the bargain is important, too.' The man looked round pointedly.

'We expect all customers to drop off and collect their pets on the appointed dates and during the prescribed time slots.'

This was too much. I piped up again. 'Presumably there's provision for unforeseen eventualities, you know, owners getting delayed at airports on their way back from holiday, that sort of thing.'

'If customers call ahead, we can always come to some arrangement,' he said smoothly. 'But we also have to be fair on those who've had the foresight to make a firm booking.' His crease-free face remained unperturbed. As we followed him back into the kennel and along the corridor, I was trying to work out what was so objectionable about him – after all, I didn't even know the man. Then it dawned on me. He epitomised the qualities I least liked in myself: an annoying know-all and control freak.

Back in reception, the women queued up to have the details of their beloved dogs entered into the database. I gave the man a perfunctory 'Thanks' and walked swiftly out.

'What an idiot, Dash! What an uptight, patronising idiot! You wouldn't have believed him.' I drove back down the rutted track and out through the gate. 'One thing's for sure, I'm not leaving you there,' I said, turning round and addressing Dash directly. Dash sighed heavily and rested her chin on her paws.

Some people just have a gift. They're born to do something and get on with it. The woman at the second kennel, Lynn, had a gift with dogs. She also had shrewd eyes, a ready smile and the slightly ruddy complexion of someone who spends most of the year outdoors. Dressed in a body warmer and wellies, her energetic manner also gave the impression that she had everything in hand. She greeted Dash and me enthusiastically, asked questions about her and showed me a wall of snapshots of doggy boarders. There were even two or three greyhounds among the photos – an encouraging sign. The kennels themselves weren't posh, but they were warm, noisy and clean. As we walked round, she regularly pushed her fingers through the bars to receive licks and talked to the dogs in an affectionate, unfussy manner. Dash bounced after her and went nose-to-nose with a few of the boarders without any hint of aggression. There was no reception area to speak of, but a central room packed with bags of dog food, bowls and assorted equipment.

'Are you busy this month?' I asked Lynn and looked round for a computer.

'Busy but not bursting,' she said and pulled a large diary off a shelf.

We checked the dates; I booked Dash in.

As if sensing the impending separation, Dash's behaviour suddenly improved. Her journey to and from the park became a fraction more sedate; her aggression towards smaller dogs more like energetic curiosity. Most striking of all, she began to poo right next to the red waste bins. I'd always found it irksome to have to follow her onto people's driveways or into the undergrowth, and then continue the walk holding a full bag of foul-smelling stuff. Now, when I saw her squatting, I even managed once or twice to slip an open poo bag on the floor beneath her and she filled it herself! I still had to tie it, of course, but it was quite a party trick nevertheless. Dash also seemed to have added to her repertoire of expressions. When Sarah and I told her off, we got an up-from-under look which seemed to say 'Who, me?' or a sidelong glance followed by a grin:

'What? I was Bitch of the Year. I can't be good at everything, you know.'

At the kennels on the morning of our departure for Egypt, we did our level best to remain unsentimental. We figured Dash had everything she needed to make her stay there a comfortable one: duvet, mat, night coat, toy, rawhide bone and a sweaty old T-shirt of mine in case she pined. Unfazed by the mass of stuff we'd brought, Lynn showed Dash to an empty kennel between an Australian cattle dog and an otter hound. Unusual but pedigree neighbours. The cattle dog, an airport sniffer between jobs, had already been there a week; the otter hound was a recent arrival. Once Dash was in and the gate bolted, we didn't looked back... or not more than twice anyway. While Sarah and I were sunning ourselves in Egypt, Dash would have a berth to herself chez Lynn.

'Dahab' means 'gold' in Arabic. The Red Sea resort of Dahab was true to its name and we'd managed to get a last-minute room in a hotel on a stretch of twenty-four carat, sandy beach. And during the week of Valentine's Day as well! Each morning, Sarah and I slept late and flip-flopped down to breakfast. Here, we sat on a terrace and ate muesli, fresh fruit, yoghurt and pastries. We sipped hibiscus tea and made cheese rolls for lunch, sneaking them into our serviettes. It was wonderful to be away; wonderful to be together. In the afternoon, we read on the beach with a backdrop of blue sea and burnt umber mountains.

We even tried snorkelling. Too skinny to be a strong swimmer, I bobbed about marvelling at the corals and fish, but after half an hour got cold and tired. My wetsuit had leaked and I was floating closer to the spiky coral wall, with no strength left to paddle away. I signalled to Sarah helplessly, who towed me back to the boat where I spent the next half hour shivering in a towel with a glass of tea. The teaspoon tinkled in the glass like a dinner bell as I shook, much to the captain's amusement.

'You need to become strong. Like your wife,' he laughed.

I nodded, my teeth chattering audibly. Sarah wasn't yet my wife but she *was* strong, the captain was right. As I watched her continue to snorkel from the warmth of the deck, I suddenly had an idea for my wedding speech. From what I'd seen at other weddings, the groom was expected to praise the qualities of his new wife. 'Strong' had to be in there, I thought. And 'kind'... and 'open'... and 'radiant'. Perhaps I could come up with something for every letter of the alphabet? Over the next few days, I jotted words down and soon had an adjective for twenty-one of the twenty-six letters. V–Z would require some more thought once back home!

Halfway through our week in Dahab, on Valentine's Day itself, we took a day trip into the desert. I rode camelback for the first time and we trekked through a canyon of multicoloured rock. Our guide had the same genial character and pencil moustache we'd come to expect as the norm. At noon, we stopped in a Bedouin village and ate flat bread baked in white-hot coals.

'You... married?' asked our guide, as we rested in the shade of a tent.

'Almost!' I replied, enthusiastically. 'Our wedding's later this year – September.'

'Children?' he then asked, as if going through a questionnaire.

'Not yet... but perhaps in the future,' said Sarah.

The guide nodded approvingly. He already had three children despite being ten years our junior.

'We have a dog if that's any good,' I chipped in.

'Ahh,' the guide said politely.

The only dogs we'd seen so far in Egypt were a few mangy strays. They roamed the streets of the town, scavenging and dodging a flung sandal or stick. By now, of course, we'd totally forgiven Dash for her poor behaviour in January. After the first flush of independence on our arrival, Sarah and I missed her terribly. We'd even decided not to mention her in case it upset us, but now I couldn't resist. I pulled out my mobile phone and showed the guide a photo of Dash.

The guide took the phone and squinted at the screen. 'Is... hunting dog?' he asked.

'No, well... not really. She used to race, you know, against other dogs.' Perhaps I was on the verge of committing a cultural faux pas? I blundered on regardless.

'She raced round a track, with other dogs, after a hare.' I put my index fingers either side of my head like hare's ears. The penny dropped; the guide grinned and showed a set of nicotine-stained teeth.

'Ah-hah! Is... great-hound?'

'Yes,' I said, relieved. 'Is great-hound. Is very great hound.'

On our last night in Dahab, we went into town by taxi. The African Cup of Nations was on TV; Egypt was in the final and had gone football-crazy. If they won, I promised the taxi driver I'd buy him dinner. The streets were packed and cafés and restaurants had put TV sets outside, linked together like Christmas lights with frayed wiring. Egypt won; I bought dinner. At the final whistle, we danced and hugged a dozen complete strangers. Taxis raced down the streets blaring their horns. Young men hung off the sides of cars and lit aerosols, shooting purple flames into the night. It was a night of national celebration – and a happy one too for Sarah and me. The next day, we were going home… and that meant a reunion with Dash.

The radio was on and I was drumming on the steering wheel and singing loudly. Sarah was doing her best to harmonise. We were on our way to the kennels and I guess you could say we were excited. Sarah and I couldn't wait to see Dash and wondered how she'd react when she saw us. Would she bark, would she jump up on her hind legs? Or maybe she'd sulk and look away, resentful at having been abandoned? Lynn, the kennel owner, met us at the entrance and reassured us Dash had been fine. She added that Dash and the otter hound had become best friends, exercising together in the paddock. She also showed us a photo of Dash she'd taken and put up on the snapshot wall.

I was impressed. 'You did well to catch her at full speed.'

'Yes, it took a few goes though! We got plenty of photos of just her tail and back legs. Anyway, let's get you three reacquainted…'

For a split second, Dash couldn't believe it. Her ears pricked up and took her eyebrows with them. Then she started bouncing up and down. She pawed at the kennel bars and turned in circles. When Lynn unbolted the gate, Dash crashed through and nuzzled my hand so hard she practically bit it. Then she dodged past Sarah and shot off down the corridor, without a lead or any of her stuff.

'Crikey, she's keen to get home,' said Lynn.

'You follow her and I'll go this way round and head her off,' said Sarah. The corridors were arranged round a central hub like spokes on a wheel. I charged after Dash, skidding on the painted floor and calling her name. After one lap of the entire kennels, Dash ran into Sarah coming the other way. Between us, we managed to get her lead on. Dash, for her part, was grinning ecstatically at the prank. Her tail thumped against our legs; we gave her a hug.

'Bloody hell,' I said to Sarah, in a combination of relief and exhilaration, 'She's just too fast. Too fast for her own good!'

Back home and refreshed, wedding preparations began again in earnest. Next on the list was the search for a suitable hotel for the bridal party and guests who'd be travelling long distance. The most promising contender was a hotel in the centre of Abingdon which sat on a sweet little promontory, accessible only by two bridges. It was delightful and looked more like a stone and brick house festooned with winter flowers than a hotel. The room that couples traditionally chose as the wedding suite was already booked, but the one above was smaller, had a sizeable balcony and a view of the River Thames. This was the one for us, Sarah and I agreed.

Buoyed up by the ease and speed of our booking, I turned my attention to finding someone who could actually marry us: the celebrant. Choosing a humanist ceremony and celebrant meant we weren't limited to a licensed venue, which was the reason we'd hired the theatre and abbey. It was only when I started to do some more research that I made an uncomfortable discovery. A humanist ceremony also meant that if we wanted our marriage to be 'legally recognised', we'd have to tie the knot at a registry office first. So that meant *two* weddings! And if the registry office was the wedding that really mattered, where did that leave the one I was busy planning for the theatre and abbey? Wouldn't it feel like an anticlimax or, worse still, a bit of a sham?

I guessed Sarah might be disappointed. Should I just come clean straight away? We still had time to cancel the venue and hotel... but what about the dream? We'd already begun to imagine ourselves in the intimate space of the theatre; in response to continual questions, we were even beginning to entertain the idea of Dash coming to the wedding, too. Was I about to turn round and declare the whole thing null and void? I had to tell Sarah, of course. The dilemma was when and how. I finally came to the conclusion that maybe it wasn't such a big deal. So we'd have two weddings. The first one at the registry office would be a formality, a technicality even. We'd turn up and sign on the dotted line, no more. For us, the second wedding would be the real thing. Our friends and family would be there at the theatre as witnesses; we'd have the reception, the meal and speeches, the dancing and drinking, the gifts, the cake – all the wedding trappings and trimmings you'd expect. So I decided to keep shtum, continue the search for a suitable celebrant and ask them to come and meet Sarah and me at home. I'd mention the legal stuff to Sarah beforehand as a casual footnote – that was all it amounted to, after all.

'WHAT?!' Sarah's face went white. We were standing in the kitchen and the celebrant was due to arrive in five minutes. I suddenly felt sick.

'What do you mean it wouldn't be "legal"?' said Sarah, aghast.

I tried to explain, flapping my hands like someone in front of a chip-pan fire.

'Humanist weddings aren't… they just aren't recognised, not in England at least. We'd have to go to a registry office first. Just a formality, you know, for the certificate…'

'A *formality*? Are you saying our wedding would be a formality?'

'No, no! That's not what I'm saying.' It wasn't, it really wasn't. But too late; the damage was done. Sarah stood there glumly. As she turned to go upstairs her eyes were wet with tears.

'Where… where are you going? The celebrant will be here in five minutes.'

'I don't care,' sniffed Sarah. '*You* can talk to her.'

She tramped upstairs with her head bowed and I heard the bedroom door shut. For a second I hovered on the bottom step of the stairs, not sure whether to follow Sarah or let her be. Then the doorbell decided for me. I stumbled through the lounge, briefly noticed Dash who'd taken refuge on her mat, and unlocked and opened the front door.

'Andrew?'

'Yes?'

'I'm Rebecca.'

'Right.'

'The celebrant… you remember? Am I early?'

'Yes… I mean no. Sorry. Come in.'

Dash immediately got up to sniff the visitor.

'You don't mind dogs, do you? She's very friendly.'

'No, not at all. Hello there, sweetie.' Rebecca bent down to stroke Dash's head.

'Will you have a cup of tea or coffee?' I asked, wondering suddenly if it wasn't a better idea to postpone or cancel the appointment altogether rather than play for time.

'Tea would be lovely, thanks,' said Rebecca, looking up. She was in her late forties, with shoulder-length strawberry blonde hair, a kind face and heavy-lidded eyes. Dressed in a skirt and jacket, the choice and cut of the fabric made her look more hippyish than was perhaps the intention. I hoped she'd be understanding, at least. While making tea, I chatted to Rebecca through the open kitchen door, half-listening to her replies and half straining to hear if there was any noise coming from the bedroom. Would Sarah come down at all? How would it look to Rebecca if the bride-to-be didn't even show?

'Of course, she's quite a handful really. Despite her sweet appearance,' I called out.

'Sorry, who is?' asked Rebecca, taking her tea as I came back into the lounge.

'Dash… the dog.'

'Oh, right,' laughed Rebecca. 'For one minute, I thought you were talking about your wife-to-be. "Sarah", isn't it?'

'Yes,' I came and perched on the edge of the sofa. 'You wouldn't think she's four, would you? Not much grey round the muzzle. And still lightning-fast given half the chance.'

Rebecca sipped her tea and looked at me inquisitively over the mug.

'Have you got any pets?' I asked, my expression starting to look like the rictus grin of a village idiot.

'Two cats,' said Rebecca and paused.

'Nice. Two cats,' I echoed and paused.

'Will… will Sarah be joining us?' asked Rebecca finally.

I jumped up and almost spilt my tea. 'Sarah? Yes, yes. She's upstairs. Just getting ready. Shall I go and check? I'll go and check. Give me a minute.' I put down my tea and backed out of the room like an actor who'd entered the stage prematurely.

'Sweetheart?' I knocked quietly on the bedroom door. 'Can I come in?' I nudged the door open and peered round. Worse than I expected. Sarah had actually climbed into bed and pulled the duvet up over her head. I tiptoed in and sat down next to the humped shape.

'I know you must be disappointed. *I'm* disappointed.'

The humped shape didn't move.

'I had no idea, honestly. I know it's a drag to have to do the registry office as well, but we can keep it really simple. Just our parents can be the witnesses. They'd love it; it'd make them feel really special. We can still have an amazing wedding the day after. Everyone will be there... at the theatre and abbey. That's what matters. Everyone can share the occasion. It's up to us to make it into what we want. I don't care if it feels like we're getting married twice – I'd marry you a thousand times if I could. I'd marry you anywhere: in a registry office, in a theatre, on top of a mountain, in the street. I don't care. I love you.'

I waited, holding my breath. Then Sarah's voice from under the duvet.

'I love you, too.'

Sarah pulled the duvet back slowly. Her eyes were red and strands of hair covered her face.

'I just want it to feel unique,' she said. 'We both waited so long to find each other. Getting married in two different places won't feel that unique.'

'Just you see,' I said. 'It'll feel twice as unique.' We kissed. I wiped her eyes.

Rebecca turned out to be the voice of reason.

'Think of it as a way of having your cake and eating it... You can have exactly the kind of wedding you want, where you want. You can write the ceremony yourselves – I'll help, of course – you can have readings, music. You can include as many elements of a traditional ceremony as you like – the giving away of the bride, the exchange of rings. You can invite whoever you want… you can even invite the dog! How about that, eh, Dash? I bet you'd like to go, too. You'd make a very elegant ring bearer, you would.'

Dash looked up at us from where she was grooming herself and licked her lips. Sarah and I were side by side on the sofa, holding hands.

'Ring bearer? Wow… now there's an idea!'

We agreed that it sounded fantastic. It would give Dash a role and a reason to be there. It could also be the perfect testament to how far she'd come, twelve months to the day after her adoption. All this assuming she behaved herself in the interim, of course, which in itself was a pretty hefty assumption. One thing was certain – there'd be no room for a four-legged liability at a wedding ceremony. Would Dash be up to it? Would she calm down enough? Would she slow down enough? The race was on.

A week later, the rift between Sarah and me was more than mended and Rebecca emailed the first draft of the ceremony. Appropriately enough considering the theatre venue, it read like the script of a play. The different speakers were indicated by name, with the equivalent of stage directions showing where they'd be standing and what they had to do. For the final stage of the ceremony, Rebecca came up with a novel suggestion. Since Sarah and I were both privy to the script, why didn't we include some 'secret words' addressed to each other but which wouldn't be heard till the big day itself? I thought it sounded like a wonderful idea; Sarah wasn't so keen.

'It's not fair – you're the creative one… I'd be worried mine won't be half as good.'

One thing we both agreed on was the exchange of wedding rings – this was to be our big symbolic moment and also the opportunity for the newly appointed ring bearer in the shape of Dash to take to the stage. No ring pillow or prayer book necessary. Fingers firmly crossed, a greyhound that six months ago had been coursing round a track, would hop onto the stage right on cue with the rings tinkling on her collar.

We estimated the whole ceremony would last about forty minutes, which was probably as much as the assembled audience (and dog) could be expected to take. So that was it. The only blank to fill in was the music, but we could do that at our leisure over the next few months.

It was soon time to dance to someone else's tune. The cèilidh band we wanted to book for the evening of the wedding had invited us to watch them in action. The venue was a hall in one of the Oxford colleges and when Sarah and I arrived, it was already full of undergraduates. Our first instinct was to turn round and flee. It was like arriving at a party to which we hadn't been invited. Not only that but everyone else at the party was so much younger than us. As we hovered at the entrance, a lively woman with grey hair and carrying a bassoon approached us. Sandy was the band leader and the person I'd spoken to over the phone about the booking.

'Glad you could make it! We're just about to start the second half. Why don't you join in and see what you think?'

Sarah and I looked at each other doubtfully. Couldn't we just observe from the side of the hall? Or perhaps this would be viewed as bad form. After all, we'd certainly encourage our wedding guests to take to the floor.

Once the music was under way, any youthful advantage the dancers had over us was counteracted by an almost complete lack of coordination. Coltish young men bounded round, crashing into each other or whisking girls off their feet. The girls thought this was hilarious, straightening their glasses and hair before clapping their hands in glee. All this despite the best efforts of the caller, a wise-cracking man with a radio mike and accordion who skipped between groups of flailing students. The Dashing White Sergeant, Strip the Willow, The Gay Gordons – Sarah and I spun and wove our way through half a dozen dances. When we forgot the steps, we made them up. Each time we met or crossed each other in the throng, our faces lit up with relief and affection. Then it was off again, jerked away until we too ended up laughing hysterically like the students half our age.

March

I thought Arnie the greyhound was big. This thing was even bigger than Arnie. It came lolloping across the grass towards Dash and me, swerved away through a patch of snowdrops and disappeared into the bushes.

Had I imagined it? Dash was mesmerised. We looked at each other like a couple who'd just witnessed a UFO. Our breaths condensed in cold white clouds. Then there it was again – bounding along a line of trees, its silky hair flowing behind it as if in a shampoo commercial. A borzoi or Russian wolfhound. Just about the tallest hound around and one hell of a commitment. An ex-racing greyhound was one thing, but what kind of person would take on a borzoi? As we rounded a hedge, I saw the borzoi was back on the lead and trotting alongside its owner like a horse on the way to the winner's enclosure. A tall black man, impeccably dressed and wearing blue wellies, waved to me as he walked over.

'Sorry about that,' he called out, laughing. 'Did he give you a shock?' He smiled broadly. His eyes glinted with a combination of brimming confidence and mischief.

'Ryan,' he said, extending a large hand.

'Who... you or the dog?' I replied, surprised by his forwardness. I was used to developing a mumbling acquaintance in the park, not being on the business end of a handshake. He threw his head back and laughed again.

'Me... me, of course,' he said eventually. 'This is Tolstoy.' He pointed to the horse-cum-dog at his side.

What a name! And to think I was worried about sounding pretentious with 'Dash'.

'Tolstoy... right,' I repeated, matching Ryan's smile.

'I've not seen you two in the park before,' he said, looking at Dash. 'Retired, is she?'

'Yes,' I said. 'Adopted her straight from the owner a few months ago. What about yours?'

'Tolstoy's eight.'

'Eight *months?*'

Ryan nodded.

'You're joking! How much taller is he going to get?'

'Another few inches, certainly,' Ryan replied. 'It's amazing. At the moment, it's as if you can almost *see* him growing.'

Up close, Tolstoy looked like a cartoon of a dog. A pair of googly eyes rolled in his head, either side of a never-ending nose. He was strapped into a harness the size of a baby walker and rocked from side to side, shifting his weight on huge white paws. Ryan had to hold on to the harness so tightly that his bicep was bulging under his sleeve. Tolstoy craned his neck forward and nuzzled Dash behind the ear. Dash panted and then leaned on him as if leaning against a wall.

Ryan and I continued to chat – after all, male walkers under retirement age were a rarity in the park. I learnt he was a stockbroker who lived in Oxford but worked in London. Home was originally the Caribbean and he'd grown up in the south of France. I felt like asking for an atlas but it was all recounted with such matter-of-fact charm that I nodded warmly. Most interestingly, Tolstoy was Ryan's *third* dog. Before getting a borzoi, he'd had a saluki and a lurcher. I didn't dare ask what their names had been in case I burst out laughing. 'Proust' perhaps? Or 'Shakespeare'? One thing was clear – here was a man who obviously knew a lot about hounds; I'd had Dash for just five months. I sensed we were going to get along. More than that, it could be the start of a beautiful friendship between the highbrow Tolstoy and the lowbrow Dash.

The single biggest wedding day expense – bar none (pun intended) – is the catering. The equation is simple. If the food and drink are good, it can make the occasion; if they're passable or poor, it can mar the day completely.

Sitting in the lounge with Sarah, Dash and me was Geoff, the third caterer we'd met that afternoon. The first two to face the 'interview panel' hadn't fared particularly well. Selma, a rounded, blousy woman, had blustered her way through the menu options but failed to impress. All puff and no pastry. She was vague about serving staff, unsure about furniture and linen hire and appeared at a loss when she learnt that the abbey had no kitchens. There was also the small matter of her email being out of action. She even had to borrow a pen to jot down notes. A definite 'no' from the panel. The second caterer to receive a grilling was an attractive young woman who came with a portfolio of photos. She certainly had plenty of ideas, but seemed disinclined to let them be influenced by what Sarah and I actually wanted. A white chocolate fondue for dessert might be all the rage, but we just weren't that keen on subjecting our guests (or their clothes) to it. The third caterer, Geoff, had made a good impression on arrival by affectionately greeting the only canine member of the panel. Dash returned the compliment by licking his fingers and sniffing his shoes. Geoff confessed to being a 'dog man' and owner himself.

'Really, what breed?' I asked.

'A Nova Scotia Duck Tolling Retriever,' he replied in one breath, as if reciting a tongue-twister.

'Sorry... a *what*?' This was a new one on me and the *All-Colour Book of Dogs* was upstairs in my office.

He smiled patiently and repeated himself, then added, 'A sort of duck-hunting dog. Ours isn't actually used for duck shoots any more but she still loves the water. A great family pet if you're out in the country.'

Geoff's catering firm was on the edge of the Cotswolds. Hardly a wilderness but certainly 'country' by Oxfordshire standards.

As he perched on the armchair opposite us, I had a good chance to size him up. Geoff was short and alert. Thick-ribbed cords and a jacket and tie gave him the air of a seventies TV comedian. When he smiled, as he did often, his eyes sparkled as if he was already two jokes ahead. Every now and again, he extended an index finger and pushed his glasses further up his nose. With him was a baggy leather briefcase from which he produced a clipboard and pen. It soon became clear he knew all the questions, and most of the answers, by heart.

'Why don't we start with you telling me about the shape of the day?' he began, disarmingly.

We'd established over the phone that Geoff already had some experience of catering at the abbey. This was another big plus in his favour. In reply to his question, Sarah outlined the rough itinerary. Geoff listened eagerly and nodded.

'And what about the menu? Have you had any thoughts?'

Our only thought was that which had informed the wedding planning so far: to keep it simple and the cost modest.

'I see,' said Geoff, sensing he'd finally been given the green light. 'Well, the first thing I'd recommend is looking at the five set menus we offer...'

I could relax; we could relax. Here was a man whose professional pedigree was obviously not in doubt. As he continued to expand on the relative merits of Prosecco versus champagne and linen, cutlery and glassware etiquette, Sarah and I sat back on the sofa like passengers in a chauffeur-driven sedan. We'd found our caterer. Dash, as if in agreement, yawned and flopped to the ground contentedly.

There were two things, however, which Geoff acknowledged he didn't provide: the furniture and a wedding cake. Inspired by his efficiency, I didn't think this would be a problem. I could search online for furniture suppliers – trestle tables for the serving and bar staff; round tables and chairs for the guests. As for the wedding cake, I sat down at my desk one morning in early March to find a torn-out magazine article in my in tray. Sarah had obviously been doing some research herself on the sly. Next to a headline which read 'Crazy about Cupcakes' was a glossy photo of a five-tiered stand loaded with mouth-watering little cakes. Each was topped by swirls of thick icing in chocolate, strawberry or vanilla. According to the article, cupcakes were 'infinitely more cute and customizable' than a traditional wedding cake. They were also a lot less messy and pricey. OK, so we'd miss out on that album-ready pose of husband and wife cutting the cake. I wasn't that bothered. When my brother Paul had got married in Barcelona, he and his new wife had cut their enormous wedding cake with a three-foot ceremonial sword. Some things just can't be upstaged. Sarah was right – cupcakes were the way to go.

We'd also made good progress in drawing up our list of invitees. Since neither of us felt it was fair for one 'side' to outnumber the other, we'd agreed to split the sixty-plus guests down the middle. The 'kiddie question', however, proved a stumbling block. To invite or not to invite the little blighters? Weddings with children in attendance can be joyous affairs. There's something about having the next generation there as witnesses – with all the hope and spontaneity they embody – which makes the day infinitely more meaningful. But children are also noisy and random. Wails during the ceremony, accidents, breakages, the extra complication of child-portions, not to mention stressed out parents usually means tears before bedtime. Child-free weddings are just that much more...

manageable. By the same token, they can also be boozy and soulless events.

After a brief wrangle – with Sarah pro-kids and me anti-chaos – we decided to invite children of close family and babes-in-arms only. If the occasion lacked anything by way of childish unpredictability, then this would be amply compensated for by having Dash along.

Being a freelancer means it's difficult to decline the offer of work... *any* work. Most phone calls go something like the following:

'Hi, Andrew. How's it going?'

'Oh, you know, comfortably busy.'

'I realise it's incredibly short notice but are you available next week at all?'

'Next week... hmm. Let me check.'

(Pause while I'm snow-blinded by my diary, empty except for a trip to the vet's with Dash and lunch with a fellow freelancer.)

'As it happens, I've actually got a window next week. What did you have in mind?'

There then follows a chat where, after a suitable amount of deliberation, I agree to do the job at whatever price is offered and by whatever deadline.

In mid-March, I received a phone call which was a little out of the ordinary. When it came to specifics about the job, the voice on the other end of the line surprised me by saying: 'Russia. A week of seminars south of Moscow. We can fast-track your visa but need an answer by tomorrow.'

Russia? A country which stretches from Europe and the shores of the Baltic Sea across ten time zones to the Sea of Japan. It has the culture of St Petersburg; the desolation of Siberia. Best of all, I was informed that the job would involve taking four successive overnight trains, the first of which followed the same route out of Moscow as the Trans-Siberian Express. But giving seminars? Editing was now my main source of freelance income and I'd not been a regular in the classroom or lecture hall for five years or more. Was I up to it? Could I bluff my way through a whole week? Of course I could. What's more, it was a once-in-a-lifetime, a dream opportunity; it was... completely impossible. How could I leave Sarah to look after Dash on her own? There was no way she could take a week off work at such short notice.

Sarah disagreed. 'Oh, no – you *must* go! Definitely. Don't worry about us. I can get up early to walk Dash before work and ask someone to drop round at lunch. I'll be back again in the evening. Dash will only be on her own for a few hours – it's just a week after all.'

It was just a week, but I also knew it would be a tough one for Sarah. It meant a week of walks in the dark, a full day's work, racing home to mix Dash's food and then back out to walk her, again in the dark. With her routine disrupted, Dash would almost certainly play up. She'd be disobedient on her walks and moody all evening. Could I really inflict that on Sarah?

'Listen,' she said, 'Dash is *our* dog, after all. Why don't you let me take over for a change?'

She had a point. Maybe the work, wedding planning *and* dog parenting had gone to my head. Sarah could handle it, of course she could. My wife-to-be was more than a match for Bitch of the Year.

Moscow was vast and completely gridlocked. The journey from the airport to the hotel took well over two hours, crawling between banks of dirty brown snow which had been ploughed to the side of the road. Every so often, over the tops, I caught glimpses of huge advertising hoardings or churches with domes like psychedelic fruit.

Since I spoke no Russian apart from the few words I'd cribbed from a guide book on the plane, it'd been arranged for me to be accompanied by an interpreter on each leg of my trip. Irina was an attractive Muscovite in her early twenties with heavy make-up, jet black ringlets of hair and an unsettling habit of giggling at everything I said. 'I live in Oxford' – this got a giggle. 'It's my first visit to Russia' – another giggle. 'I recently adopted a greyhound and am getting married to my girlfriend in September' – an absolute fit of giggles ensued. God help her, I thought, if I say something genuinely funny. She'll probably have a heart attack.

By the time we got to the hotel it was almost midnight and I was keen to get some sleep. Irina reassured me that the university faculty where I'd be giving my seminar the following day was just round the corner from the hotel. I'd talk for an hour about language teaching, field questions and then schmooze with the head of the faculty over lunch. What could be simpler? She even drew me a map and said she'd be waiting at the entrance. I thanked her; she giggled; I went up to my room and slept heavily.

The alarm on my phone had been ringing so long it had switched itself off. It was now too late for breakfast and, if I didn't get a shift on, I'd miss the start time of my seminar as well. I threw on my clothes, double-checked I had my handouts in my bag and scampered downstairs and out of the hotel. According to Irina's map, the university faculty was no more than 100 metres from the hotel.

After a sprint which even Dash would've been proud of, I arrived at an imposing square edifice from the Soviet era... but where was the entrance? And where were the teachers and students, for that matter? Perhaps I had the map upside-down? I paced quickly around the side of the building and, breezing through an open gate, found myself in a small courtyard. Directly opposite was an archway with a set of steps leading up. Those large, lit windows on the first floor must be the classrooms. Also directly opposite me – and barring access to the steps – was a strange Wendy house with a metal roof. I stared at it for a few seconds before realising it was a dog kennel. A battered metal dish the size of a washing-up bowl was on the ground next to it with dark patches on the concrete where the water had been sloshed out. Surely a university building didn't need a guard dog? Were the students that unruly?

At any rate, I was already late and would have to get past it to reach the stairs and classrooms. I took half a dozen confident but quiet steps; something stirred in the kennel. I stopped and put my head on one side to listen. Nothing. If I was quick, I could skip past and race up the steps. Suddenly, there was a loud bark followed by the blur of a black and tan shape hurtling towards me with its teeth bared. At the same instant, every single hair on my body stood on end. I pirouetted and sprinted back in the direction I'd come, losing a shoe in the process and almost falling over. Behind me there was the sound of dragging metal like a ship's anchor being let down, followed by a thud. The barking continued unabated.

Having reached what I hoped was a safe distance, I glanced back to see a dog which could only be described as a cross between a Rottweiler and a grizzly bear. I made a mental note to check in the *All-Colour Book of Dogs* for a breed of 'Siberian bear-dog' if I ever got back to the UK alive. For now, the beast was straining at the end of a heavy metal chain fastened to the kennel. When it barked, I could see the vivid pink of its gums and bright white fangs. Slobber dripped from its massive jaws which made it look rabid or, at the very least, a messy eater.

Most distressing of all, there at its feet, was the cast-off shoe I'd lost in the chase. One of a pair of black Yves St Laurent loafers that were going to be my wedding shoes. The problem now was how on Earth to get it back? Although I'd made a reasonable start in training Dash, I was certainly no 'dog-whisperer'. The creature in front of me didn't look like it would respond to anything except a blow from a hefty club. Taking care to keep well out of range, I crouched down and held out my hand; it strained even more wildly to get at me: a Friday-night drunk being held back by mates. As it reared up on its hind legs, I noted with mild interest that it was a bitch. And I'd thought Dash was aggressive in the early days! This bear-dog was a real bitch and no mistake. I tried making a shushing sound and then took another baby step in its direction. The barking redoubled in volume and ferocity. No, it was no good. I was already late for the seminar. Reluctantly, I'd have to abandon my shoe to Cerberus.

After walking quickly and slightly uncomfortably back to the hotel and asking at reception, I eventually found the faculty building 100 metres in the *other* direction. Irina was standing at the entrance looking worried but waved when she saw me.

'You're late,' she giggled.

'I know,' I said. 'I'm *really* sorry – I had a bit of a… well, an encounter.'

She glanced down at my shoeless right foot. The navy blue sock was already dusty.

'Don't ask,' I said, shaking my head grimly in frustration.

Irina clapped her hand to her mouth and, for once, didn't giggle.

Before stepping in front of the audience of 150 teachers, academics and postgraduate students, I decided to remove my remaining shoe. Call it the symmetrical approach. If I acted completely normal, I reasoned, perhaps they wouldn't even notice. My socks were dark, after all. Maybe they'd look like the slimmest of slip-ons and I'd get away with it. Affecting a kind of hippy nonchalance, I ambled into the lecture theatre, mounted the stage and then snuck behind a large lectern.

Thankfully, the seminar was a great success. Ninety minutes on *The Peculiarities of English Idioms* flew by and afterwards, the head of the faculty remarked how much he'd enjoyed it: 'Yes, especially the decision to lecture in your socks. Most *peculiar*, I must confess.' The final ignominy came when Irina presented me with my missing shoe, courtesy of the caretaker from the bear-dog's building. Apart from scratch marks on the leather and a large hole in the heel – presumably where it'd been carried back to the monster's lair – it was surprisingly intact. Whether it was still smart enough for the wedding, however, was debatable.

A week later, I was lying on the top bunk of a Russian train compartment. On the other bunks were three fellow travellers, all fast asleep and snoring. Through a gap in the blind I could see out the window – miles of luminescent snow broken only by ranks of black pine trees. It was late, very late. The past seven days had gone by in a blur of talks, meals and bizarre but entertaining encounters. Each evening, I'd been loaded onto a train by my interpreter-cum-companion for that particular city and thundered off in a new direction. I'd found my compartment, introduced myself to my fellow passengers in awful Russian and then fielded their curious questions which were often in excellent English. They were delighted to hear I was enjoying my first visit to Russia, and even more delighted to sample my supplies of tea and organic chocolate. This went on till the early hours, at which point they'd strip off, haul themselves onto their bunks and pass out until breakfast. By the time I'd wrestled to get my clothes off and my pyjamas on, while still under the sheets, I was exhausted myself. I was also desperately homesick.

I missed Sarah immensely. A week away from home had given me the chance to reflect on our story so far. I remembered when we'd first got together – a Saturday evening in September two and a half years before. Nothing about the day had suggested it would change my life. It was reasonably warm; I was happy. I was holding down a half-decent job and trying to buy a flat. My dad was alive but unwell. When I walked into the party in east Oxford, I might have even seemed a bit cocky – saluting friends and stashing my beers in the fridge. Sarah was in a small group outside in the garden. I remembered strolling out and seeing her – a tall, upright woman with a naturally beautiful face. Those cheekbones. When she spoke, her voice was low and soft, making me think of a yoga teacher. She had the same aura of calm. We chatted. At some point, we moved back into the house and stood in the kitchen, not opposite each other, but side by side. I was intensely aware of how close our bare arms were. A hair's breadth... then less than a hair. For a week afterwards, we texted each other love notes. We met for a drink and went for a meal – our first date at Oxford Thai.

Not that it was that simple. Sarah already had a boyfriend. I spoke to my parents when next in Stafford. After years of floundering around, I'd finally met an amazing and beautiful woman... but she was taken. They listened to the story sympathetically. Then my dad, a Yorkshireman and never normally one to get confessional, cleared his throat.

'When I first met your mother, she was engaged.'

'You've never told me that.'

He nodded. Mum smiled.

'All right, so there wasn't a ring on her finger. But she was promised to some other bloke.'

'What did you do?'

'Well, I waited.'

'Waited till what?'

'Till she saw I was a better proposition. You know, the gentle suitor stuff.'

'But… but wasn't that a bit awkward?'

'A bit.'

'What your father's trying to say is that it was awkward for me,' chipped in Mum. 'It left me with a choice to make.'

'Right. But you made it, obviously.'

'Yes, and don't regret it… well, most of the time, that is!'

Dad, weak as he was, laughed at this and stuck his tongue out at Mum like a naughty child.

I'd returned to Oxford with a renewed sense of hope. If Sarah and I were meant to be together, then it would happen. I'd play the gentle suitor like my dad advised. The boyfriend – who Sarah later claimed was only a casual fling – was duly nudged aside. The way was clear for our autumn love to bloom.

And what about Dash? Did I miss her during my Russian trip? For six months we'd been constant companions, often no more than a few metres apart. Some days at home when the phone didn't ring, Dash was the only soul I talked to for eight hours straight. My waking hours were shaped by her needs, from her walks and feeds to putting her to bed. They say a dog can have only one master. Dash had two – a mother and a father figure. Ironically, the roles had been reversed. I'd become her mother figure; the one who fed and dressed her, who disciplined her if she stepped out of line; the one who she ran to if hurt or in trouble. Sarah had taken on the role of father figure – always ready with a smile and stroke – whose return from work was a cause for celebration. It meant an end to a day of dozing and boredom for Dash. As soon as the side gate slammed shut, Dash would jump up and stand at the conservatory door. She stretched and wagged her tail when she caught sight of Sarah; she pawed the glass and whined. Sarah's homecoming was the signal for the good times to begin – a noisy kitchen, cooking smells and scraps, followed by the warmth of the lounge and the comforting drone of TV. Sometimes the parenting parallels were comical. After a day when Dash had misbehaved – stubbornly refusing to toilet at lunchtime or having a go at other dogs – I readily handed Dash over to Sarah as she stepped in the door, with maternal-sounding complaints such as 'She's been impossible today, you take her,' or 'I've had it up to here with her this afternoon'.

During my week away, Sarah reported Dash had been a model dog, no less. Typical.

It was the first outing for Sarah, Dash and me since my return from Russia and we'd chosen an aristocratic destination – Blenheim Palace. A walk there is a double pleasure. Besides the fresh air and sunshine, there's the sheer space and beauty of the grounds. Swathes of lush grass, lakes and islets, bridges, clumps of shady saplings and enormous oaks as old as the palace itself. Most striking in March are the daffodils. Thick clumps of them are everywhere – yellow trumpets sounding the arrival of spring.

It was a fine day and a good time to try Dash without her muzzle again. How could she possibly be aggressive towards other members of the animal kingdom in a setting like this? Sarah and I strolled the paths hand in hand; Dash roved ahead on the flexi-lead with the white tip of her tail flicking from side to side. We chatted about the wedding. With six months to go, it felt like things would only get busier from here. Spring and summer were sure to shoot past. Still, we'd already booked the venue and hotel; we'd met the celebrant, found our caterer and sent out our invites. We'd even seen our cèilidh band. Not too bad for three months' work. That said, the lack of a proper engagement ring still played on my mind, and there were the wedding rings to find, too. Sarah still proudly wore the 'holding ring' she'd dug up in December, but I felt I owed her something more permanent.

Down a long straight drive was Blenheim Palace in all its baroque splendour. I adored this view – the spreading arms of its architecture, the way the sun reflected off the golden stone walls. I could even imagine driving through the huge wrought iron gates, tossing the footman the keys to my Jag and skipping up the steps. Sarah and Dash would be at the doorway to greet me – one wearing a diamond-studded ring, the other a collar of soft leather.

'Hang on,' said Sarah, 'I need the loo. You wait here with Dash and I'll nip to the café.'

So much for the daydream. I sighed and lay down in the grass. For once, instead of standing round aimlessly, Dash lay down too. I put my head back in the grass and gazed upwards. Nothing but blue sky and birdsong. Dash wriggled so she was resting against my leg – one man and his dog; no muzzle. A picture of tranquillity. I drifted off and only came round when Sarah returned and kissed me awake.

The route back to the car passed through Woodstock, the posh town on the edge of Blenheim Palace grounds. We knew about the jeweller's but hadn't planned to go. Dash, it seemed, had other ideas. She gazed through the glass and wouldn't budge. I looked in at the window myself to see a tasteful collection of rings, earrings, bracelets and necklaces. Suddenly I was aware of eyes looking back at me through the glass. Or not so much looking at me as looking at Dash. A woman leaned forward, smiled and beckoned us to come in, but again she seemed to address the gesture to Dash. Bemused, I turned to Sarah. What was going on? Some kind of animal communion? Sarah shrugged. Then the woman opened the door and said hello. This broke the spell and Dash, never one to turn down the offer of an open doorway, promptly walked into the shop.

Christel Weiss was in her forties but had a twenty-something figure. Her jewellery was chic, her hair styled and her green eyes those of a fairytale fortune teller. When she spoke, she had the trace of a central European accent which made her seem even more mysterious.

'What a gorgeous dog. Sorry, I just had to meet her. She is a she… isn't she?'

I nodded enthusiastically. 'Yes, she's a greyhound. Dash… her name's Dash.'

Christel, it transpired, was keen to get a dog. She'd built up the jewellery business herself and worked six days a week, often finishing late in the evening. A dog would be the perfect companion, she felt, but up till now she'd only ever had cats. She'd set her heart on a Bernese mountain dog, a puppy, and had already been in touch with a suitable breeder abroad. They'd informed her that no puppies would available for a month, so in the meantime, she was considering other breeds. Did we think greyhounds would be suitable?

'Well, they're certainly lazy… if you're looking for something to hang out in the shop,' I said.

'And funny too,' added Sarah. 'Dash has all sorts of charming little quirks.' She told Christel about roaching and Dash's comedy run.

'They're easy on the maintenance front,' I said. 'Teeth-cleaning twice a week but a bath just once or twice a year. They groom themselves really – I suppose they're quite like cats in that sense. Very clean, quiet and even a teeny bit aloof.'

Christel was nodding and her eyes shone even brighter. I felt I should perhaps give her the complete picture.

'There are downsides though. With so many adults up for adoption, it's hard to get one as a puppy. Then there's the whole walking on the lead thing… and how they get on – or not – with small dogs or cats. Not to mention squirrels.'

Christel frowned. I gave her the abridged version of some of Dash's antics in the park.

As we spoke, Dash leaned against my leg and started to whine softly. I asked Christel whether she'd mind if we let Dash off the lead. There was nowhere to go in the shop after all – display cabinets at one end and a curved counter-cum-workbench and a consultation table at the other.

'Be my guest,' she said, with the same bewitching smile we'd seen through the window. I unclipped Dash's lead and she did a circuit of the room, sniffing as she went.

The conversation turned to jewellery. Christel made most of the pieces in the shop herself. As well as a high-tech lamp and magnifying glass, the workbench had all sorts of metalworking tools scattered over it: files, pliers, buffers, a soldering iron. Since we'd not exactly come into the shop of our own accord, I felt I could be a bit cheeky.

'Tell me, how much does it cost to make a diamond ring these days?'

'Well… that depends on the budget,' laughed Christel, 'and that in turn informs the diamond and the metal.'

I looked at Sarah. This sounded interesting. So interesting that we decided to let Christel in on the fact that we were getting married in September. We also mentioned the fact that Dash might well be our ring bearer.

The budget for the engagement ring was £500, which I'd pay myself, and we were hoping to get both wedding rings for two hundred and fifty each from the joint budget. That gave us a total of a grand to spend. Would that amount buy even *one* ring in Christel's shop? She assured us it would and, if we were artful in our choices, could just about be stretched to buy all three! Time to take a seat at the consultation table. By now, Dash had finished sniffing the perimeter of the shop. Ever so casually, she slipped past the table and stuck her head into a floor-mounted safe, the door of which was ajar.

'Dash! Come out of there!' I shouted. 'Sorry, she's not a jewel thief. Just very inquisitive.'

Christel laughed and reached round to stroke Dash. Dash rested her chin on Christel's forearm and gazed at her with chocolate eyes.

'So, let's just go over it again,' said Christel, looking at her notes on a little pad. 'For the engagement ring: single yellow diamond, raised setting. The ring itself made of palladium.'

We nodded. After hearing the low-down on the type of diamond we could actually afford, Sarah had decided to go for something unusual. I knew from the bit of research I'd done back in November that coloured diamonds were considered 'impure'. The structural defect itself determines the colouration, and means they can come in a range of rainbow colours. The diamond Sarah had chosen was a bright yellow – a springtime yellow; a daffodil yellow. It would be a memento of a lovely day out at Blenheim Palace as well as our Big Day in the future. It was sunny and happy whereas the colourless diamonds we saw seemed too ice-cool. The raised setting would have the effect of making the diamond look a little bigger than it actually was. As for the metal, palladium, we were assured, was an alternative to platinum. It was pale like platinum; it was hard like platinum; it was cheaper than platinum. Christel continued her summary.

'And two bands for the wedding rings, again palladium. Sarah's will have a curve... to accommodate the raised setting of the engagement ring next to it. Andrew's will have some sort of... design. Am I right?'

I'd sat patiently for the past half hour, murmuring approvingly while Sarah had made her choices; I'd even taken Dash for a stroll round the block – not out of indifference but because I didn't want Sarah to be rushed into a decision. When it came to my turn, I knew I wanted something simple but personal. Instead of a highly polished ring, I opted for a brushed, matt look. Christel had said that palladium, unlike platinum, discolours at high temperature. This meant it could take a simple design. I liked the idea but would have to give the design itself some thought.

Sarah and I chatted giddily on the drive home. Neither of us could really believe it. Three bespoke rings... in one afternoon! The engagement ring would be ready to try for size in April. At the next consultation, I'd tell Christel about any ideas I'd had for the design of my wedding ring and we'd proceed from there.

'And all because of you, Dash! Good girl!!' cried Sarah, turning back to look at her.

I angled the rear-view mirror in time to see Dash sit up serenely on her haunches, as if for a round of applause.

The paws of Tolstoy the borzoi were resting on my shoulders. I was nose-to-nose with a giant.

'What have you been feeding him – fertiliser?' I said sideways to Ryan as Tolstoy continued to give me the eye.

'Tolstoy, down,' said Ryan and smiled broadly. Tolstoy got down.

'The usual stuff,' he said in answer to my question, 'beef stew, sausages, biscuits, chews…'

Ryan and I had arranged to take a walk over Oxford City Golf Club and it was the first time I'd seen Tolstoy for a month. Dash was now completely dwarfed in comparison. The two dogs looked like different species rather than different breeds. As we walked up the overgrown footpath towards the golf course, Dash pulled on the lead to keep in front. She took two steps to Tolstoy's one, but still refused to take second place to a mere puppy – even one as gargantuan as Tolstoy. On reaching the top of the path, we all paused to catch our breath. The fairways of the golf course stretched out in every direction, deep green corridors trimmed to perfection.

'Are you really sure it's all right for the dogs to race about on here?' I asked Ryan.

'Sure,' he reassured me, oozing confidence as usual. 'I've been up here dozens of times. There aren't many golfers at this time of day anyway. Hounds need a good sprint off the lead or they'll have too much pent-up energy. I'm telling you, Dash spends way too much time on the lead as it is. That's probably why she's funny with other dogs. Essentially, it's fear. Snap first and sniff later. That damn muzzle you used to use probably didn't help either.'

I hadn't expected the lecture but took Ryan's advice on the chin. As a three-time dog owner, I thought he should know what he was talking about.

'What if… what if they don't come back?' I asked weakly.

'They'll come back,' said Ryan. 'You've told me yourself that Dash's recall has improved no end.'

'Yes, but that's in the garden!'

Ryan gave a dismissive wave of his hand, so I gave in and finally unclipped her harness. She and Tolstoy immediately trotted off with their noses sweeping for scents.

As we walked after them, I felt a little surge of confidence and kinship. Ryan and I were roughly the same age. Here we were: two hound owners out for a stroll like old pals. Feeling I could open up a little, I talked about my recent trip to Blenheim, choosing the engagement ring and the fast-approaching wedding.

'That's quite a story', he smiled. 'Are you sure you're ready?'

'Ready for what?'

'Married life.'

'Yeah – why shouldn't I be?'

'No reason. Rather you than me, though.'

Ryan went on to reveal he'd already been engaged to three separate women and broken it off each time. I couldn't decide whether he was being deliberately insensitive or just plain honest. Perhaps I should say something to defend the institution, given the fact that in six months I'd be a card-carrying, ring-sporting member of the marriage club myself. I was just about to speak up when Ryan beat me to it.

'Check out the dogs!' he said, nodding his head.

Dash and Tolstoy were coursing down one of the fairways. Tolstoy was taking long, free-flowing strides, but Dash was quicker. I suddenly felt a buzz of pride and adrenalin.

'Go on, Dash!' I shouted. 'Looks like she's got him licked.' I turned to Ryan triumphantly.

Ryan scoffed. 'I should hope so. Tolstoy's giving away more than four years to Dash. Anyway, she'll overshoot if she's not careful.'

By now Dash was two lengths in front and heading straight for the flag of the putting green as it fluttered in the breeze. Two golfers, the size of spent matches in the distance, were deliberating over their putts. A black streak shot across the green. The golfers looked up and then stared back down the fairway in amazement. Tolstoy had pulled up short and was already trotting in our direction.

'Time to test that recall of yours,' said Ryan gleefully.

'DA-ASH, COME!'

Dash slowed and looped back round towards us. As she bisected the green again at top speed, I could see one of the golfers raise his club and shake it in outrage. Was he thinking of taking a swing at her? He would be better off trying to connect with a comet.

April

Sarah and I were off to The Dogs. A return trip to Oxford Greyhound Stadium, the scene of Dash's glory days. It was the first and last stadium she'd raced in and the sporting home of Bitch of the Year. We'd been given a pair of freebie tickets by Peter, Dash's ex-owner. I could barely contain myself.

Diligent to a fault, I researched how to bet the day before. The most important indicator of how a greyhound will run is its form guide, with the results of the last few races of each dog included in the racing programme for the evening. If the form shows that a dog has been clocking up regular first and second places, it'll obviously be a sound proposition for a flutter. Other important factors include a dog's age and the grade of race. Generally speaking, a male dog reaches its peak at about two years old, with bitches peaking a year older at three. In the UK, greyhound races are divided into nine grades: A9 (the lowest) to A1. These function roughly like the divisions in football, with A1 being the equivalent of the Premier League and the grade where you can expect to see the fastest, fittest hounds.

Of course, as with any kind of betting, there are also the odds to consider. Despite being reasonably numerate, I'm embarrassed to say I still don't completely grasp the system. To this day, I've got no idea whether a dog – or a horse for that matter – with odds of 15/8 is more likely to win than one at 9/4. I remember my dad would regularly bet on big sporting events, the foremost of which was the Grand National. Over breakfast, the family would be shown a double page spread of runners and riders from that morning's newspaper.

'Lady and gents,' he'd say to my mum and us three boys, 'choose your mounts'.

We would pore over the form and 'um' and 'ah', before doing what ninety-five per cent of the population probably did – make our selection according to the horses' names or the jockeys' silks. Funny names and favourite colours were just far easier to understand.

Although we couldn't take Dash herself to the greyhound stadium, Sarah and I did invite a couple of friends, and their dog-loving kids. The parents, Sheila and Pash, travelled a lot for work, so having a family dog was unfortunately out of the question. Their two youngest children were identical twin girls of ten. Long blonde hair, clear complexions and bright, blue eyes – they looked like a pair of Alices in Wonderland. The elder brother, George, was thirteen and going out on a Saturday night with his parents – and worse still, with his parents' friends – was perhaps a bit of an ordeal. To mitigate this discomfort, he spent the entire evening in a camouflaged hooded top. The hood was zipped up under his chin, leaving a drainpipe-sized hole through which he could communicate.

'Hi, George,' I said into the hole as we stood in the stadium car park.

'Hi.'

'How's school?'

'OK.'

'Still top of the class?'

''Fraid so.'

As we all strode off in the direction of the entrance, I couldn't help wondering what to expect. I'd known very little about greyhound racing until adopting Dash, but vaguely associated it with colourful language (plenty of it), booze (in abundance) and cigarettes (chain-smoked). Had we made a mistake bringing children along?

Upstairs in the two-tiered grandstand we discovered a swish-looking restaurant at one end and a lengthy bar at the other. The side of the grandstand that faced the track was a huge wall of glass so spectators could follow the races without even venturing outside. Banks of TV screens blazed overhead, some showing live action from other stadiums and others with the odds for the first race of the evening. The bar end was already crowded; the smell of beer and chips overpowering. Large groups of men in collared shirts stood round eyeing up equally large groups of women. It was more like a nightclub than a sporting venue. There were hen and stag parties in full swing, with the usual regalia of L-plates, miniskirts, Stetsons and fancy dress. It was bustling, bright and raucous. In contrast, the restaurant end was more sedate and favoured the older patron. Most diners were smartly dressed, with more than a few outfits looking like they'd been dusted off from the nineteen eighties. At least one elderly gent was wearing head-to-foot tweed and a bowtie.

'What do you think?' whispered Pash as he sidled up to me. 'It's a bit lairy at the bar end for the kids... and we didn't book a table in the restaurant.'

I suggested we look downstairs. Pensioners with pots of tea at bingo-style tables; kids running round while parents chatted or laughed with friends; groups of workers from the nearby Cowley car plant, still in their overalls and standing in clumps. This was more like it. I was starting to see that there was something for everyone at The Dogs. We'd begin here and then move outside to the terrace once the races got under way.

Over a beer, I examined the racing programme. Twelve races were scheduled – one every fifteen minutes – which meant a total of seventy-two dogs would charge over the finishing line during the course of the evening. I pondered how much money the assembled crowd would bet, and how much of that sum actually went towards the long-term welfare of the dogs themselves. Before coming, Sarah and I had actually questioned whether, as bona fide retired greyhound owners, we should be putting money into the industry's pocket at all. But curiosity had got the better of us. Seeing such an important part of Dash's past would help us understand her present, we felt.

As he dealt two-pound coins across the table, Pash gave his kids a potted guide to the evening's entertainment. It turned out he knew more than I did, explaining they could bet inside at the Tote, the 'official' bookmakers, or outside by the track with the 'independents'. The difference, he explained, was that the odds tended to change quicker with the independents and they might get a more favourable starting price, and consequently a better return on their money if they backed the winner. Still zipped into his hooded top, George nodded like a robot receiving operating instructions.

'There are four main types of bet,' Pash went on. 'Win, Place, Forecast and Trio. Win is self-explanatory – you choose which dog will come first. Place is when you choose two dogs you think will finish first or second, in either order. Forecast is the same, but you predict the correct order. Finally, Trio is…' The twins had started to spin their coins on the table top and glaze over.

'Well, a Trio is… unlikely,' he said with a wry smile.

George was now holding the open programme up to the hole in his hooded top as if hoovering the information off the page.

The first race was an A1 grade over 450 metres, which meant the calibre of dogs would be respectable.

'Why don't you and I bet on the same dog?' asked Sarah, a bit baffled by the form notes.

'No way,' I replied. 'It's every man, woman and child for themselves tonight.'

'Spoilsport!' Sarah pouted and gave me a playful smack with her programme.

I settled on a greyhound called Sutton Gem. She'd come first or runner-up in three of her last five races. At two years and nine months, she was the perfect age for a racing bitch. Of course, I had to choose a bitch for my first bet – not only was Sutton Gem black like Dash, but, according to the breeding info, she actually shared the same father or 'sire' as Dash, Droopys Woods. Sutton Gem's starting price was 3/1 – not the favourite, but not a long shot either. Perfect. We decided to make our first bet inside at the Tote. As we queued up, Sarah told me she'd noticed one of the dogs in the same race was actually trained by Ron, Dash's trainer. She said she was backing it out of 'loyalty for the kennels'. I wavered – perhaps I should do the same? – but then decided to stick to my guns. Besides, Sarah would accuse me of copying her. I duly put my two pounds on Sutton Gem to win. Start boldly, I thought, none of this Place or Forecast nonsense.

As we went outside to the terrace clutching our betting slips, we were buffeted by a blast of cold air. Unseasonably chilly for April, it didn't seem to prevent most of the other punters outside from standing around in T-shirts and cropped tops. This was obviously where the hard core hung out, but there was also an excitement and bristling good humour that had been lacking inside. Four independent bookies stood on boxes next to a low brick wall at the front of the terrace. The odds boards were propped up behind them like placards for a golf sale. Each bookie was busy in the last few minutes before the race started, calling out the bets to an assistant who wrote them down in a ledger without looking up. Though not yet dusk, the large, lozenge-shaped track itself was already floodlit at the bends, with a gantry of lights above the finishing line. I looked over to the other side of the track, to the patch of ground where Sarah and I had first met Dash over six months ago. The same collection of trainers' vans and trucks was parked in a line. What would have happened if we'd decided not to take her? Would she have been any less happy? Would we have eventually got a different dog… or given up the search altogether? The tinny sound of trumpets over the public address system interrupted my train of thought. The dogs were about to be paraded in front of the grandstand.

The first dog was a black male, wearing a loose white overcoat, presumably to keep his muscles warm until he was put into the trap. The handler paused and lifted up the overcoat to show the racing jacket to the clerk of the course – a white number one on a red background. The clerk nodded with a smooth formality and beckoned the next greyhound, a big grey male. A peculiar fact about greyhounds is that, despite their name, they're not often grey. Officially classed as 'blue', this one was a slate colour which made him seem all the more attractive and ethereal. He was also the joint favourite. Next up was Sutton Gem – my chosen bitch and the Dash lookalike. She pranced and pulled at her lead; she licked her lips inside the wire muzzle. I felt confident I'd backed a sure-fire winner. Two more greyhounds passed and then Ron's greyhound, handled by Peter himself. Sarah and I wanted to wave at him but thought better of it.

'That's Dash's original owner,' I pointed out to the twin girls. They'd been round to our house a few weeks earlier and had met Dash in the garden.

'Why did he give Dash away?' one of the twins asked.

'Because she retired from racing,' I replied to both of them, as if they were one double-headed entity.

'Wasn't she any good?' asked the other twin.

'Yes... but he wanted to find a nice home for her,' I said, wishing I'd never started the conversation in the first place.

By now the dogs had been walked to the trap – a long, cage-fronted box which could be wheeled quickly on and off the track. Leads, collars and overcoats were removed and each dog was put into the correct compartment. The handlers then scurried off as if a bomb was about to explode. Silence. The twin girls bounced up and down like organ stops; George's hood pointed in the direction of the trap.

Over the public address, a nasal voice shouted 'Haaaare comiiiiing!' and from behind the trap there was a whirring, rattling sound like a large train set. Then the 'hare' itself came into view. I'd expected it to have ears, at least! The thing that came round the bend looked like the torn-off sleeve of a fluorescent orange jacket, travelling at about 40 miles an hour. As soon as it passed the trap, the cage-front flew up and the dogs shot out. The crowd shouted. The sight was exhilarating, so much so that I immediately forgot which number dog I'd backed and had to check the programme. Number three: Sutton Gem, wearing white. There was jostling at the first bend but already two dogs were clearly out in front. The front runners hurtled down the far side of the track, all four feet off the ground at times like I'd seen Dash do on her first solo run off the lead. Two bends later and it was all over... in less than thirty seconds.

The joint favourite had led from the start and gone on to win. Sutton Gem had come in next to last, who knows how many lengths behind. Despite the race being over, I noticed that the dogs sprinted past the winning post, racing round to the far side of the track. The hare was covered and the handlers hurried on to collect their charges. Win or lose, the dogs seemed to have enjoyed it – their tails were held high and thrashed from side to side.

An inauspicious start to my greyhound betting career. Sarah's pick, Ron and Peter's dog, had come in third. The choice of Sheila and the twins had come second; Pash and George had both backed the winner. Pash was grinning broadly and shouting 'Well done, son!' down the black hole of George's hood. Of course, there's always the next race. This time, I placed my bet with one of the independent bookies – a squat man in a long brown overcoat which made him look like a pepper mill. He took my two-pound coin and tossed it casually into a battered metal dish, giving me a numbered betting card in return. My run of bad luck turned into a streak. Fifth place again. Any consolation on hearing that George had only backed the second-place dog was denied when he revealed he'd made a Place bet.

'This doesn't mean that my pocket money will get cut, does it?' came a voice from the depths of the hood to his parents.

Some improvement came in the next race in the form of a striped dog or 'brindle' by the name of Lazy Jim, which came in second. Stubbornly, I'd refused to do anything but back it to win outright. By the time of the race after that, any idea of studying the form had gone out the window.

I'd reverted to the childhood approach of funny names and favourite colours. Call it Angie was a tiny black bitch, even smaller than Dash at 22 kg. She was no bigger than a Whippet and scampered jerkily when her handler paraded her. This was her first ever race at A9 – the lowest grade of race and the preserve of juveniles, novices and hopeless cases. The remarks in the programme for Call it Angie's solo trial the month before consisted of one word only: 'Green'. She looked frightened and it melted my heart to see her plight. I put five pounds on her to place; she came in last. George, the boy genius, had backed the favourite for a small return. I was no longer enjoying myself.

'I'm going to take a little wander,' I said to Sarah and the others. 'Think I'll pass on the next couple of races.' They went inside to warm up and I strolled round the track in the direction of the paddock. Away from the bright lights of the grandstand, the paddock was darker and quiet. Handlers were walking their dogs round a large patch of grass. Some dogs stopped to pee; others relieved themselves of a heavier load in what must have been the equivalent of pre-race nerves. But did they actually get nervous? Were they even aware of what was demanded of them?

I imagined Dash in the same situation. Would she paw at the door of the paddock kennel in excitement like she used to do in the crate when I came downstairs in the morning? As she skipped out, would she yawn that excited jaw-wrenching yawn she does when we're about to go on our afternoon walk? Perhaps she would be given a massage as a loosener – corkscrewing her tail with delight and craning her neck round to gaze at the handler. Did she sense when it was time for her race? I could see her now – keen to feel the firm sand of the track under her feet and parade past the grandstand like a gladiator before a fight. But greyhounds are not fighters, not even Dash. They are elegant, noble beasts, their shapes are signatures done with a flourish. Everything about them flows, from their neat heads to their deer-like necks; their powerful shoulders and deep, barrelled chests; their slim waists and power-packed legs; their dainty, furry catlike feet.

''Ello there!' It was Peter. He was out in the paddock and had seen me dreaming through the railings.

'What you up to then?' he asked.

'Oh… nothing,' I said, collecting myself. 'Just thought I'd come over and say thanks for the tickets. It's been really good to see where Dash used to race.'

'No problem. You won any yet? How's the bettin'?'

'Rubbish,' I said. 'Put it this way – if the bookies paid out on last place, I'd have made a fortune.'

'Ah, you don't wanna let that worry yer. It's all a bit of fun in the end.'

I thought about mentioning the wads of £20 notes I'd seen one punter hand to the bookie. Shocked, I'd watched the punter during the race as he stared fixedly at the pack of greyhounds as they entered the home straight. Whichever dog he'd backed, his face barely registered the result… but he hadn't gone to collect any winnings afterwards.

'You and Ron got any more dogs running tonight then?' I asked, changing the subject – embarrassed at coming across as a forlorn adolescent.

'One in the nine-fifty nine,' replied Peter. 'Stands a real chance an' all.'

'What's its name?'

'Yahoo Sara,' he said. 'Black and white bitch.'

'Nice name – almost the same as the wife-to-be,' I said, not sure if Peter caught the allusion.

Back at the grandstand, the kids looked tired and Sheila was checking her watch.

'Almost ten o'clock. I reckon this'll have to be our last race,' she said.

After making a month's pocket money in an evening, George opted to hold onto his winnings and sit the final race out. Sarah and I finally joined forces and bet on her namesake to win. Yahoo Sara duly obliged. First out of the trap, she never looked like anything but a dead cert. As she crossed the line, I was shouting so loudly I spat my chewing gum out by mistake. All this, and Yahoo Sara had slouched in sixth in a race just the week before. I'd discovered the world of greyhound betting was unfathomable.

On the Sunday morning after our visit to The Dogs, I walked into the conservatory and pulled up the blind with a dramatic flourish. Dash stuck her head out of the cocoon of her bed; she pricked up her ears. Something was up, something was very up. The back garden had disappeared under a duvet of pure white.

Dash sprang to her feet and stood at the door. Then she barked and jumped on the spot, either in fear or amazement.

It's just possible, I thought, that this is the first time she's ever seen snow. Who knows what kind of outdoor view she got when kennelled in her youth, and she would certainly never have raced in it. I led her outside and she sniffed circumspectly at the bright, white scene. Soft flakes filled the sky. It was like being inside a giant snow globe. A snowflake landed on her nose; Dash went cross-eyed as she inspected it. Friend or foe? A long pink tongue extended and licked it off. Cool, refreshing… even tasty. Snow was cold and wet but it was obviously all right.

Florence Park had been relocated to Lapland. The paths had disappeared and trees had grown to twice the size, all wearing snowy overcoats. Everything was smooth and pure and dazzling white. Sarah and I had woken up early and as soon as we'd seen the snow clambered into warm clothes, buckled Dash into her winter coat and headed out. Dash immediately set to foraging for smells and scents preserved from the previous day. There was absolutely no one else around; no one else awake it seemed. We let her off the lead.

It was the deepest snow for years. Fluffy to the touch, it quickly compacted into smooth balls the size and weight of peaches. I threw one at a tree trunk and it crumbled on impact.

'Take that!' I shouted at Sarah, launching another snowball in her direction.

'Ow!'

She grabbed a handful of snow and lobbed one back in reply. I ducked and threw another, which hit her square in the back as she turned around.

'Ow!! Not fair,' she cried, laughing, and floundered off through the snow in an attempt to find cover.

I needed a more worthy opponent. Someone lightning fast; someone with four legs rather than two. Dash was still rooting around in the snow a few metres away. I took aim at the red double 'D' stitched on the side of her coat. The snowball whistled over her back; she didn't look up. Another one missed her by a whisker, but the third smacked against her backside. She jumped sideways and stared at me in the canine equivalent of shock.

'Dash, catch!' I shouted and lobbed another snowball towards her.

She lifted her nose like the gun of a clay pigeon shooter and followed the snowball as it arced towards her. Then she bounded forward, opened her mouth and snapped her jaws shut. The snowball exploded, leaving a frosting of powder covering her face. By now, Sarah had rejoined us. She threw one herself and we burst out laughing when Dash repeated the trick. The funniest thing was Dash's dazed expression when the snowball disappeared. She'd followed its flight path and felt it connect, but where was it now? It was all too much. In a crazy spurt of excitement, she did her comedy run and then leapt sideways into a bank of snow, disappearing completely. Two seconds later, she burst out and charged towards us like a runaway snowplough stuck in top gear. Her eyes shone with a zesty gleam, her tongue hung out and her tail flexed from side to side in a blur. No doubt about it, she was a very happy girl.

'Have you ever wondered how we managed before we got Dash?' asked Sarah. The three of us were navigating a path through the snow on our way back home.

Dash had arrived on the scene and despite the difficulties, she'd made us both much happier. We had to admit it. We'd grown to love her and, in her own way, we were sure she loved us too.

'Why can't I help you choose the wedding dress?' I complained to Sarah.

'You just can't. You'll have to wait till the day.'

'What about my tie? You've already seen that.'

'It's just a tie. I won't see your suit if you don't want me to.'

'At least tell me what the colour will be.'

'White… or off-white.'

'And the style?'

'Simple.'

'OK, if you won't tell me about the dress, then what about the shoes?' I pressed her.

'I haven't decided yet.'

'Well, don't forget we've got the same size feet. If they're too uncomfortable on the day, we can always swap over!'

Sarah laughed but I could see she wasn't going to crack. This was one area of the wedding planning which was clearly off limits. Just when I was looking forward to getting to grips with the difference between chiffon and brocade. Instead, I'd just have to content myself with finding an appropriate suit. For the first and perhaps the only time in my life, I was going to splash out and get something bespoke.

The door of the tailor's in London's Savile Row made a shushing sound as it opened. A Persian rug, a chandelier and gilt-framed mirrors; shop assistants like footmen immaculately attired with clipped heels and clipped smiles – it was all instantly intimidating. I even noticed a deer's head on the wall. I realised I didn't have a clear idea what kind of suit I wanted and was afraid I'd come across as foolish. Thirty seconds later, the door made a shushing sound as I walked back out. I'd made an awful mistake. I was out of my depth and, more importantly, out of my class.

What now? I'd come to London especially to get a suit and, hopefully, a shirt as well. I'd even organised a dog sitter for Dash to give me the day off. The only thing I'd got for my wedding outfit so far was a tie. Admittedly, I was enormously proud of it and hadn't been able to resist showing Sarah. It was silk and thick as pitta bread, with an embroidered design in pink, red and brown. Sarah had liked it so much she suggested we use it as an unofficial swatch for the wedding colour scheme. It's a bold groom, however, who attends his wedding in nothing but a silk tie and boxer shorts. I simply had to get a suit and it had to be a good one. Surely there must be some middle ground between bespoke and off-the-peg? I decided to phone a friend. I hadn't seen Charles since the New Year visit to Camber but was sure he'd know what to do. He was a doctor, after all. Sure enough, a few minutes later, I had the name of a tailor's in Piccadilly.

'Ask for Maurice,' Charles had advised. He'd recently bought a suit there himself and been impressed by the quality, not to mention the reasonable price tag.

I imagined Maurice would be French, greying, a little stooped perhaps, with half-moon glasses and a tape measure round his neck. I wasn't even right about the tape measure. Maurice was in his mid-twenties, Dutch, and sharply but not showily dressed in a black suit with scarlet lining.

'What we do here isn't exactly bespoke,' he said in excellent English, 'instead we carry a range of unfinished suits which can be tailored to meet your requirements. If you'd care to come with me...' He swept down a set of spiral steps like a junior Count Dracula. On a clothes rail which ran the entire length of the basement room hung a variety of suits organised by size, fabric and colour. Maurice pointed out some of the salient differences – 'for a September event, I'd recommend a mid-season suit of light wool' – and then disappeared to let me peruse the collection. Feeling a lot more relaxed, I picked out a suit to try on. As soon as I glanced round for Maurice, he appeared again with an effortless smile.

Half an hour later, I had both my suit *and* shirt. The suit was pale grey with the suggestion of a check pattern; the shirt off-white with red buttons and stiff, double cuffs. Both would need alterations, however, and Maurice had pirouetted round me with pins, noting the measurements on a palm-sized computer he'd conjured from one of his sleeves.

'And would you like a monogram stitched on the shirt?' he asked at the end of the operation.

'A monogram? Oh, like my initials, you mean?'

'Three letters or numbers,' Maurice replied.

I thought for a moment. Here was my chance for a neat little surprise for Sarah.

'How about a combination of letters *and* numbers?'

Maurice nodded his consent.

'In that case, I'd like "A4S" – Andrew for Sarah.'

'It's not that I don't want to go, it's just that it's a long way.'

After a busy week which had included the trip to the tailor's in London, I was tired and whinged like a teenager. Teesside *was* a long way. Sarah had friends there she hadn't seen in months and the plan was to drive the 250 miles from Oxford on Friday night so we could make the most of the weekend. The plan was also for Dash to tag along.

After five hours on the road, we were still stuck on the northbound M1. The traffic was nose-to-tail, as was Dash, curled up on her mat in the back of the car. We'd already made one stop to feed her in the corner of a service station car park. As she tucked in, there was a sudden downpour, turning the food in her bowl from mush to gravy. I'd stood over her with an umbrella as she finished, feeling faintly ridiculous.

Finally, at one o'clock in the morning, we arrived at the house of our hosts in Stockton-on-Tees. Mel and Rich were an all-action couple. Mountain biking, trekking and camping were their leisure pursuits of choice. Mel was another friend Sarah had made while teaching English in Thailand. She'd since made the jump out of teaching and landed in human resources. Warm and sociable, it suited her down to the ground. Rich was more laid-back, doing just enough work to free up time to play his electric guitar and add to the collection of tattoos, which snaked their way up his arms and across his broad back. Mel and Rich weren't married and neither wanted kids. A dog would be great, they confessed, but full-time jobs made it difficult.

'Well, think of Dash as yours for the weekend,' I said. 'A greyhound on loan.'

Mel and Rich took me at my word. The next day, they took us for a walk on the North Yorkshire Moors. Rich led the way, wearing only a T-shirt and shorts despite a brisk wind. Round his beefy neck hung a pouch with a map and in his hand, let out to its maximum length, was Dash's flexi-lead. Dash made full use of the slack she was given, plunging into clumps of coarse grass and then bobbing up again moments later. If she thought the park was a storeroom of smells, then the moors were an emporium. Her nose never lifted more than an inch off the ground – sniffing and sneezing from one crazy scent to the next. Strands of sheep's wool caught on barbed wire were mysterious clues. Every rabbit hole was subjected to intense scrutiny; every dropping catalogued. When Rich let her clamber over rocks or up steep banks, I couldn't help sucking my teeth. Did he realise Dash wasn't that robust? Built for a life on the flat, one slip and her spindly legs could snap! That night, Dash crashed out on her mat at the foot of the stairs and uttered not a peep, whine or roo.

On the Sunday, Mel and Rich suggested an amble along the beach of the town of Redcar, followed by fish and chips. Sarah and I were already stiff from the day before and sorely tempted to head directly for the chippie. Dash, however, was up for fun. As soon as we stepped onto the promenade, she fluttered her nostrils in the sea air. Every hair on her slender body seemed to stand on end and she danced about on her white paws, eager to know which way we were going. Down on the beach, a low wind whisked off the top layer of sand, making it difficult to see without squinting. Dash must have had camel blood in her – she forged ahead, untroubled by the stinging grains.

'Why don't we let her off the lead?' said Sarah.

I looked round. At regular intervals along the beach, were weather-beaten, wooden groynes; behind us was the high beach wall; in front, the sea itself. No possible means of escape for a hound with wayward tendencies. I unclipped Dash's lead and she immediately set off at a swift pace in the direction of the water, only to reverse promptly when a brown wave rushed to greet her.

'Don't worry, Dash! It's only the sea, you've seen it before. Remember New Year at Camber?'

I remembered New Year at Camber and her 'attack' on the Cavalier puppy only too well. Dash had now been muzzle-free since our visit to Blenheim Palace in March and her behaviour had shown a steady improvement. Most of the time when I called her, she came. If sent to her mat or bed, she went there and stayed. She hadn't assaulted the furniture for months. If I could only work out why she was still testy around certain dogs.

We idled along in pairs, chatting about the wedding preparations. Dash, meanwhile, had got as far as the first wooden groyne. It came up to her chin and she stood looking over it like a horse over its stable door. As I watched, I saw her tail begin to wag slowly; then suddenly a lot faster. In one leap, a Dalmatian appeared, hurdling the groyne and Dash together. Dash spun round in pursuit. The Dalmatian had a head start but Dash was gaining with every stride. As she drew level, she growled and barged it into the water. The Dalmatian, a chunky specimen, crashed back out of the surf. He seemed to enjoy the experience. Dash closed in again for a second broadside. This time, the Dalmatian swung his rump and Dash was the one who got bumped aside. She barked in excitement, dodged back and forth boisterously; the Dalmatian galloped off like a commuter train intent on making up time.

The four of us stood there watching. 'You know,' said Rich thoughtfully, 'it's like Dash doesn't know how to play.'

I nodded. 'You're right. That's it. That's *exactly* it.'

We were absolutely cockahoop. The engagement ring was ready and looked incredible. Christel, the jeweller, smiled at us across the table. Sarah was beaming and held out her hand for me to inspect. Dash also took the opportunity to give it a sniff. The metal gleamed; the yellow diamond shone fiercely.

'Gorgeous,' I said. 'Are you pleased?'

Sarah was more than pleased. She looked like her head was spinning.

'I don't want to take it off.'

'You don't have to,' I replied nonchalantly. I'd already sent Christel a cheque for the ring in advance. This way, I figured, the magic of the occasion wouldn't be sullied by having to fumble with payment. Sarah was obviously thrilled with this act of gallantry.

It was now time to tell Christel the idea for my wedding ring. Since I hadn't told Sarah either, I was a little nervous about how it'd be received.

'Bear with me,' I said to Christel. 'On our last visit, you said the metal, palladium, discolours at high temperature.'

Christel nodded.

'So if you drilled into it, it'd change colour – right?

'Right,' she echoed. 'Exactly which colour depends on how high the temperature is, but it'd probably go a sort of grey-blue.'

'Making it stand out more?'

Again, Christel nodded.

'Well, all I'd like is three dots drilled into the ring,' I began, inclining my head slightly like a storyteller. 'Not too large or too far apart.'

Sarah looked puzzled. I glanced at her and told her with my eyes to be patient.

'This represents the number of years Sarah and I will have been together on our wedding day.'

Christel smiled; Sarah smiled broadly.

At the risk of coming across as a smart-arse, I continued. 'It's also a letter in Morse Code.'

'Which letter?' asked Sarah.

'Guess,' I said. 'Dot, dot, dot.'

She thought for a moment and then unknitted her eyebrows and smiled even more broadly.

'S… is it S?'

Now it was my turn to nod.

'Ohhh – S for Sarah!' she exclaimed, reaching across impulsively and stroking my cheek. Keen to get in on the act, Dash jostled between our seats at the table and waved her nose in the air. Sarah and I looked down at her and laughed.

'And you know what often comes right after a dot in Morse code? It's our very own ring bearer: a dash!'

May

Dash was about to step out in her spring collection. Among this season's must-haves were a classy collar with diagonal stripes and a showerproof coat. Like a lot of women, she fell between two sizes. Too big to squeeze into the coat for 'Large Whippet'; too little to fill out the one for 'Small Greyhound'. In the end, I opted for the greyhound size in pale pink. There was something demeaning, I felt, about dressing Dash in a different breed's coat.

Dash couldn't have cared less. As I tried to get the coat hole over her long nose, she fidgeted and bobbed her head like a child at the barber's. It was held in place with two ties which looped under her hips and, because they were so long, had to be tied on her back in a large floppy bow. I stepped back to check the effect. She looked the gift-wrapped horse of a jousting knight. Still, better than getting soaked to the skin, I thought. Dash was not a fan of the rain.

After eight months, I'd built up a formidable repertoire of dog walks. There were short walks, long walks and marathon walks; wet walks (with shelter), hot walks (with shade). There were dog-free walks (if Dash happened to be in confrontational mood), there were people-free walks (if I was). Even with such a variety of places for Dash and me to take our morning or afternoon constitutional, the default was still a lap round Florence Park. By now, Dash and I had met just about every dog and owner who frequented it. Each pairing had their own little routes and habits, as unswerving and predictable as the hands on a public clock. Some, like Casper the Old English sheepdog and his lookalike owner, Tony, seemed to be in the park permanently. Tony was a mine of local knowledge and we'd sometimes do a lap or two together. One morning, he even told me the history of my own terrace and every house in it. He knew where each outside toilet had once stood, the passage that linked the back gardens where coal had once been delivered, the sheds which had served as bomb shelters and were now demolished. He knew what had been behind our garden wall before the DIY superstore had been built, and what had been there before that. If I wasn't careful, a twenty-minute walk turned into a ninety-minute history lesson. I had a full-time job to do after all – a desk to get back to, emails to answer and a phone that *sometimes* rang with the offer of work.

Dash, of course, adored everyone and was adored in turn. Her particular favourites among the dog walkers were what Sarah and I affectionately nicknamed 'The Mobility Brigade'. These were the old-age pensioners who scooted around on electric buggies while their equally decrepit dogs followed on behind. As soon as we were within a few feet of a buggy, Dash would charge up and thrust her nose into the lap of the delighted pensioner. They would lavish strokes and treats on her, and shower us both with chat. Trips to the doctor, trips to the shops, trips to church – their world consisted of a series of battery-powered sorties. Each member of the Mobility Brigade shared a nodding acquaintance, with the buggies sometimes pulling up alongside each other like cabbies discussing a fare. If the weather was harsh, they'd cross with nothing more than a gloved salute from a pile of woollens and mufflers. Olive, an old campaigner with rouged cheeks and a tartan deerstalker, was one of the fastest. In her wake, she trailed a wheezing Pekingese with all the character of a feather duster. Olive surged round the park on her buggy like a runaway shopping trolley, hailing the other dog owners. Once, she'd caught me unawares and whizzed past just as I was bagging Dash's poo. With the lead in one hand, I raised the full poo bag in the other hand in a kind of awkward wave. Thinking I must be proudly showing her the fruits of Dash's labour that morning, she stuck her thumb up in approval before moving off like the Queen inspecting the armed forces. When Olive did hit the brakes and stop to chat, she wasn't shy of giving her opinion, particularly about other dog owners.

'It's not right,' she'd say about one dog owner, curling her lip in disgust, 'letting that dog hump her leg like that. No discipline – that's what it is.'

Olive reserved her sternest words for Bertie, another of the Mobility Brigade. Bertie's buggy was a clapped-out model with half a dozen wing mirrors, making it look more like a mod's Vespa from the sixties. His bulldog waddled ahead of it like an overweight bodyguard while Bertie drank tea from a flask and puffed cigarettes, letting them hang from his toothless mouth till they'd turned to ash on the front of his tracksuit. His approach was the cue for Olive to grit her teeth and change direction, wrenching her buggy round and careering off the way she'd come. Minutes later, I'd catch sight of both Olive and Bertie in the distance on another path, like two Daleks locked in a game of deadly pursuit.

With Dash now well known in the park by both owners and dogs, it became easier to experiment with letting her off the lead. In the more isolated areas of the park, I'd unclip the lead and watch her roam along happily, snuffling her nose in bunches of flowers. As soon as I caught sight of an unfamiliar dog, I'd clip the lead back on so Dash could approach the stranger at a modest speed. If she successfully greeted the other dog, I unclipped her again and she trotted off. Encouraged by this and outings further afield with Ryan and Tolstoy the borzoi, I began to let Dash off the lead more often.

One afternoon, I happened to bump into Kate and her giant greyhound, Arnie. They were on their way to meet Sally in the park. Sally had finally got her *second* greyhound and, keen to meet the new arrival, Dash and I tagged along. It was warm and the park was busy. Sally was waiting by the bandstand with Jess, her first greyhound – black all over – and a new black and white greyhound, obviously a male. Apart from looking exceptionally lean, 'Rocky' was settling in fine. Sally had already walked him off the lead without a problem.

'Rocky's great,' she said, 'a real sweetheart. I think he takes his cue from Jess in terms of confidence. No problem at all.'

Dash sniffed both ends of the newcomer and seemed to approve.

With three of the four greyhounds now off the lead, I couldn't help feeling sorry for Dash.

'Why don't you let her run with the others for a bit?' suggested Kate.

'Yes, you should – she'll be fine,' added Sally reassuringly.

'I'm not sure,' I murmured. 'I still don't completely trust her.'

Was that how I appeared then – an anxious parent, the one greyhound owner too cautious to risk letting his dog run free? Perhaps they were right. Perhaps this was the breakthrough moment. After all, what was the worst that could happen? I was sure Dash wouldn't run off with the other greyhounds close by.

'OK, OK,' I said, unclipping the lead. Dash immediately shook herself from nose to tail and the other three greyhounds crowded around her in welcome. We all set off at a slow walk. I was on edge at first, but slowly relaxed. I chatted and laughed. When it came to using a poo bag, I found I didn't have to restrain a dog with one hand and twist backwards with the other. It was all so much easier and so much more relaxing. I could imagine meandering around for hours on end; thinking deep thoughts, occasionally glancing up to check on Dash. So this was what it was *really* like to walk a dog in public. This was freedom… this was a dream.

'Arnie!' Kate's shout rang out. Dash had taken off after a squirrel and the massive white blur of Arnie was in pursuit. Close behind was the new greyhound, Rocky, with Jess bringing up the rear. All four were going flat out as if back at the track – the race was on. Dash charged through a flowerbed, knocking the heads off a row of primroses. The other three greyhounds followed in her floral wake. The squirrel had received a generous headstart but safety in the shape of the nearest tree was still a dozen hops away. Dash lengthened her stride, skirted a toddler, who wobbled unsteadily, and crashed past a rhododendron bush. The squirrel reached the tree and shot up the trunk like a streak of lightning in reverse. Dash danced up on her hind legs as Arnie, Rocky and Jess arrived to stake their claim. They had the tree surrounded. Everyone who'd witnessed the chase was staring at the dogs, and then at us. Parents scowled and called their children to them; a jogger looked backwards while continuing to run forwards. The three of us arrived at the tree, breathless, and put our respective dogs back on the lead. Dash was panting and her eyes were bright with pleasure.

'I don't know what got into Arnie,' said Kate. 'He's never been that bothered about squirrels before.'

'Rocky's new,' said Sally, puffing, 'but I thought Jess would've known better.'

'It's Dash's fault – she set them all off,' I confessed. 'Must have been pack mentality or something, I don't know.' What I did know, however, was that it was embarrassing.

'Still, it was just a squirrel,' said Kate, who could see I was on the verge of giving Dash a stern reprimand.

It wasn't the squirrel I was worried about. What if Dash had crashed into the toddler, or run into a tree herself?

At that speed, who knows what would have happened? Maybe the cold, hard fact of the matter was that, once she'd taken off in pursuit of something small and furry, Dash just couldn't be trusted to stop. Full stop. We stood there awkwardly before Sally spoke.

'Give her another try. Go on. Even Jess was just the same at the start – OK, maybe not quite that fast… but… wow, you should be proud of Dash.'

Pride was the last thing I felt at that moment. But I *was* determined, I hated giving up on anything. We unclipped the leads and walked the dogs back to an open, grassy space and sat on a bench. The four greyhounds lay down around us like the lions in Trafalgar Square. Peace was restored; the sun shone; the dogs panted.

Then suddenly Dash was off again. She sprang to her feet and, in a chain reaction, the other three dogs followed. In the far distance, a fuzzy white puppy was circling its owner and yapping. Target sighted. Air Marshall Dash headed straight for it, flanked by Wing Commanders Arnie and Rocky. Flight Squadron Jess closed in behind.

'Dash, come!' I boomed, jumping to my feet.

By the time I arrived, the owner, a woman in a pink shirt, had picked the puppy up and was hugging it to her chest. The four greyhounds stood round her with their tongues hanging out.

'I'm really sorry,' I said, feeling sick and frustrated at peddling the same line for the umpteenth time. As I spoke, a dark stain spread over the woman's shirt. The puppy had peed itself. My dog had made another dog pee on its owner out of fear. If I'd been embarrassed about the squirrel incident, I was mortified by this one. The woman herself was shocked and upset. My offer of paying for her shirt to be dry-cleaned was rebuffed and I took this as my cue to disappear. I felt like crawling out of the park. Dash trailed behind me like a rag on the end of a tow rope.

The wedding was off. Or at least Dash's part in it. If she couldn't be trusted to behave herself in the park, what hope was there for her as ring bearer during the ceremony? All it needed was the sighting of a squirrel or puppy at the venue and she'd wreck months of planning in just a few seconds. A ring bearer wearing a muzzle? No chance. Dash's number was definitely up. It was finally time to call in the experts. As much as it felt like an admission of defeat, I would contact a dog behaviourist. Before picking up the phone, however, I rehearsed the spiel in my head.

Take one: 'Hello. I hope you can help. I'm afraid I've got a small problem with my greyhound. She's sometimes a little bit over-eager when off the lead.'

No, no. Too tentative and apologetic.

Take two: 'Hi there. I'm sure you can help. My greyhound's been belting round the park and chasing everything on four legs.'

No. Too much the other way. Just the facts – keep it informative.

Take three: 'How do you do? I'd like to invite my greyhound to my wedding but she's got a tendency to pursue small animals. I was wondering…'

Hopeless. The behaviourist would think I was a total crank. Talk about stating the obvious – my greyhound was behaving like a greyhound. Why was I surprised? It wasn't Dash's fault, of course. I just had to face up to the fact that she was programmed differently from the 'ideal dog' I'd grown up wanting, the dog that always obeyed my every command. She was also different from other greyhounds. Dash was Dash, a champion bitch. When she chased something, she had that much more chance of actually catching it. The idea of her being ring bearer at the wedding was a crazy whim. I should put it out of my mind and stop being so hard on her. What she really needed was a confidence boost. A small and achievable challenge rather than a mountain to climb.

'So, you're saying Dash has won?'

'That's right. A studio session all of her own.'

I couldn't believe it. The timing was perfect. A week after the debacle in the park, I took a call from the press officer of an art gallery. I'd entered Dash for an online competition – a chance to get her picture taken by a world-famous dog photographer, and she'd won! Here was an ideal opportunity to raise my self-esteem as a dog owner after Dash's disgrace the week before. Perhaps the camera flashes would even remind her of her racing days on the winner's podium.

The confirmation arrived the following day. I tore the envelope open and read the letter aloud to Sarah at breakfast. Dash was to report to the gallery in two days' time. The session would last an hour and result in a number of portraits, the best of which would be displayed in the gallery itself. Not just any album-sized print either. This would be a high-quality, glossy print almost half a metre square.

'What do you think of that?' I asked Sarah.

'Fantastic! We'll have to groom her beforehand. She'll need to look her absolute best,' she said excitedly.

I read on. The photographer, Cherie Hatter, was 'the photographer of choice for celebrities and their dogs'. Among the roll-call of famous names she'd snapped were the Norfolk terriers of the Duke and Duchess of York and a trio of pooches belonging to fashion designer, Alexander McQueen. The fee for her services normally ran into the thousands – about half our wedding budget, in fact – but we'd be getting them for free. Then the bombshell. In the small print at the bottom of the letter, it stipulated that only one person was able to accompany Dash. Not only that, but for the duration of the session Dash would be expected to sit.

Suddenly downcast, I looked at Sarah.

'*You* should go,' she said graciously and without hesitation. 'You're the one who entered her for the competition after all.'

'Are you sure?' I said.

'Positive. Besides, it'd be difficult for me to get the time off work.'

I could see she was making the best of it. What a sweetheart.

'But, but… what about the sitting stuff?' I said pathetically, after a pause. 'She's never once sat properly since we got her. I don't even know if she can.'

It was true. Due to their lanky legs and muscle-bound rump, greyhounds rarely sit like a 'normal' dog. Would this disqualify Dash from her photo session? The only alternative was to train her to sit conventionally and I had forty-eight hours to do it.

The art gallery in West Bromwich looked like a massive grey box with windows made out of jelly. It was modern all right. Inside, the floor was patterned with swirls of colour. Everything was plastic or metal and spookily lit. If I didn't happen to have an invitation, it was the last place I'd think of bringing a dog. Despite all this, Dash seemed delighted to be there. It was an outing and – for her – any outing was a splendid idea. Her toenails clicked across the floor as we walked up to a bright orange reception desk.

'We're here for the photo shoot,' I said to the receptionist, before adding, 'This is Dash,' and nodding my head towards her.

The receptionist, a slim young man in an even slimmer tie, leaned over the desk to look at Dash.

'Nice,' he said casually. 'I'll call Kathleen, the press officer. Have a seat over there.' He pointed to a cluster of white plastic chairs which looked more like pieces of abstract sculpture than furniture.

'Thanks,' I said, 'I think we'll stand.' I'd been working intensively with Dash and didn't want to overdo it before our big moment. After two days training, Dash could just about manage to sit. It was actually more of an upright stoop which she held for twenty seconds or so before keeling over. I was hoping, rather optimistically, it would be enough to get away with it.

Kathleen, the press officer, was a bright-eyed young woman with a mass of red curls. She shook my hand and then knelt down to stroke Dash under the chin.

'Isn't she sweeeeet?' she said in a slightly sickly, high-pitched voice.

'She has her moments,' I replied, smiling.

'Well, the photo studio is up on the second floor. Will Dash be OK in the lift?'

'Er, yes, I think so.'

As we waited for the lift, Kathleen told me what to expect. 'I think you'll like the artist. Cherie's got an amazing rapport with dogs. Have you seen much of the artist's work?'

I said I'd seen a few pieces online and was very impressed.

'They seemed quite painterly,' I added, sensing it would go down well with someone who used the word 'artist' as much as Kathleen did.

'Yes,' she breathed, 'some of them look like they're done in oils. Particularly the ones of black dogs on a black background.'

The lift door pinged open and Kathleen walked in. I followed, leading Dash, who suddenly had second thoughts and pulled back. Mindful of a repeat of the episode with the gate at New College, I quickly stepped forward, wedged the door open with my foot and scooped Dash up in my arms and into the lift.

'Still lots to learn,' I said, smiling at Kathleen. Kathleen smiled back. Dash, meanwhile, was looking over my shoulder at the greyhound in the mirror on the back wall of the lift. Her ears pricked up and she furrowed her brow.

'That's you, Dash,' I whispered in her ear. 'That's your other half.'

Kathleen laughed and repeated: 'Isn't she sweeeeet?'

The artist, Cherie, was a study in black. Dyed-black hair, thick black glasses, a black jacket and combat trousers and a pair of thick-soled skateboard trainers, also black. When she spoke, she surprised me with what I took to be a soft American accent, but which I later learnt was Canadian. She was having a bad day, apparently. Fifteen minutes earlier, she'd dropped her extremely expensive camera on her extremely expensive laptop. The camera was fine, fortunately, but the 'Enter' key of the laptop had come off – a fact she was not pleased about. She was also jetlagged, gesturing airily towards a couch as if she'd just flown into the country on it.

The studio itself was built into the corner of one of the large gallery spaces and was completely blacked out. Except for the couch, the only piece of furniture was a small table with the now damaged laptop on it. Fixed to one of the walls was a wide roll of matt-black material, which extended downwards and covered the floor. A small cross of white gaffer tape had been stuck in middle. Opposite this were two large square lamps which were bright enough to light a football pitch. I made conversation while she had her back to me, fiddling with the detached laptop key.

'So, how long are you in the UK?' I asked.

'Just a week,' she replied. 'I'm planning a retrospective here at the gallery for the Fall. If I can shoot a few portraits to fill in some gaps, I'll be happy.'

So that was where Dash came in. I waited for some sign from Cherie of the 'amazing rapport with dogs' that Kathleen had mentioned. So far she hadn't even greeted Dash.

'So you've not done a portrait of a greyhound before?' I asked, mildly surprised.

'No, unbelievably. This'll be the first. Most of my celebrity clients tend to have the fancier breeds, you know, Shar-Peis, poodles, pugs…'

'What about you? You must have a dog.' I felt it was a fairly safe assumption.

'Chihuahua.'

'Called…?'

'Titan.'

Cherie turned round. 'Now, do you just wanna let Dash off the lead so she can have a good sniff? I tend not to make a big hoo-ha about saying hello to the dog, if I can help it.'

I unclipped Dash's lead and she roved round the studio with her nose to the ground. The white cross of tape aroused most interest. This had obviously been the hot spot for a dozen different canine behinds. I cleared my throat and felt like I should get an apology in early.

'She's not great at sitting, I'm afraid.'

'No?'

'No. She does that funny squat that greyhounds do. I've tried to train her to sit normally. She may take a while to get it right.'

'Well, we've got an hour,' said Cherie resolutely. 'All it takes is one good shot.'

The first task was to get Dash correctly positioned on the white cross.

'Does she need to be right on top of it?' I asked over my shoulder.

Cherie was now kneeling between the two square lamps with her camera poised.

'Yup. X marks the spot,' she replied out of the side of her mouth, the rest of her face obscured by the camera.

On the fourth attempt, Dash lay down slap bang on the cross. From here, all I had to do was to get her to sit up. I held a treat in front of her nose and raised it slowly between her eyes and over her head.

'Sit.'

Dash sat up, snaffled the treat and then collapsed forward onto her chest.

I tried again. And again. And again. The lamps made the studio incredibly hot. I was starting to sweat. This time Dash held the pose, about as comfortable as a stuffed penguin.

'Stay,' I intoned, holding my hand out and backing away till I was behind the kneeling Cherie.

'You'll have to lie flat so you don't block the lights,' she whispered to me.

I lay down, still holding my hand out at Dash.

'Stay,' I repeated, from the prone position.

What happened next took no more than a couple of seconds. There was a loud squeak which seemed to come from the camera; Dash sprang towards Cherie just as the lamps flashed; Cherie rocked backwards on her knees and fell over my trailing legs, flailing her arms to regain her balance. In doing so, she hit both lamps which wobbled precariously on their stands but didn't... quite... crash over.

'Christ!' said Cherie, when she'd got her breath back.

'It was the squeak,' I said. I was so shocked myself I didn't have time to get embarrassed. 'Where did it come from?'

'It's on the side of the camera,' said Cherie. 'It's supposed to get the dog's attention just before the shot.'

'Sorry, she's mad about squeaks – all her toys have a squeak. Maybe we should try it without next time. I think we've got her attention by now.'

'I think maybe we have,' said Cherie sardonically. She soon regained her composure and an amused not to say artistic smile flitted across her lips.

When it arrived a week later, the head-and-shoulders portrait was stunning. Larger than life-size, Dash was gazing back out of the darkness. Her ears were cocked, revealing a flash of pale pink in each. Front on, her nose was foreshortened but ended in the same black blob, shining like wet liquorice. The effect wasn't exactly 'painterly', it was more like a forensic close-up. Every hair, every whisker was visible. Even the two lamps used in the shoot reflected in her eyes like strip lighting off snooker balls. It captured the racing side of Dash's character perfectly: poised and intent; ready to fly. There she was, staring straight into the camera, forever waiting for it to squeak.

I was hopeful some of the success of Dash's portrait session would rub off on our search for a wedding photographer. A friend who'd recently got married had advised us that this was one area not to stint on. If you're putting your heart and soul into planning a wedding, then you want the photos to do it justice. Initial research online suggested that the age of the wedding album was over. We could now expect a CD of the day containing thousands of digital photos. If we so desired, these would chronicle every event from the bride getting dressed in the morning to the closing of the bridal suite door in the evening. Neither Sarah nor I were keen on such a 'reportage' approach. For this reason, we didn't fancy shaky video footage either. We felt it would be fine for the photographer to start snapping away from three o'clock at the ceremony itself, along with all the other guests.

Crispin was born and raised in Oxford. Judging from his smooth skin and tuft of brown hair, it wasn't that long ago either. When I'd spoken to him on the phone, I guessed he was in his thirties, at least. The man sitting alongside Sarah and me in our lounge looked barely out of his teens. The shoulders of his jacket looked as if he'd left the clothes hanger inside. His neck stuck out from his shirt collar like a plant cutting in an overlarge pot. Even his shoes were roomy. Based on my experience with Cherie, I imagined most 'serious' photographers wore black. Crispin was wearing head-to-toe turquoise. He'd set up his studio straight from college and had already done a full year of weddings.

'Let me show you some images from one in September last year.'

As he scrolled through his portfolio, Dash sniffed round the edge of the laptop. The pictures showed an attractive couple in the grounds of an Oxford college. Pageboys hovering like cherubs on a green lawn; a red-faced uncle laughing heartily; the married couple themselves embracing beneath a dramatic skyline; even the odd 'ambient' shot thrown in – the radiator grille of a Roller complete with large bow on the hood ornament.

'Lovely,' said Sarah, 'but ours is going to be a bit less formal.'

'For a start, the ceremony's in a theatre,' I added.

'No problem,' said Crispin briskly. 'If you give me the contact details, I'm happy to reconnoitre the venue in advance. All part of the service.'

What was also part of the service was the provision of *two* photographers.

'Call it a pincer movement,' chuckled Crispin. 'I find it really works in getting good coverage and a lot more naturalness to some of the shots.'

By now, Dash had switched her attention to sniffing Crispin's long bony fingers, which he waved in front of her nose like doggy chews as he spoke.

'Dash, stop pestering,' I said curtly.

'Don't worry,' said Crispin, extending a slim hand to stroke Dash's forehead. 'She's lovely, very photogenic. Will she be coming to the wedding?'

'No,' said Sarah and I almost simultaneously.

'Shame,' said Crispin politely.

'Yes,' I said. 'The truth is, she's fine at home but when she's out and about she gets a bit... a bit... what's the word?' I looked at Sarah blankly.

Sarah raised her eyebrows and then looked at Crispin, who took it as his cue to speak: 'Er... hyper?'

June

Hot dog! Summer had finally arrived and Dash was determined to spend most of it sunbathing. After breakfast, she'd stand at the conservatory door and whine plaintively. This was her cue to be let out into the garden where she'd find a comfy spot, lie down and soon start to pant as if she'd just run the race of her life. With her black fur hot to the touch, she'd eventually rouse herself and come inside to take on water. Then it was out again to 'tan' the other side. This went on until noon when, slightly sun-crazed, she'd roach with her legs in the air and try to bite her own tail. One morning, I came downstairs to find her completely covered by a bedsheet which had drifted off the washing line. Blissed out by hours in the sun, Dash lay underneath it like a hospital patient in traction.

In early June, I took a long, hard look at my accounts. I'd now been freelancing for a year and it was time to grapple with my first tax return. Owning a greyhound, I discovered, can be an expensive business. Though Dash's adoption hadn't cost a penny, I worked out she was now setting us back an average of £50 a month in food, vet's fees, insurance and sundries. It was hard to see where I could economise in terms of food and vet's fees. Due to their liveliness off the lead, insurance is an absolute must for greyhounds. Admittedly, I'd probably overdone it in terms of sundries. Dash was now the owner of three coats, two collars, two tags, two leads, a muzzle, a neckerchief, two mats, one dog bed and over a dozen toys. Added to this was her 'maintenance kit' of grooming mitts, poo bags, treats, toothpaste and toothpicks. Since owning Dash was a pure unadulterated pastime, I couldn't even write any of this stuff off as a business expense.

If dog ownership was proving expensive, then getting married was likely to break the bank. With three months still to go, the expenses were mounting up. According to the Love Budget spreadsheet, we'd already spent £8,500 of our projected £10,000 budget. Now that cheques had actually been signed, the profligacy of blowing such a dizzying amount of cash on one day made me feel distinctly uncomfortable. The food and drink was the big spend but we could hardly invite guests to our wedding and then give them breadsticks and tap water. The price of the venue hire and the celebrant were fixed. I'd already haggled with Crispin the photographer and the cèilidh band had actually come in cheaper than budgeted. Even Sarah's dress looked like it would cost us less than anticipated. But somehow we'd completely forgotten to factor in gifts for the bridesmaids and helpers. Then there was the expense of putting Dash in kennels for the duration. All this and we still had to find some funds for the honeymoon.

Sarah had taken charge of the honeymoon since it was a discreet task which she could do during odd moments of the day at work. We'd already discussed the idea of a 'two-parter' – something short and sweet in the UK straight after the wedding itself, followed by something not so short and hot, hot, hot once we'd recovered. Our sights were set on Cuba if the budget had some slack in it; India if it was stretched to breaking point. Maybe it was time to tell Sarah that I didn't think we'd be able to afford the suncream, let alone the price of a flight and hotel.

Sarah herself was remarkably sanguine: 'Oh, the wedding budget doesn't include the honeymoon, does it? Not if we're going later anyway.'

Whether this was an accounting trick or not, it reassured me we still had a chance of bringing the whole thing in for our target of ten grand. The idea was that we'd have three months' earning time after the wedding before we went away as Mr & Mrs. We'd book the flights and hotels by credit card and chip away at the payments over the autumn. We'd still take a 'mini-moon' straight after the wedding itself, but it would be a long weekend in Bath. A session at the thermal spa was on the cards. By the time the wedding was over, we imagined, a battery of detox and de-stress treatments would be all we were good for.

One Sunday afternoon, Sarah and I were sitting in the garden. Sarah's dad, Harry, had laid a patio of flagstones the summer before and Dash was at our feet, toasting herself on the warm stone. It was quite a suntrap, framed by a passion flower which covered the garden fence and, in an act of rampant colonisation, had mounted the top and proceeded to scale the neighbour's pergola. We'd always got on well with the neighbour. So had Dash, who regularly poked her nose over the fence in search of strokes. Once, in her enthusiasm to be petted, she'd got her head wedged between the bars of the adjoining gate. She stood there helplessly for five minutes, like a convict in the stocks, until we were able to twist her head sideways and pull her free.

This particular Sunday, with three months to go till the wedding, Sarah and I were having trouble prioritising the tasks. Was it too early to set up the gift list? Should we get chair covers *and* swags? Did we need to organise a cupcake tasting? These were the questions that had sent me into a spin. Just then, there was a rustle behind the bench where we were sitting. Dash, still in the prone position, jerked her head upright. Another rustle. Dash suddenly lunged between our feet with her jaws wide open. Then, there was a swishing sound, and just as quickly she went into reverse, crashing into a large plant pot. At the same time, a brown and white shape shot up the passion flower and into the neighbour's garden. Dash rebounded off the pot and stood up on her hind legs at the fence, her head moving quickly from side to side like a top-flight tennis umpire.

We'd always wondered how Dash would get on with cats. Up to now, we'd only ever glimpsed them in the distance on our walks, departing swiftly via a hedge or melting into the evening shadows. Online, I'd actually seen photos of unmuzzled greyhounds and cats sharing the same sofa, even cuddling up together. Again, it all seems to depend on the particular greyhound. There are those that will show little interest and can be considered 'cat-safe'; those whose curiosity will only be aroused once the cat moves but are essentially 'cat-correctable'. Finally, there are those that will pull you off your feet in an attempt to have a close encounter of the feline kind. No prizes for guessing which category Dash came into: 'cat-uncorrectable-not-to-say-incompatible'. It was half an hour before she lay back down again, and despite a scratch sustained on the nose, she spent the rest of the afternoon staring intently at the spot where the cat had been hiding.

'She's definitely one in a million,' laughed Ryan, the owner of Tolstoy the borzoi, when he heard about the episode on our next dog walk. 'I've seen some dogs in my time but Dash is wired. Imagine what she must've been like on the track.'

'Hmm,' I said unenthusiastically. The success of Dash's racing career hadn't exactly made the transition to family pet an easy one.

'You could always fasten a bell to her collar,' Ryan said in a sudden brainwave. 'If cats wear one to scare birds, then Dash could have one to scare cats. That's logic for you.'

'Hang on, wouldn't they just think she was a bigger cat? Besides, she'd end up with some kind of identity crisis.'

'Rubbish,' said Ryan and then, after a moment's thought, added: 'Some cows have bells anyway.'

'Yes,' I replied without missing a beat, 'but that's because their horns don't work!'

With this, Ryan and I fell about laughing. Dash and Tolstoy, who'd been walking on ahead, turned round to watch us and then looked at each other as if mystified.

Dash and I were spending way too much time together. We got up at the same time, ate at the same time and shared the same group of doggy friends. Even our constitutions had become disturbingly similar. She had bad teeth; I had bad teeth. I had the occasional bout of dandruff and flaky skin; she was rarely free of it. She had a motion twice a day; suddenly so did I. The latest parallel became apparent when I heard sudden gasps for air coming from the kitchen. It sounded like a death rattle. I charged downstairs to see Dash lying on her back, her eyes wide with fear. Her chest heaved in bouts as she struggled to breathe. Panicky, I rubbed and patted her between the shoulder blades. Could she have swallowed something? Surely she'd cough it up on her own if she had. I wasn't sure what else to do – I'd never attempted the Heimlich manoeuvre on a person, let alone a dog. After a few seconds, the gasps subsided and her breathing returned to normal. She rolled onto her side and looked up at me as if surprised at all the fuss. The third time it happened in as many days, I took her to see Mr Barker, the vet.

'Tell me the exact nature of the attacks,' he said in his no-nonsense manner.

I recounted what I'd heard and seen, giving the time of day and duration.

'Now describe any dog walks you've been on recently. The flora and fauna, as well as her behaviour.'

I told him what I could remember of our last few sorties, mostly to Florence Park. Not much was new – the smell of tree blossom heavy in the air; bright little rings of daisies; the park keeper on his lawnmower, making the first cut of summer. Dash hadn't done anything out of the ordinary. Mr Barker listened while looking out of the window. He then tugged briefly on his tufty beard and turned to examine Dash again. He checked the whites of both her eyes and looked up her nose. He cleared his throat.

'Hayfever,' he said. 'In a word.'

'Oh,' I said. '*I* get hayfever, too.'

He looked at me as if that meant I should have known the answer all along.

'I can give her a course of allergy-relief tablets but the best remedy is to keep her away from tall-stemmed or swaying grasses. Check the weather forecast before you go on your walks to see if the pollen count is high.'

So the park in all its summertime glory was to blame. When I thought more about it, Mr Barker was probably right. Dash had a particular fondness for sniffing at clumps of tall grass before marking them with a dribble of pee. I'd also noticed she sometimes even ate the stuff, but had assumed this was a seasonal quest for roughage.

To make life easier for both of us, I started to walk Dash along the river instead. One afternoon while padding along the towpath, Dash's ears shot up and she froze in a way which could only mean one thing. Another greyhound in the vicinity. The greyhound in question was a skinny, fawn-coloured creature, tethered by a rope to a bench. Sitting on the bench with one hand resting on the greyhound's back and holding a can of beer in the other was a large, unshaven brute of a man in his mid-fifties. He was wearing a bandana and had a thick gold hoop in each ear. His sleeveless shirt showed both arms adorned with tattoos; his jeans were three-quarter length, with white cotton threads hanging down in a straggly fringe. All in all – the can of booze and the greyhound aside – he looked like an amateur pirate. Slowly, and with great effort, he got up from the bench as we approached. It looked like it was the first time he'd been on his feet for hours.

'Ex-racer, is she?' he said gruffly.

'That's right,' I replied, a little wary. 'Yours, too?' I gestured at the fawn-coloured greyhound, which showed no sign of wanting to greet either me or Dash.

The pirate ignored my question. Instead, he walked unsteadily towards Dash, patted her on the head and then took hold of one of her ears. Dash herself didn't seem to mind. The pirate turned her ear inside out and squinted.

'Paddy, is she?' he asked.

'Sorry?'

'The tattoo – is she Irish or English? Two means she's a Paddy. Just one and she's English.'

'Oh,' I said, cottoning on. 'Just one… in her right ear. She's English, well, Scottish actually.'

The pirate fumbled with Dash's other ear and nodded to himself.

'English!' he exclaimed triumphantly, before tottering backwards onto the bench. This was obviously enough activity for one afternoon, and he settled down with an expression somewhere between a grin and a grimace.

The very next afternoon by the river, Dash and I bumped into the pirate again. This time, I waved at him from a distance but he seemed not to notice. Too sozzled perhaps. When we got within a few paces, he hauled himself to his feet.

'Ex-racer, is she?' the pirate growled with a leer.

I looked at him and frowned. Were we about to go through the same routine? Undeterred, he stumbled towards Dash and started to fumble with her ears.

'Paddy, is she? Ah, no... here it is.'

'What about yours?' I asked, in an attempt to change the script.

He looked at his own greyhound, which still wore the rope lead round its neck like a noose.

'She's English!' he exclaimed, clenching his fist as if in defiance.

'Uh-huh... what's her name?'

'Emma.'

On hearing her name, Emma the greyhound pricked up two tattered ears and turned to face us inquisitively. Her lean frame showed most of her ribs, her muzzle was grey and she had dark stains under both eyes, making her look even more mournful.

'How old is she?' I asked.

The pirate suddenly became maudlin. 'She's gettin' on, she is... she's nearly there.'

I didn't know what to say next, so bowed my head. Dash started to whine. The pirate suddenly reached out and clapped a paw-like hand on my shoulder. His bottom lip trembled.

'You know,' he sniffed, 'Emma's all I've got.'

I sensed he was about to blub and reached out to pat his arm. As I did so, he wailed and pulled me towards him for a hug. It was hard to say which was worse – the stench of stale beer or the sensation that he was squeezing the life out of me. After a few seconds that felt like minutes, I managed to break free.

'Ah, well. You're lucky to still have her then,' I said, trying to recover my composure. 'Anyway… we should probably push on with our walk.'

Despite the pirate's crushing embrace – and my speedy retreat – I did feel a solidarity of sorts. He was the only other male greyhound owner I'd ever met. He also had a female dog, a bitch. I shuddered at the thought of what else we might have in common. Dash was important, granted, but she wasn't *everything*. I had Sarah; I had my family and friends; a house; a job. True, I'd only had Dash for nine months. I should count my blessings. Given that a healthy greyhound can live to twelve or thirteen, things would undoubtedly be different after so many years. By then she'd be part of the furniture, part of me even. How do you say goodbye to part of yourself? People you love leave a hole when they're gone. Dogs certainly aren't people, but they're not mere objects either. Dash had moods and expressions. She had character. The addition of sardines in her food bowl or the sight of the grooming mitt was a cause for joy; being left alone when Sarah and I went out was a cause for sorrow. I pondered this on the walk home but the only conclusion

I came to was to change my route along the river. It would be too painful to run into the drunken pirate and Emma the greyhound again.

Strictly speaking, Oxford City Golf Club was off-limits to non-members, and that included greyhounds. The lure of the long, landscaped fairways, trimmed hedges and neat greens was irresistible, however. Via an overgrown path which Ryan had shown us, Dash and I were able to gain access without going anywhere near the clubhouse. At the top of the path, I peered cautiously round a hedge as if we were about to step out onto a busy motorway. The little black wedge of Dash's head did likewise. Her mouth was gaping open and her ears pricked up. The grass was lush and wet with dew. There was no one about – it was still too early for even the keenest of Saturday morning golfers.

Mindful of Dash's disgraceful behaviour in the park only last month, I'd decided not to tell Sarah about my plan to let Dash loose on the golf course that morning. Some things, even between fiancés, are best kept secret. If Sarah had her way, we wouldn't let Dash off the lead at all. Besides, she was going for a final fitting of the wedding dress and I didn't want to distract her. We'd now had Dash for nine months and getting her to behave like a 'normal' dog – one that could be let off the lead in public without being a total liability – had become a mission of mine.

With the usual frisson of last-minute nerves, I unclipped Dash's lead and we stepped out onto the golf course.

Thankfully, Dash didn't bolt; neither did she gallop off round an imaginary greyhound track. Instead, she trotted alongside me with her tail bouncing merrily from side to side. When she stopped to sniff, she quickly looked up to check where I'd got to. After a couple of minutes, I called her to me and put her back on the lead. A minute later, I let her off again. The same story – she behaved impeccably. I couldn't believe I'd finally cracked it. At last. We managed to walk for a full half-hour without incident. I was ecstatic.

On the way back to the path and with Dash off the lead, I suddenly stepped on something hard and stumbled. A golf ball. It was plugged deep in the long grass like a bird's egg in a nest. Wiping off the dirt, I realised it was brand new. It felt cool and hard in the palm of my hand. Strange for a golfer not to look for it more carefully, I thought. How long had it lain there lost and forgotten? I looked up, wondering which direction it had come from. That's when it felt like someone threw a bucket of ice-cold water over me.

Dash had completely vanished.

'I've lost my dog,' I said in a voice like that of a six-year-old.

For a second, the woman police constable behind the window of thick glass didn't reply. It was early evening on a Saturday and perhaps she was expecting something a little more exciting to walk into the police station. Her blonde hair was pulled back tightly and her face was unsmiling, but a bridge of freckles which crossed her slim nose and both cheeks suggested she might have a softer side. She sported a crisp white shirt with a neat chequered cravat and black epaulettes.

'You'll be wanting the dog warden then,' she said at last.

'Right. Where is he?'

She raised a plucked eyebrow before replying: 'Down at the pound where he always is. The police don't deal with stray dogs – that's the council's job.'

I must have looked particularly crestfallen.

She cast a glance at the lead which I'd had with me all day and put on the desk. The lead that was now no longer connected to Dash.

'Hold on a sec,' she said, stepping away from the window to a computer terminal at the side. She made a few clicks with a mouse and then lifted a shiny black phone.

'Jim? Hi, it's Stella from Cowley HQ. I've got a gentleman here who's lost his dog. You picked up any strays today? OK… I'll ask.'

Constable Stella rested the handset on her shoulder and turned to me.

'What breed is it?'

'Greyhound,' I replied quickly.

'Greyhound,' repeated Stella down the phone. The dog warden, Jim, was obviously jotting down the particulars.

'What about a name tag?'

'Yes,' I said smartly. 'With her name and phone number. She's got a tattoo in her ear as well. Dash, she's called Dash.'

'Tattooed female answering to the name of Dash,' said Stella into the mouthpiece. 'OK, Jim. Speak in five.'

Stella put the phone down and stepped back to stand at the window. 'Take a seat,' she said, indicating a trio of lime-green chairs that were bolted to the floor. 'The warden will phone back when he's checked the pound.'

I sat down heavily and looked round. The walls were decked with posters and leaflets giving advice about knife crime, carjacking, drugs, mobile phone theft. It all made the streets of genteel Oxford feel like Mexico City. There was nothing, however, about what to do when a greyhound disappears into thin air.

'What time did you lose her then?' Stella asked. In my inspection of the walls, I'd failed to notice she was still standing at the window.

'About seven-thirty this morning. On the golf course.'

Stella frowned. 'That's private property up there.'

'I know, I know,' I said, somewhat exasperated.

In view of the circumstances and my frazzled demeanour, Stella obviously decided to drop the trespassing charge. Instead, she drummed her nails lightly on the metal hatch set into the desk.

'You look worried,' she said.

'Very,' I replied, rubbing the side of my face wearily. 'I've only had Dash nine months. My girlfriend's still out there looking. She's with a couple of friends who've also got greyhounds, you know, sort of trying flush her out with dogs of the same breed.' I'd called Sarah earlier that day after a couple of hours of panicked, fruitless searching. She'd cycled to the golf course straight from town and suggested we recruit the help of Sally and Kate, fellow greyhound owners from Florence Park.

'She wouldn't have found her way back home, would she?' asked Stella suddenly.

'Not a chance,' I replied. 'Too far and too many roads. If Dash tried to cross a road on her own, she's had it,' I said, leaning my head back against the wall and squinting up at the strip lighting.

'Not got much road sense?'

'None whatsoever.'

A pause of a few seconds followed while I tried *not* to think of Dash dodging traffic.

'Bit of a cat person myself,' mused Stella. 'Less fuss, you know. When people lose a cat, they put up a "Lost" poster. You thought of trying that for your dog?'

'No, not yet.' I'd been out all day, with only a can of Coke for lunch. The next step was to call in at home, grab a bite to eat and then rendezvous with Sarah and the others to continue the search before it went dark.

Suddenly, the phone went. Stella let it ring twice and then picked it up.

'Hi, Jim. And?' Her eyes brightened as she turned to face me. 'Your lucky day. He's picked up a greyhound... no name tag though. What colour's yours?'

My heart leapt and I jumped to my feet. 'She's black, black with a white chest.'

Stella put the phone to her ear again and then frowned. 'This one's mostly white,' she said, 'with a brown patch on its back.'

'No, that's not her. Dash is black.' My heart plummeted. I hung my head. 'She's black,' I repeated as if it could change the colour of the greyhound in the warden's pound. A vision of Dash's little black head, chocolate eyes and glossy nose came into my mind. I'd lost her. She was gone, for sure.

Stretched by a roadside somewhere or trapped in a thicket of brambles. I felt utterly hopeless.

'Sorry,' said Stella. 'I hope she turns up.'

'Me too,' I said, suddenly realising this was what I wanted more than anything.

I turned to go and stood in front of the automatic doors, which refused to open.

Stella coughed politely. 'Er, the button's on the side.'

I sighed and pressed the large button helpfully marked 'Push'. The doors relented and slid open on the mild June evening.

I was plodding down the hill towards home when my mobile rang. It was Sarah, who sounded breathless.

'Get home quick. No time to explain. I'll meet you on the way.'

What did she mean? Had someone found Dash? Was she dead or alive? I broke into a run, the dog lead still clasped firmly in one hand like a relay baton. Five minutes later, I rounded the corner of our road. Then a shout behind me – Sarah was standing up out of her bike saddle and pedalling furiously. She drew level and reached her hand out; I squeezed it. As we spoke, the words came out in gasps.

'The guy... from next door called... about Dash.'

'Is she... OK?

'Not sure... but he says she's in the garden.'

I nodded and put on a burst of speed; Sarah raced alongside. Then I vaulted the railings in front of the house. Sarah jumped off her bike and let it fall to the ground. From the other side of the wooden gate, the one we'd had built on the advice of Peter, came a high-pitched and frenetic whining. Dash?! Was she hurt? I threw open the gate and Sarah and I rushed through together, almost getting jammed in the process.

Dash came at us like a black arrow. Then she reared up on her hind legs as if to give us a hug. It was hugs all round. And tears of relief, too. We couldn't believe it.

'Dash, Dash, Dash. We thought we'd lost you!'

Dash pawed at us wildly and licked our faces. Then she went into a manic version of her comedy run, circling us like a demented clockwork toy. She seemed more than fine. We tried to grab hold of her but she squirmed free and changed direction, her tongue hanging out sideways like ham from a sandwich. This reunion was better than winning any race; better than catching the hare even.

That evening, once things had calmed down – which took quite some time – Sarah and I tried to piece together exactly what had happened. When I'd lost sight of Dash that morning, she must have simply wandered off the golf course. While I was shouting myself hoarse for the next couple of hours and quizzing each group of golfers I ran into as to whether they'd seen a small black greyhound, Dash was methodically retracing her steps in the direction of home. This was the last place we'd thought to look. Somehow, she'd managed to navigate two back roads, a busy main road, a pedestrian crossing, a garage forecourt, a side street and then found our house. All this unscathed. To think I'd been impressed the September before when Dash had stopped outside the house on the way back from the park!

It transpired the guy from next door had come home at lunchtime to see Dash standing forlornly by the side gate.

Finding it strange that neither Sarah nor I was with her, he'd let Dash into the garden and closed the gate after her. Later, when we still weren't back and Dash had been loafing around in the garden for over five hours, he called Sarah on her mobile. The rest, as they say, is local history and one for the 'solved' section of the dog warden's case files.

In terms of yet another lesson learnt by letting Dash off the lead, this time I'd experienced the despair of actually losing her for several hours; not something I wanted to repeat in a hurry. On the other hand, there was the realisation that maybe she was both smarter and much more attached to us than we'd given her credit for in the past.

'You know,' Sarah reflected some days later, 'she certainly knows where home is now.'

July

I raised the gun and aimed at Sarah. She giggled and ducked behind a tower of crockery. We'd taken the afternoon off and were in a department store doing our wedding gift list.

The store assistant had shown us how to add gifts by 'zapping' the barcodes with a laser gun. Sarah and I had begun by trooping round together. A set of china dinner plates: zap. Egyptian cotton towels: zap. We worked our way through 'Home & Garden', 'Electrical Appliances' and 'Sport & Leisure'. We had considered doing something different with our wedding list – donations to charity or, as one friend had done, asking for a book from each guest to build up a personalised library. This was all very well, but at home there was chipped crockery and utensils that we'd been using since our student days, and bed linen that was now threadbare. It was difficult to pass up the opportunity to replace some of this old stuff.

After an hour of dutiful zapping, however, we got bored and decided to split up. Each of us had a laser gun and was ready to use it. Pursuing each other round the store, we dodged behind displays or ran up escalators. If something got zapped by mistake, it would have to stay on the list. We finished by giving each other ten minutes to zap as many ridiculous things as we could. We'd then reconvene over a coffee in the restaurant to see how well (or badly) we'd done.

'A television – what's so strange about that?' asked Sarah, sipping her coffee.

'This isn't just any old TV,' I replied, raising an eyebrow. 'This is a digital home cinema system. A snip at just two and a half thousand pounds.'

Sarah almost spat out her mouthful of coffee.

'OK,' I said. 'Maybe not. Try this instead. Adjustable sew-easy valet dress model – full figure.'

'Price?' said Sarah in a nasal, officious-sounding voice.

'One hundred and twenty-seven pounds, zero pence.'

'Pah,' she said, contemptuously. 'Listen to this: Ten-foot Trampoline with Bounce Surround – guaranteed to give a growing family years of fun.'

'Not bad,' I acknowledged. 'Dash would certainly love it...'

'Speaking of which,' interrupted Sarah, 'how about this last one? The Swimming Dog Toy. He comes with his very own pair of goggles, a towel and – wait for it – an adoption certificate.' She winked teasingly.

'Unfair,' I pouted. 'There's only room for one dog in our life. The mere fact she hates water and would probably sink like a stone doesn't make her any less lovable.'

Indeed it did not. After misbehaving so frustratingly in spring, Dash was having a fine start to the summer. She'd proved she could not only walk off the lead, but was able to find her way home again solo. Impressive stuff. So much so that Sarah and I had thought about rescinding our decision to ban her from the wedding. I'd chatted to Ryan about it on one of our dog walks together.

'It's an analogy, if you ask me,' he said. 'You want to let Dash off the lead in the same way you want to let go in life... but you're always frightened about what'll happen if you do. Here you are, trying to control a force of nature. You've got to give in to it instead.'

'Nonsense,' I said. 'You're just jealous because you wanted a hound and you've ended up with a horse!' The growth of Tolstoy the borzoi had continued unabated. He was now twice as tall as Dash.

'No, it's true,' scoffed Ryan, undeterred. 'It's the same with this wedding stuff. You're trying to plan everything down to the last detail. Step back a bit.'

'What do you mean?' I said.

He pulled a face. 'Well... it's not normal to get so... so involved.'

'Actually, it's a question of having the time,' I countered. 'I'm just more flexible than Sarah when it comes to work. Besides, she's doing more than you think.'

'Like what?' he asked.

'Like her wedding dress and shoes,' I said. 'And the flowers... and the menu and drinks... and the entire honeymoon, in fact!'

'Fair enough,' said Ryan, raising both hands in mock surrender. 'I'm just saying you need to take it less seriously, that's all.'

That evening, I asked Sarah: 'Do you think I'm doing too much for the wedding?'

'Doing too much?' she echoed. 'No, I think it's amazing. I can't believe how much you want to do. You're so organised – it's great!' She came over and gave me a soft little kiss on the lips.

'Oh. Well. Right,' I mumbled.

'What makes you ask that anyway?'

'I don't know. Just a thought.'

She paused. 'Maybe you *do* get a little obsessive about it sometimes. But that's who you are and that's why I love you… that's why we both love you.' She nodded at Dash who was lying on her mat and fixing us with an adoring gaze. As if on cue, Dash got up and padded over.

'Group hug', I announced and we crouched down to Dash's level. Dash stuck her head in the air and leaned against us contentedly.

'Tell you what,' said Sarah brightly. 'I'm supposed to get in touch with Geoff the caterer soon to arrange a tasting. Why don't I fix it up for next week? We'll go together. It'll be lovely and relaxing. It won't seem like hard work at all.'

A large kitchen on an industrial estate seemed an unlikely venue for a romantic dinner. Geoff was delighted to see us, however, and was wearing the same seventies jacket-and-tie combination as when we'd first met him, only this time with the addition of a serviette over his arm like a high-class waiter. He'd laid a tablecloth and two place settings over a metal worktop and left a large bowl of water at the entrance for Dash.

'Hope you don't mind if Dash stays out here,' he said apologetically. 'Not even my own dog's allowed in the kitchen – health and safety and all that.'

As if to show she too was prepared to compromise, Dash lapped a few mouthfuls of water before lying down.

'Right then, let's get this wedding tasting under way,' said Geoff with a smile and disappeared momentarily, only to return in a large white apron.

'Are you playing all the parts yourself this evening then?' I asked good-naturedly.

'Indeed, I am,' Geoff replied, pushing his glasses up the bridge of his nose. 'The staff prepared the food this afternoon, but I like to handle the clients myself.' He segued smoothly into previewing the menu we'd chosen.

'Here's a basket showing the selection of breads,' he said, placing it in front of us. 'Typically, we'd serve these with butter roses and olive oil.' With his other free hand, he levered open a large fridge door and produced a plate of chilled butter roses. Then, as if with a third hand, he poured me and Sarah a glass of sparkling water each.

'Are there any alternatives to butter roses?' enquired Sarah as we started to munch on the bread. 'It's just that they're a bit... I don't know, a bit dated.'

'No problem,' said Geoff, smiling politely and producing another plate from the fridge with equal dexterity. 'How about butter "swirls" instead?'

These met with Sarah's approval, as did the cold starter: roasted aubergine and peppers interleaved with feta cheese.

It *was* delicious, but just as I was into my third mouthful, Geoff adroitly whisked away the plate.

'What's going on?' I whispered to Sarah when Geoff's back was turned.

'It's just a tasting,' she whispered back. 'You're not supposed to finish everything!'

'Oh, right!' I dabbed the corners of my mouth with a serviette in the hope that such a sophisticated gesture would make me look less ravenous.

For the main course, we'd chosen pan-fried lamb fillet with a port and redcurrant sauce.

'So this was par-cooked earlier and now I'm just finishing it off,' explained Geoff. 'That's what we'll do on the day to get round the limited facilities at the abbey.'

The port and redcurrant sauce mingled with the natural juices of the lamb, which was so tender it almost melted. We murmured our approval and, while Geoff had his back turned again, I slid a slice off the plate into my serviette.

'I'll just go and check how Dash is doing,' I said and wandered casually out of the kitchen. Still lying where we'd left her, Dash twitched up an ear like a satellite dish. Her nose followed.

'Here you go, Dash. What do you think?'

Dash gobbled down the piece of lamb as if it was her last meal.

The veggie main course option was porcini mushroom, spinach and Parmesan tart. I decided not to repeat the serviette trick this time but, quicker off the mark, did manage to eat three of them before Geoff could swipe the plate.

'For dessert,' announced Geoff, 'you chose summer berries in dark chocolate nests. Now I can serve this with clotted cream… or crème fraîche, if you prefer.'

'How about we try one of each?' I asked Geoff. I felt I was getting the hang of this tasting thing.

'I'll leave you to mull it over for five minutes,' said Geoff, placing the desserts and two glasses of red wine in front of us while deftly lighting a candle. It was a sweet little touch, which we appreciated. Getting the food right was a big relief. Sarah and I sat back and enjoyed the dessert.

When Geoff returned, he'd divested himself of the apron and was back to his role as head waiter.

'Well – how did we do?' he asked expectantly.

'Perfect,' Sarah and I replied in unison, before I added cheekily: 'Just the bill and we're done, thank you.'

As well as being good company, Ryan was actually an antidote to the stress of wedding planning. It was also good for Dash to spend time with Tolstoy the borzoi. At first, his irrepressible playfulness had confused and perhaps even annoyed her, but now she took it in her stride. When they ran off the lead together, it was side by side and there was no barging.

One Friday afternoon, we were making our way along a narrow path flanked by banks of nettles. We'd talked solidly for over an hour, keeping an eye on the dogs before putting them back on their leads. Suddenly Ryan looked up and frowned.

'Uh-oh.'

He nodded his head towards a figure approaching us along the path. A lean bloke in his twenties in baggy jeans, T-shirt and, despite the mild weather, a woollen hat pulled down over his ears. Barrelling along by his side – jutting head, cropped ears and docked tail – was a Dobermann pinscher. Instead of the usual mix of black and tan, its fur was the reddish colour of raw liver. It had a loose, thick chain round its neck and was off the lead.

With the path not wide enough for three dogs to pass comfortably, Ryan ushered Tolstoy off to one side. I followed suit, standing behind him with Dash. As the pair drew level, the Dobermann growled threateningly in our direction. The bloke in the woollen hat kneed it roughly and yelled at it to keep moving.

'Why don't you put it on a lead?' said Ryan sharply.

The bloke stopped.

'Eh?'

'You heard me. Put it on a lead if you can't control it.'

When it came to speaking out, it was fair to say that Ryan was no shrinking violet. He also had the big arms and broad chest to back it up. Once, when we'd met up for lunch, he'd complained to the waitress that his steak was inedible. The chef himself had come to our table and, after five minutes of raised voices and finger-pointing, was dispatched to the kitchen to make a fresh meal.

'Eh?' the bloke in the woolly cap repeated, sticking his chin out angrily. He then gave Ryan a mouthful of abuse, the gist of which was that he'd treat his own dog how he saw fit. His right eyelid drooped and the eye was a strange grey colour as if it'd been damaged in a fight. Or maybe his own dog had done it? The Dobermann began to bark aggressively. I suddenly felt distinctly uncomfortable.

Without any trace of amusement, Ryan smiled at the bloke and stepped towards him. This set off a domino-effect. The Dobermann lunged at Ryan, who sidestepped it swiftly, unfastening the lead on Tolstoy's harness as he did so. Missing its initial target, the Dobermann continued forwards and snapped at Dash's throat. Dash dodged away, barging me into the nettles. Then something quite extraordinary happened. Tolstoy sprang round behind the Dobermann and mounted it. The Dobermann tried to shake him off but Tolstoy's paws were the size of a goalkeeper's gloves and rested heavily on its back. Tolstoy was having a fine time, thrusting his flanks in and out energetically. His burgeoning manhood was most definitely on display. It was at once appalling and peculiarly comical.

After another raft of insults – Ryan's dog was 'queer' and as crazy as its owner – the bloke bawled at the Dobermann to follow him and stalked off down the path.

I was shocked and silent. My hands were covered in nettle stings and felt red hot. Dash's ears were pressed flat to her head and she was trembling violently. A smear of the Dobermann's saliva coated her neck just below her collar. Fortunately, the skin was unbroken. Ryan himself was livid.

'You know, it's the dog I feel sorry for. A trained Dobermann's perfectly safe. That idiot's turned his dog into a weapon!'

The only one who seemed unperturbed by the encounter was Tolstoy, whose mouth was wide open in delight.

A couple of days later, Ryan phoned me at home.

'Listen, I just thought I'd let you know I'm leaving Oxford at the end of the week.'

'Really? That's a bit sudden, isn't it?'

'To be honest, it's been on the cards for a while. I'm sick of it here and what happened the other day has pushed me right over the edge. Oxford's just too parochial.'

'Oh. Where are you off to then?'

'London. I've found a place near Richmond Park. I'm guessing four square miles of parkland should be just about big enough for Tolstoy.'

'I'd say so. Richmond Park's got deer in it, hasn't it? You'd better watch he doesn't bring you back some venison when you're out walking.'

There was an awkward pause. I wasn't quite sure how to finish the call. Ryan spoke first.

'Well, look after yourself. It's been fun. I've enjoyed our dog walks.'

'Me too.'

'Say goodbye to Dash from Tolstoy. Oh… and good luck with the wedding. Don't forget you're actually supposed to enjoy yourself, you know!'

So that was that. I'd lost a new friend. More importantly perhaps, Dash had lost her running mate.

In late July, I started jogging to get myself 'wedding fit'. Naturally, I took Dash with me – I got the exercise I needed; she got her afternoon walk. I soon discovered, however, that she had a frustrating habit of burying her nose in the grass every other stride. Either that or bouncing along beside me and making the whole thing look too easy. She'd have to wait at home instead.

One Thursday, I decided to run at lunchtime. Forty minutes later, I arrived back at the conservatory door panting and dripping with sweat. Oddly, Dash wasn't there to greet me. I'd become so used to her welcome routine of stretching, bowing and wagging her tail that I was suddenly concerned. I squinted through the glass door to her mat in the kitchen. Perhaps she'd taken refuge there from the heat of the conservatory? No, I couldn't see her. Panicking, I put the key in the door. It was unlocked. My blood ran cold. Had I forgotten to lock it before going out? Surely there was no way Dash could have opened the door *and* closed it behind her afterwards. But what if someone had got in? What if they'd stolen her or, worse, left her poisoned on the kitchen floor?

I rushed into the conservatory and turned the corner into the kitchen, fully expecting to see Dash stretched out and breathing her last. The kitchen was dark, cool and... empty. I called her name two or three times but still no sign; I opened the door to the lounge and looked in; I walked back outside and checked both neighbouring gardens, calling her name again as I did so. By now, I felt sick with worry. Where had she got to? What should I do? I decided to call Sarah at work – Sarah would know what to do. I stood in the kitchen and quickly punched in the phone number. When Sarah eventually answered, I didn't waste time with small talk.

'Dash has disappeared again.'

'What?! Where?'

'I don't know. I went out for a run and left the conservatory door unlocked. When I came back, she wasn't here,' I said breathlessly.

'Wait a minute. Was the door actually open when you got back?' asked Sarah.

'No.'

'Then she couldn't have opened it.'

'Correct.'

'So she's still in the house somewhere.' Sarah was beginning to sound like a private eye.

'Look, I've checked,' I said. 'She's definitely gone. Someone must have taken her.'

Sarah paused. 'Why?'

I was beginning to get hysterical. 'How do I know? She was Bitch of the Year, wasn't she? Maybe they wanted to use her for breeding.'

'But she's been spayed,'

'Yes, *we* know that...'

Just then I heard a soft 'thump-thump-thump' coming from upstairs.

Dash had always been a ground floor dog. In the beginning, we'd fitted a stair-gate to stop her going upstairs. It wasn't that we wanted to shut her out; we just didn't want her rooting round the bedrooms and my office. What we didn't know, at least initially, is that retired racing greyhounds can't actually climb stairs. Accustomed to living life on the flat in kennels, they simply never encounter them. Once we'd learnt this, we removed the stair-gate – safe in the knowledge that upstairs would remain a dog-free zone where Sarah and I could read, sleep or work unmolested. Now, after ten months, it looked like Dash had taken it upon herself to 'access all areas'.

'Hold on a second,' I whispered to Sarah, still on the end of the line. I put the phone down and started to creep upstairs. After the first few steps, the stairs turned sharply and the rest of the flight continued upwards.

'Thump-thump-thump.'

There, on the very top step – her tail beating crazily against the wall and looking incredibly pleased with herself – was Dash. Relieved to have actually found her, I didn't know whether to praise or chastise. She'd obviously gone in search of me or Sarah. If she couldn't find us downstairs, perhaps we'd gone upstairs instead? The fact that Dash had watched Sarah leave for work that morning via the conservatory door, followed by me at lunchtime the same way, was immaterial.

'Dash! You clown!'

She danced on her front paws and her tail started to wag even faster.

'Come down!'

She put a paw forward and then drew it back as if on the edge of a gaping abyss. After she did the same with her other paw, it suddenly struck me. She'd learnt how to go up... but not to come down.

'Stay,' I said and darted back down to the kitchen to fill Sarah in. What a relief.

I went back upstairs and stopped halfway. Perhaps instead of just picking Dash up, I should teach her to get back down by herself?

'Come here, Dash,' I said, holding out both hands.

Dash crouched and put a paw on the next step down.

'Good girl!'

She then quickly retreated, spun in a circle and barked. This was going to be harder than I thought. I went downstairs again and returned with a handful of treats and a bathroom towel. I placed a treat on each step from top to bottom, like bits of bread in a fairy tale. Dash leaned forward and her nostrils quivered. She could smell the treats; she could see the trail. She slowly extended a paw. With her body flat to the ground like a stalking panther, she cautiously picked the treats off one by one. As she reached the right angle turn, I deftly slipped the towel under her belly like a hammock and swung her round. She managed the last few steps in one bound and then pranced round the kitchen in a lap of honour.

What this now meant, of course, was clear. The cat was out of the bag; the dog could do the stairs. From this point on, nowhere would be sacred. I imagined trying to get some work done with Dash tailing me everywhere. If I went downstairs for a cup of tea, she'd come too. When I went back up to my desk, she'd be hot on my heels.

The gravity of this impressed itself on me even more once I discovered what Dash had got up to during her brief sojourn upstairs. A stack of files in my office had been knocked over; the bin was also on its side, its contents strewn over the floor. An empty biscuit wrapper had been shredded as if it was top secret data. In the bedroom, Sarah's clothes had been pulled off a chair; the sheepskin rug at the foot of the bed had been attacked and large tufts of wool pulled out.

Worst of all, there was a suspiciously dog-shaped depression on the duvet and short black hairs on both pillows.

That evening, Sarah and I held a council of war. Were we about to let Dash into our bedroom as well as our hearts? Would we surrender the last dog-free enclave or confine her to quarters? It seemed a shame to punish Dash's ingenuity – here was something she'd learnt to do on her own. Let's be honest, it was one of the very few things she'd ever learnt to do on her own. After much discussion, we agreed that, above all, what Dash needed was boundaries. 'Good fences make good neighbours', to quote the poet Robert Frost. So it was, with the turn of a screw and a heavy heart, I put the stair-gate back. Upstairs would have to remain off-limits. No dog hairs in the bedroom; no wet nose under my elbow at work. August was going to be a busy month, after all. It was a month for a hen and a stag, not a dog that didn't know its place.

August

'What's happening to Dash at the weekend?' asked Sarah.

I'd already got the message that she wanted *me* to disappear while she had her hen party. Mistakenly, I'd also assumed it would be fine for Dash to loaf about at home.

'She's a girl, isn't she? She can stay here with you.'

Sarah frowned. She wanted to let her hair down with her friends, not worry about the dog.

'You know what she's like – she'll get in the way. Can't you take her somewhere for the weekend?'

'Like where?' My mum was on holiday; my brothers were busy.

'I don't know. A trip or something.'

'A trip? What kind of a trip? It's not as if she's got any family we can suddenly drop in on!'

The sign on the roundabout read 'SLOW' but I put my foot down. It was Saturday morning and Dash and I were on our way to Scotland. My flippant comment to Sarah about

Dash's 'family' had set me thinking. On the first page of her stud book we'd been given was the name and address of Dash's breeder: Mr McQueen, Stockroom Farmhouse, Ochiltree. There were also the names of Dash's 'dam' and 'sire', True Swallow and Droopys Woods. There was no contact number for Mr McQueen so I couldn't phone ahead. I didn't even know if he still lived there. Sarah thought I was crazy to risk it, but what the hell? I now had a weekend to kill. While Sarah was tearing it up with her fellow hens, Dash and I would be on a journey of discovery. If anything was to help me understand Dash better, I felt it would be a journey back to her roots... to the place where she was born.

The sun shone relentlessly, making a greenhouse of the car. I was beginning to regret that I didn't have air con. Dash lay on the back seat and panted heavily. I glanced back nervously, mindful of the warning posters I'd seen as a child: 'DOGS DIE IN HOT CARS'. Stopping at a service station after three hours on the road, Dash took on more water than the average elephant. Before we set off again, I soaked an old towel and spread it over her like a cold compress. I ate my sandwich in between gear changes, saving a piece of cheese for Dash. She snapped at it greedily and resumed panting.

The Scottish border came and went. As we pressed on, a dozen scenarios filled my head. What if the breeder really didn't live there any more? What if he did live there, but refused to see me? After all, what kind of oddball drives 350 miles on the off chance of meeting his dog's breeder? It was whimsical to say the least. If he did agree to see me, would he even remember Dash? She was just one pup. He'd probably bred hundreds over the years. But I'd already gone too far to turn back and I was becoming more excited with every mile.

The motorway narrowed to a dual carriageway, bypassed small towns and eventually became a single-lane road between hedgerows. It was four o'clock by the time we arrived at the Ayrshire village of Ochiltree: low stone cottages lining a single main street. According to the red circle on the map, the farmhouse was just past a church at the edge of the village. We were about to find out if six hours on the road had been worth it. My backside was sore and my heart was racing. Finally, we were here.

I had to confess I was disappointed. The 'farmhouse' looked suspiciously like a bungalow. Was this it? The birthplace of Bitch of the Year? Then suddenly the sound of barking. Greyhounds? I grabbed the stud book, unclipped Dash from her car harness and led her out. There was no number or name on the door and, when I knocked, no reply. I knocked louder; nothing. I looked down in disbelief at Dash, who returned my gaze and pricked up her ears. Had we driven all the way from Oxford only to find the breeder wasn't in? Determined not to give up, I walked purposefully round the side of the bungalow. Against a garage was a kennel made of rough wooden planks. The shapes of two dogs were visible inside. I held my breath. Dash's mother and father? Surely the breeder wouldn't mind if we had a quick peek, I thought, seeing as we'd come all this way. Dash seemed to agree and pulled me eagerly towards the kennel.

'Hello?' a voice called out from the open garage. An old man was sitting in a deck chair, shielding his eyes from the sun with a paper.

'Hello,' I said, striding forward with my hand out. I'd been so focused on the kennel that I hadn't even noticed him. 'Mr McQueen?'

The old man paused thoughtfully, before replying.

'No.'

'Oh. This isn't Stockroom Farmhouse?'

'No,' the old man said again. 'The farmhouse is over the way.'

'Sorry, where exactly?' I asked, leaning forward and suddenly embarrassed at my intrusion.

'Follow my finger,' he said, chuckling and pointing behind me.

I couldn't understand how I'd missed it. Nerves perhaps. The bungalow was obviously no farmhouse and the dogs in the kennel were a couple of mongrels. After seeming unfriendly at first, the old man had got up from the deckchair and walked with us back to the road, still in a pair of slippers. He pointed again, patted Dash gently on the head and smiled. In the distance, partly screened by a few tall trees, was a large farmhouse.

The approach road was long and overgrown. By now, Dash was sitting up on the back seat. The trees gave way to fields of lush grass on either side. In one of the fields a small group of fawn and white dogs were bounding through the long grass and then, at the sound of the car, froze and looked in our direction. Greyhounds! The sight of them so young and without collars made me think of baby kangaroos.

Dash now stood up and pushed her head over my shoulder and out the car window. She sniffed the air enthusiastically.

'What do you think, Dash? Is this it? Is this home?'

The farm buildings were arranged around three sides of a yard with a walled rockery in the middle. On the right were a small barn with a blue corrugated roof and a long, low cowshed with two doors, one of which was open. Opposite these was an outhouse with a pair of crooked windows and a chicken coop on the side. The chickens themselves were roaming freely in the yard, pecking or standing circumspectly on one leg. In front of us was the farmhouse itself. Its tall buttressed side and high windows gave it the look of a church. All of the buildings were of the same pale granite and on the sturdy side of weather-beaten.

As I parked beside the rockery, I saw a woman's face appear in one of the farmhouse windows. I got out, holding the stud book. This time, however, I opted to leave Dash herself on the back seat till I was certain we were in the right place. Moments later, the woman I'd seen at the window came round the side of the farmhouse. She was in her late thirties and dressed in an open-necked blouse and jeans. Long brown hair framed an attractive face with a good complexion but her blue eyes looked slightly alarmed.

'Hello there. Are you Mrs McQueen?' I said, trying to sound as warm and friendly as possible.

'Aye, I am,' she replied in a soft Scottish accent.

I introduced myself, explaining I'd come all the way from Oxford to see her husband about a greyhound.

'Is Mr McQueen at home?'

She looked past me and nodded.

'Yes… but he's just feedin' the dogs for now.'

I turned my head in the direction of her gaze to see the door of the outhouse swing outwards with a kick. A tall, well-built man stepped out holding a large metal dog bowl in either hand. On seeing me and my car, an expression of disapproval flashed across his face, quickly replaced by one of enquiry directed at his wife.

'He's come about a dog,' Mrs McQueen called to her husband, then added 'all the way from Oxford.'

Mr McQueen's bottom lip dropped, as if unsure whether to speak or spit. I stepped towards him, holding out the stud book in my defence.

'I'm really sorry to turn up out of the blue,' I said. 'I would've phoned ahead if I'd had your number. I adopted a greyhound bitch last year – she's here in the car.' I opened the stud book. 'According to this, she was whelped here. I wondered if I could chat to you for twenty minutes.'

'About what?' Mr McQueen said, with a hard edge to his voice.

'About her… the bitch,' I replied.

He looked at me up and down searchingly and then at his wife.

'OK, OK… but I've to feed the dogs first.' He strode past me swiftly and through the open door of the cowshed.

'Will you be wanting a cup of tea?' Mrs McQueen asked me.

'Oh, thanks very much.' I perched on the wall of the rockery. When Mr McQueen returned, I got up again and extended my hand.

'Mervyn,' he said unsmilingly and returned my handshake firmly. He joined me on the rockery wall and I put the stud book down between us like a peace offering. Up close, he was a handsome man with shaggy black hair going grey at the fringes. His nose had been broken and one of his front teeth was chipped. He was wearing large mud-spattered wellies, old jeans and a T-shirt which would have been beige if it wasn't so bleached by the sun.

'What did you say the bitch's name was?' he asked, glancing at the car and frowning.

'Her racing name was Beautiful Energy. Do you want to see her?'

He thought about it. Then he pursed his lips and gave a half-nod.

I opened the car door and Dash, who'd been whining to be let out, shot past my waiting hands and took off in the direction of the stone barn. By the time I caught up with her and clipped the lead on, she was straining to sniff under the barn door.

'Sorry! That wasn't meant to happen.' I shouted back over my shoulder to Mr McQueen. He looked at us doubtfully.

Mervyn McQueen, it turned out, remembered Dash well enough. He spoke guardedly at first, but once onto the subject of her whelping and bloodline, he began to open up. Dash's grandfather had been Top Honcho, a famous Irish stud dog and 'none better', but her dam, True Swallow, hadn't fared so well.

'Did next to nothing for the pups. There was some sickness in 'em. Only two of the litter made it… her among 'em,' he said, indicating Dash, who was leaning against one of his wellies and gazing at the barn. He reached down and idly scratched Dash's chest in a gesture which seemed second nature.

'Is True Swallow still alive?' I asked.

'Still alive but no' here,' he said. 'Down south. Not up to much now though she threw some decent pups in her time.'

'And the sire, Droopys Woods?'

'Died in Ireland. This summer, I hear. He'd be gettin' on now.'

In my naivety, I'd hoped Dash's parents would still be with the breeder, living together in a happy family. It was obvious that this was not how it worked. Greyhounds were matched, mated and then moved on in a sort of canine speed-dating roadshow. The pups were then reared until about three months old and sold or given away.

Mrs McQueen returned briefly with two cups of sweet, milky tea and the conversation turned to Dash's track record. Despite professing not to be interested in 'them websites', Mervyn was aware of Dash's success in Oxford. I sensed he was beginning to soften slightly and asked how he thought she was looking.

'In good nick, aye,' he acknowledged. 'But five's hardly ancient for a greyhound.'

'Do you think she knows where she is?' I asked. 'You know, that she's come full circle to where she was born?'

'Nah', said Mervyn without hesitation. 'She'd be no more than ten to twelve weeks old when she left here.'

I paused, a little upset. Another romantic notion shattered.

'I'm thinking of making her ring bearer at my wedding next month,' I suddenly blurted out. Something approaching a smile formed itself on Mervyn's lips, which he masked by raising his mug of tea. Feeling slightly more at ease, I mentioned some of the problems I'd had with Dash over the past year – the muzzle, her aggression towards other dogs, her obsession with squirrels.

'They're no' dangerous,' Mervyn said, suddenly stern again. 'I've got greyhounds runnin' round here in the fields with hens an' geese. Listen, I'm no' sayin' that if a pack o' dogs are in a field and a rabbit pops up, they won't chase it… or take it. But they're no' dangerous. That stuff is just a myth… a hoax.'

I half expected him to swear. Instead, he reached down to his feet and picked up a small pebble. The sound of whining and barking which came from the barn had been getting louder during our conversation. Without changing position and in a single fluid motion, he lobbed the pebble high behind him. It clattered off the blue corrugated roof and the whining stopped immediately.

Spots of rain seemed to signal that our chat was at an end. I wanted to ask if I could look round but then thought better of it. I'd already pushed my luck. Instead, I thanked him for his time and his wife's tea and loaded Dash into the car. As we trundled back down the approach road, Dash refused to lie down on the back seat. Instead, she stood looking out of the rear window, remaining there for a good five minutes after we'd reached the main road.

'Safe journey home,' was all Mervyn had said as we left. The sun had been replaced by ominous grey clouds, so I took his words as some kind of grudging benediction.

The plan was to drive back to Oxford via the Lake District. Dash and I would stay overnight in a dog-friendly B&B and then take a lakeside stroll on Sunday morning. I figured the change of scene would give me chance to clear my head in preparation for the final month of wedding planning. Since it was still only late afternoon, I decided to take a different route back.

'Black Craig', 'Windy Standard', 'Cairnsmore of Carsphairn' – this is the roll call of mountain peaks that border the Southern Upland Way. The views from the winding road were sublime. A rainbow materialised in the distance; clouds cast shadows over heather-green hills. Dash lay curled up on the back seat in a foetal position, meditating – I liked to think – on the visit to her place of birth. Her eyes were shut and her breathing slow. By now, I was tired, too. The adrenalin of the drive north was replaced by a kind of dreamlike trance as we drifted south. I wondered what Sarah would be doing and how the hen party would be going. By now, the craft class would be finished – Sarah had wanted to have a go at making pottery – and the hens would be having a cocktail before going into town for a dance. A good head taller than her friends, Sarah was already striking but wearing her glad rags and make-up, she'd be simply stunning. I couldn't wait to see her and tell her about the day's adventure. I'd taken a risk and it had paid off.

BOOM! S-S-S-CRUNCH! YELP! OW-W-W! I'd driven off the road in a daze and the front of the car struck a road marker. My seatbelt held firm, but Dash's car harness was too slack and she slid off the back seat into the footwell. For a fraction of a second that felt long enough for the mountainside to crumble, I sat stunned behind the wheel. I was OK... but what about Dash? In a cold sweat I undid my belt and helped her scrabble free. Perhaps she'd broken something? I couldn't tell. Surely she'd show more sign of being in pain if she had? She looked at me questioningly and then stuck her paw out for a stroke. She was OK. After I'd breathed a sigh of relief, I got out to assess the damage to the car. The front bumper was smashed and hanging off. The striped road marker which we'd hit had bent like a lollipop stick and was wedged underneath. It looked like I could reverse the car to free it, but the tyre had burst. I wouldn't get far. Great. What an idiot! One moment's inattention and I'd wrecked the weekend. I wasn't about to start changing a tyre on the side of a mountain road in Scotland. Instead, I got my mobile out to call for breakdown help. No signal. What now? I'd passed the nearest village twenty minutes earlier. How long would it take to walk back... and what about Dash? Should I take her, too? I imagined her tottering along on her spindly legs. No, the safest thing was to wait for the next passing car. Seeing us in trouble, they'd stop and either give us a lift or phone for help on our behalf when further ahead.

I put the hazard triangle on the road behind the car and waited. Dash was comfortably ensconced on the back seat again, licking her paws. Another fine mess I'd got us into. After a few minutes, it started to spit with rain, then big single drops burst on the windscreen. I jumped back into the car, barely in time to avoid a soaking. The rain hammered down; it drummed on the roof. Just when I thought it would stop, it started to hail. I leant over to stroke Dash, as much to reassure myself as her. She looked at me with her dark chocolate eyes. Hopelessly overwrought and drained, I started to sob.

'Aye, make nae bones aboot it, they're a damn fine breed.'

Of all the breakdown truck drivers in all the world, I had to get the greyhound fancier. Craig was a burly man, Glasgow-born, with pockmarked skin and a cracked laugh. Two hours after hitting the road marker, Dash and I were perched in the cab of his truck.

Once the hail had subsided, we'd been picked up and ferried to the next village by a father and son in a Land Rover. From there, I'd called the breakdown service. Craig had arrived and taken us back to the stranded car. The car was more damaged than it first appeared. The front corner of the chassis had partly caved in and, added to that, the spare tyre had been in a pitiful state and judged to be practically useless. There was no option but to load the car onto the truck and drive us all the way back to Oxford. So much for our plan to overnight in the Lake District.

Craig wouldn't hear of Dash remaining in the pranged car, so I lifted her up into the truck's cab and passed the seatbelt through her harness. A couple of minutes into the journey, she stretched out and put her head across my lap to study the driver.

'O' course, Shawfield's nae a great track... but it's aw we got by way of somethin' official.'

Craig recounted that there was only one greyhound stadium in the whole of Scotland: Shawfield, just south of Glasgow. The rest of the racing took place on unlicensed 'flapping tracks'. I suddenly remembered the fate of Dash's brindle-coloured brother, True Joe. I'd completely forgotten to check with the breeder so asked Craig if he'd ever heard of him.

'"True Joe" ye say?' Craig thought about it then shook his head, ruminating: 'Brindle males are the ones to watch though. Greats the like o' Mick the Miller and Pigalle Wonder. Brindles both.'

'And black bitches like Dash here, how do they usually fare?' I asked.

'Unless they're at the top o' their game, a bitch'll always struggle,' he conceded. 'Only a wee handful's ever won the Derby doon south. Dolores Rocket, now there was a lady though. Only bitch to crack the double o' the Derby an' St Leger...'

Under different circumstances, I would've happily listened to Craig for hours but after the day's events, I was exhausted. As he continued to list the greats of the greyhound world, I stifled a yawn and drifted off into an uncomfortable sleep.

By the time we arrived at Oxford, it was two o'clock in the morning. The house was dark – Sarah still wasn't back from her hen party – so I sat in the lounge, bleary-eyed and cradling a mug of strong tea. At that point, even Dash called it a day and wandered off to curl up in her bed. An hour later, Sarah returned wearing a pair of pink, fluffy cat's ears and looking ever so slightly the worse for wear. After she'd got over the shock of finding us back a day early, we swapped stories. Sarah had had the most wonderful time with her friends. The room where they'd done the craft class had been decorated with bunting and dozens of photos.

'Baby photos, school photos, snaps from Thailand and my old teaching days – I don't know how they did it,' she said, wiping her eyes.

It was touching to see her so moved. I wondered idly if my stag party would prove as emotional.

I'd had some pretty clear ideas about the stag party even before I'd had any for the wedding. Since I'd secured the use of Charles's coastal house in Camber in January, I'd also had plenty of time to refine the plan. The idea was to keep the weekend uptempo and outdoors for the most part. There'd be some wild drinking, of course, but there'd also be a run on the beach, barefoot five-a-side football and a ride on a miniature railway.

The attendees were a small but select bunch: my two brothers, the two best men and half a dozen close friends from school, college and Oxford. Since it was a strictly men-only affair, unfortunately that also meant no Dash. She'd just have to stay with Sarah in Oxford. Besides, Sarah was having a trial run of her wedding hairstyle at the salon that weekend. She'd need an objective opinion from another female when she got home.

Surprisingly perhaps, the highlight was a visit to a nature reserve at nearby Dungeness. Something a bit different than the average stag outing. When we were growing up together, my brother Mike had often taken me out birdwatching in the local woods and marshes. He was an enthusiastic and informative guide and I knew he'd make the visit come alive.

When a dozen of us trooped into the visitor centre behind him, an elderly woman behind the desk looked up but didn't smile.

'Afternoon,' Mike said cheerily, leaning on the till. 'My name's Mike Dilger. I'm on the TV.'

To be fair, he *had* done some TV work in his time – natural history stuff for an early evening slot.

'This is my brother,' he said, indicating airily behind him without looking round. 'He's getting married in a fortnight and these are some of his... his wedding guests.' He studiously avoided the word 'stag'.

The woman pursed her lips and cast an eye over us.

'I was hoping you could do us some kind of deal,' Mike continued, 'seeing as I'm such a staunch ally of the bird world.' He paused.

'What TV programme did you say you were on again?' the woman asked.

Mike grinned. 'I didn't.'

The woman's face slowly cracked into a smile.

'Well, I can let *you* in for free but your... entourage... will have to pay half-price.'

We sat in the dark, musty bird hide like excitable boys on their first day at school. The binoculars passed from hand to hand with the occasional whisper. Suddenly Mike himself picked something out on one of the gravel islands.

'It's a crane,' he announced, surprised. 'Hold on. Two of them, I think. There, near that little island. Quite a rarity. How about that?'

I got the binoculars and trained them on the island. Moving through the shallow water on stick-thin legs, the tall grey birds were clearly visible. Every now and again they bent to pick at something with their beaks. They were exquisitely poised and methodical. Neither strayed far from the other, like an old married couple tending the garden.

Back at Charles's house late that same evening, the atmosphere was considerably noisier and boozier. I slipped outside to phone Sarah in Oxford before she turned in for the night.

'Hi, how's it going?'

'Oh, hello!' she said sleepily, already in bed. 'You shouldn't be ringing me, should you?'

'Why not?' I asked.

'I don't know – isn't the stag supposed to have a bride-free weekend or something?'

'But I was missing you…'

'I miss you, too. Are you having fun?'

'Plenty. Great weather, too. How's the hound?'

'Oh, Dash is fine…'

'And… ?'

'And fine. That's it. Morning and afternoon walks, two bowlfuls of food gone in less than a minute. You know, usual stuff.'

'Nothing to report, then – no mishaps?'

Sarah laughed softly. 'You sound like a worried parent on their first weekend away!'

'Oh.'

'No, it's sweet,' she laughed again.

We chatted some more – two soon-to-be-weds – and chirruped our goodnights.

Less than a month to go till the wedding! The final phase of the planning was under way and I'd drawn up lists of duties for 'key players' on the big day. Tentatively, I'd put 'Looking after Dash' on Mike's list. It was still up in the air whether Sarah and I would actually relent and risk Dash attending.

To be fair, Dash's behaviour when out and about had continued to improve. This was largely due to two tactics I'd employed on our walks. The first was rewarding Dash with a treat after every 'positive' interaction with another dog. If she sniffed and wagged, she qualified for a biscuit in the shape of a bone; if she stalked or snapped, she got nothing but a stern reprimand. One morning, she even let a little white Jack Russell balance on its hind legs and kiss her on the nose. A few months earlier, this kind of encounter would have been unthinkable.

The second tactic was routinely giving Dash a run off the lead on our afternoon walks. Since she was so 'hyper', she obviously needed more exercise. I'd learnt to my cost that this was impossible in Florence Park. Too many obstacles, distractions and furry temptations. The golf course was an option but I was always a little nervous of losing her again.

Recently, however, I'd come across an enclosed grassy field by the river that was ideal. It was the size of a football pitch, fairly flat and, best of all, completely empty. A tailor-made greyhound paddock. On one side of the field was the river, fronted by a wall of bulrushes. On the other side was a robust hedge and line of low trees, which screened off the field from view and made it feel even more exclusive. I'd try to arrive there at the end of the walk, when Dash was already warmed up. After checking and double-checking the coast was clear, I'd unclip her harness and turn her loose. For the first few seconds, she'd make a show of idly sniffing the grass. Then, with no warning or signal, she'd suddenly burst into motion as if from the trap, running two or three full laps of the field at top speed, her body gliding over the ground and her legs scissoring until they were a blur. This was the 'fix' she needed and was usually enough to tire her out. A tired greyhound is a happy one and, in Dash's case, a happy one was that much more tractable.

On the last Friday in August, I arrived at the field earlier than usual. Bright but with a slight breeze, it was the perfect weather for an afternoon sprint. I scanned the perimeter of the field. Everything in order. I reached down to unclip Dash's lead and at that precise moment, another dog walker appeared. In all my previous visits to the field, I'd never seen so much as another dog's poo let alone a dog walker. I'd got used to thinking of the field as my own private patch. Suddenly here was someone else who probably thought the same. Not only that, but this person – this intruder – had *two* dogs eager to let off steam. I strode over for an introduction. The other dog walker was a blonde, fluffy-haired woman in her mid-forties. She was wearing the kind of quilted jacket, silk scarf and horsy trousers which look preposterous on anyone outside the Royal Family.

'Do hope we're not interrupting,' she said as we approached.

'No, no,' I replied, trying to sound generous. 'We've just arrived ourselves.'

'Yes, it's a perfect little spot for the dogs. We've been coming here for a while.'

I sensed she was staking her claim but didn't rise to the bait. Instead, I watched as Dash greeted the woman's two charges. One was a woolly labradoodle the colour of caramel and the other a rough-haired lurcher with pale eyes. The greeting passed off peacefully; I quickly rewarded Dash with a biscuit.

'So you don't mind if I let my two off as well?' the woman asked.

I could hardly say no. 'Mine's not great at playing, I'm afraid. She'll probably harass yours and try to race them.'

'Oh, that's fine,' the woman said dismissively, waving her hand. 'They can look after themselves anyway. The lurcher's pretty much uncatchable.'

I raised an eyebrow and looked again at the lurcher. The coarse hair of its coat disguised a beautifully sleek but powerful body. I remembered reading in the *All-Colour Book of Dogs* that the lurcher was 'the poacher's favourite'. A tough tearaway. All the natural advantages of a breed which combines the best of the greyhound with something more solid.

'Be my guest then,' I said to the woman and unclipped Dash's lead. I felt like a gunslinger who'd just called the sheriff's bluff.

The dogs milled round each other, sniffing intently. The labradoodle circled behind Dash but the lurcher went nose-to-nose. Dash's top lip twitched as if not altogether at ease. Suddenly the lurcher dropped down on its front paws and barked. Dash pushed her ears back and looked surprised. Echoing its partner in crime, the labradoodle barked as well. A classic pincer movement. Dash was stunned. So stunned that she failed to react when the lurcher and labradoodle sprang away and started sprinting round the field. Instead, Dash looked at me; I stared back at her. I'd never taught her commands like 'Go!' or 'Start!' or 'Chase!' I'd spent all my time teaching her *not* to charge round after other dogs. Had it finally had some effect? Had I succeeding in knocking the champion racer out of her?

Dash suddenly shuddered as if struck by a bolt of lightning and started to run. Within a few strides she was flying after the other two dogs. The labradoodle was first in her sights. It didn't run so much as bound along. Dash was fast; Dash was a black fox, a vixen with a head like the point of a blacksmith's anvil. She closed in on the labradoodle, she jinked – one, two – and overtook it, then put in a fresh burst of speed.

I glanced sideways at the fluffy-haired woman and bit my lip to hide the smile. She made a face as if to say: 'Well, *that* was hardly a surprise.'

By now the lurcher was several lengths clear. It ran with a smooth, fluid motion, well within itself. Dash's head dipped;

she sped up. She was a black flag streaming in the wind; a black banner at the head of an army as it charged over the hill. Five lengths became four; four became three. Then the two dogs reached the first corner of the field. The lurcher slowed down into the bend, cornered neatly and accelerated away. Dash overshot and had to use her tail to brake. It circled wildly like a loose rudder and her flanks brushed against the hedge as she spun away.

Now it was the woman's turn to smile. Her lurcher was too strong. Her lurcher was too clever for a greyhound bitch – a greyhound whose glory days on the track were over, whose trophies were gathering dust.

But Dash was off again in pursuit. Her head had started to nod madly and her stride lengthened. The lurcher seemed to be running backwards, drifting against the tide. The length of two dogs separated them… then one… then none. Dash was close enough to bite the lurcher's tail. The tip of it flicked in her face like an aristocrat's glove. Dash was defiant. Her tongue lolled sideways out of her mouth and she became an engine, a burning black engine, hot to the touch. The pistons pumped; the exhaust roared. But the lurcher was strong; the lurcher was strong and clever. In 20 metres they'd be at the next corner. The lurcher forced Dash wide. If Dash wanted to overtake, she'd have to do it at high speed and then swerve in time to avoid the trees. I sensed the danger and stepped forward anxiously. If I called Dash now she could still stop in time… but Dash was past hearing. She surged past the lurcher and into the lead. The trees were just metres away. Too late. Her tail started circling… too late.

Too late. She slammed her front paws into the ground and swerved, hitting the trunk of the first tree side on. A sharp and terrible yelp like a scream. Dash bounced off the tree and I started to run. What had I done? What had *she* done? Had she broken her leg? Or worse, much worse? Dash staggered forward and yelped again, holding her left back leg in the air.

'Wait, Dash! Don't move. Stay!'

She started to limp towards me.

'Don't move. Stay!'

Then, as if she'd been caught by a sniper's bullet, Dash twisted sideways and flopped to the ground.

September (again)

'There's a transverse tear in the gracilis muscle. Also severe ligament damage to the near hind toe; associated bleeding and nail bed damage. Likely prognosis: permanent injury to the muscle; scarring and reduced movement in the toe. I can't rule out the possibility of amputation of the toe if it gets worse but I'd say, for now, she's an extremely lucky greyhound.'

Mr Barker looked over his glasses and frowned at me, then looked sideways at Sarah to make his point. I sank back into the plastic chair, consumed with guilt but also relieved.

Dash's toe had blown up like a pool ball. She couldn't walk; she could barely stand.

'She'll need a course of painkillers, antibiotics and anti-inflammatories to start with, as well as footbaths in Epsom Salts twice daily,' Mr Barker continued.

I nodded dumbly and fondled Dash's ear. She leant against me heavily, with her bandaged back leg held in the air like evidence in a courtroom.

'Bed rest till Monday; very short walks on soft ground for a week after that... and don't even *think* about exercising her off the lead for a while. Four weeks from today would be my estimate, and that's a conservative one.'

'Don't feel too bad, honey,' said Sarah after we'd collected the medicine. 'It wasn't your fault... or not entirely.'

I shrugged and pushed my chin out hopelessly. The adrenalin rush of the accident had worn off and I felt awful. I had a pounding head; my back and arms ached. After her smash, I'd picked Dash up and run with her to the nearest road. I didn't stop to trade pleasantries with the fluffy-haired woman or her two dogs. I'd phoned Sarah and then the vet. Sarah had just arrived home from work and jumped in the car to pick us up. We'd wrapped Dash in a blanket to keep her warm. The blood from her damaged paw was a brilliant, scarlet red and had stained the back seat. The blood from my face had drained away and I'd hardly said a word. After less than twelve months and with the wedding just round the corner, I'd damaged our lovely greyhound. Sarah had gone easy on me in saying it wasn't 'entirely' my fault. It was totally and utterly my fault. I'd treated Dash like a toy – pitting her speed against that of the woman's dogs in a pathetic attempt at point scoring. I was a bad dog owner, an awful parent. I was inconsolable.

But these things happen. Any dog owner will tell you; any greyhound owner especially. There's a saying that goes: 'Don't always keep your dog on a lead if you want it to be attached to you.' The paradox is clear: dogs live to run free – if you let them go, they'll love you for it. Yet with greyhounds at least, unless you're extremely careful, they can risk their lives. Far worse things happen at the track. During races, some dogs are thrown clean into the air after hitting the rail or the boards. The most common racing injury is a broken leg but a neck can also snap like balsa wood. There's no getting up from an injury like that. The call goes out; the trackside vet arrives and puts the screaming dog to sleep with a lethal injection. The carcass is removed without fanfare or photographs. And that is all. Greyhounds are bred for racing; like it or loathe it, the sport goes on.

'So we're sure?' Sarah checked. 'We're *really* sure?'

Yes, we were sure. We had just one chance and wouldn't forgive ourselves if we missed it. In the space of a year, Dash had become indispensable. Injured or not, she was coming to the wedding. More than that, she was going to bear the rings and take part in the ceremony itself. I was going to make it happen. But to add to the surprise, we wouldn't tell a soul till the day. What could go wrong? Well, with everything else Sarah and I had to think about – plenty. At this stage of the game, however, so much seemed to be left to chance that one more thing made little difference.

Well before the big day itself there was a to-do list as long as a bride's train. It was now far too much for me to handle on my own, and both Sarah and I were becoming increasingly harried. At breakfast we ticked things off; at dinner we drew up a new list for the following day. We were multitasking and rarely still for ten minutes at a time. All this was extremely unsettling for Dash. She registered her concern by repeated bedwetting. Early in the evenings, as much as two hours before her usual toilet time, we would find her lying in a telltale dark stain. It was as if she'd just 'leaked', as if she couldn't be bothered to move or even whine. When we told her off and showed her the stain, she would lower her head and saunter off in the canine equivalent of a shrug. Her frustration with our new routine wasn't confined to dirty protests either. She took it out on her toys. One evening in early September, the stalwart red rubber chicken known as Pullet finally expired. Dash succeeded in severing the last of its rubber legs and the squeak went. The fact that she also had to have her jaws prised open and the offending lump of rubber hoicked out ruined any solemnity. For fifteen minutes, she'd been chewing vacantly on it like a football coach chewing on a piece of gum.

Disruptive as all this was, we were inclined to forgive Dash everything. In the aftermath of her injury and bed rest, she'd hobbled round the park showing off her bandaged leg. If it had been a plaster cast, it would have been decorated with signatures and messages of sympathy. All the dogs sniffed it; all the owners asked concerned questions and wished her a speedy recovery.

'You can bet speedy is the one thing it'll be,' I replied. 'That's her all over.'

Every bride wants sunshine on her wedding day. So does every groom – if only for the sake of the bride. The weather forecast for mid-September looked far from encouraging and Sarah and I were beginning to get anxious. A downpour would put an end to the idea of canapés and fizz on the riverside lawn. There was no way the budget could stretch to a marquee. Or even a medium-sized gazebo. Umbrellas? A possibility. But how could you hold an umbrella, a spinach tartlet, a glass of Prosecco and a conversation at the same time? Rain would mean the photos would have to be taken inside too. Worse still, what if it rained *and* was unseasonably cold? There wasn't much in the way of heating in the theatre or the abbey. Come to think of it, the long gallery where the meal would be served didn't even have glass in the windows! There were blinds which could be drawn down at dusk but this wouldn't stop a bitter wind if it chose to blow through Abingdon that day. Sarah suggested telling the guests to bring shawls and coats.

'Hmm. And mufflers and gloves, too,' I added.

In the end, we decided that goodwill, booze and body heat would have to do. Some things are in the lap of the gods – and not just the napkins.

No matter how far in advance you ask guests to RSVP, some only get round to it a week before the wedding. Some never get round to it at all but take it for granted that you know they're coming. Eight days to go and at last we had the final numbers: fifty-seven adults (twenty-eight men; twenty-nine women), five children, five babies... and one dog. That made sixty-eight hot bodies in total. The theatre could seat a maximum of seventy, so Sarah and I breathed a sigh of relief. As far as special dietary requirements were concerned, there were twelve vegetarians, and novelties included one person with wheat intolerance and another with an abhorrence of red peppers. I sent the breakdown to the caterer – another big tick on the to-do list. The fact that we knew our total number of guests meant it was time for that great lottery, the no-win situation to end them all: the seating plan.

Sarah and I started off with a pencil and paper. After using up half a rubber in the first fifteen minutes, we took to writing the names on Post-it notes. By the end of the evening, we were sitting on the floor like two kids squabbling over the pieces of a large yellow jigsaw. It wasn't that there were any sworn enemies or rabid ex-wives who couldn't sit together – just an infinite number of permutations. Dash hadn't helped by persistently stepping all over the Post-it notes, which attached themselves to her tail and paws. We finally agreed it was best to look for pairs of guests who had one big interest in common. They couldn't fail to discover it during the course of the meal.

'Do you think this is how Buckingham Palace does it for state banquets?' I asked Sarah idly. 'Or international summits?'

'I think they're probably easier,' she replied, puffing out her cheeks and then sighing.

In the end, we had to settle for the fact that everybody had something in common. They knew either Sarah or me. As long as children were with their parents, and partners or spouses were on the same table, we couldn't go far wrong.

Now all we had to do was get the seating plan in a form that guests themselves could understand. The usual thing is some kind of board resting on an easel. Guests mosey into the dining room, consult the board and discover who they'll be stuck with for the next couple of hours. At the table itself, there's a place card to make sure they don't try to wriggle out of the careful pairing they've been put into. The first change Sarah and I wanted to make was to have guests' first names only. As soon as you add surnames, it all gets a bit stiff and formal. The other change was that instead of place cards, Sarah had wanted badges. In fact, I'd already gone as far as buying a badge maker.

Since going to the greyhound track in April, I'd been intrigued by the different coloured racing silks worn by each dog. Perhaps these could be used for the table numbers and seating plan? Sarah wasn't sure.

'Isn't it enough that Dash is coming to the ceremony without letting her take over the meal as well? Besides, it'll ruin our colour scheme.'

I persisted. The idea was that if you were table one, the number would be white on a red background; table six, red on black and white stripes. The only problem was that there are only six dogs – and therefore only six different silks – in greyhound racing. At the wedding, there'd be eight tables with eight guests on each. I looked again at the seating plan. Could we squeeze everyone onto just six tables? This time Sarah put her foot down.

'No! That'd mean ten and a half people per table...'

She was right – it wasn't going to work. Then I made a discovery. Greyhounds race in groups of six in the UK but in the States and Australia they race in groups of eight. Not only that, but some of the silks were pink, orange or had peppermint stripes. Why not take an 'internationalist' approach and combine silks from different countries? This time Sarah gave in. Just so guests got the greyhound reference, I also asked a designer friend to add a photo of Dash in the corner of each table number – a noble profile with her ears pricked up.

Wednesday the seventeenth of September was the day before the civil ceremony and my last as an unmarried man. It was also my last day at work for a while. I sat at my desk and tried hard to concentrate. Sarah was already on leave and the wedding planning had finally become a genuine double act. I must admit I was relieved. By lunchtime, Sarah had been to the salon to get her nails done; collected a carload of drinks from the wholesaler (wearing gloves to protect her nails) and nipped into town to buy eight pink orchids as centrepieces for the tables.

All I had to do was wrap up my work by four o'clock. At four, I walked Dash for twenty minutes – a gentle amble round the park on the lead. At half past, I set off to pick up my mum, who was due to arrive by train at ten to five. Military precision. This was the start of a sequence that needed to follow on like a line of tumbling dominoes.

Mum was in good spirits despite the journey. Travelling by train at rush hour can be an ordeal – even more so if you're a diminutive seventy-three-year-old and lugging a suitcase the size of a treasure chest. I loaded both into the car and we crawled home through heavy traffic.

'So, how do you feel?' she asked. 'Everything ready?'

'Yes and no,' I replied. 'I might have a job or two for you tonight... if it's no bother. How do you feel about folding a few napkins?'

'Fine. How many is *a few*?'

'Sixty-seven,' I said, trying to look apologetic.

Sarah and I had clean forgotten and I was already on 'badge-making duty' that evening.

'No problem. Great!' said Mum.

It suddenly dawned on me she had expected to help, demanded it even. Her youngest son was getting married and she'd do everything she could to make the occasion go smoothly. I was touched.

That evening, the lounge looked like a haberdashery. Mum was busy folding napkins, Sarah was cutting lengths of ribbon and I was stamping and sealing badges. Dash lay roaching on her back, with her legs stretched out. Each time I finished a badge I balanced it on one of her outstretched paws. We all carried on until nine in the evening when we had a couple of surprise visitors. Sarah's parents. The hotel had messed up their booking and there were no rooms free that night. Of course, the odd mistake can happen at any hotel, but this was the fifth or sixth problem that our guests had reported. So far, bookings had been taken in the wrong name *and* for the wrong kind of room *and* for the wrong dates.

'How hard can it be?' I asked the hotel receptionist, gripping the phone tightly. 'So what are they supposed to do? Sleep rough?'

She said she didn't understand what I meant. I made a mental note to tell her... but *after* the wedding and in triplicate. Exasperating.

At last, at long last, it was The Big Day – or at least the first big day of two. Although Sarah and I would be legally married by the end of it, we were treating it more like a dry run for what we considered the real thing. After breakfast, the first task was to take Dash to the kennels. Her surprise entrance would be at the theatre tomorrow. Today at the registry office, it was all about Sarah and me.

'Well, Dash,' I said to her in front of Mum. 'It's off to the kennels for a few days. No place at a wedding for an injured dog like you.'

Dash looked up at me and placed a paw on my shoe. With the bandage now removed, the only indication of her leg injury was a dip in the muscle and a delicate limp.

'Ahh, she doesn't want to go,' said Mum. 'She wants to be part of it all.'

'Yes,' I said. 'I bet she does…'

I clipped on the lead and Sarah winked at me slyly as she bent down to hug Dash. The traffic on the road was light and the weather was already warming up. Amazingly, luckily, it seemed we just might get bright sunshine for both days. It would be more than lucky, in fact, it would be a minor miracle. I said what approximated to a prayer of thanks and promised never to complain about British weather again as long as I lived. If it just stayed fine for these two days, it was OK by me if it sheeted down for the next forty. As we pulled into the backyard of the kennels, Dash's ear flicked up and she sniffed through the slit of the open window. Familiar territory. Lynn greeted us at the door and Dash's tail went into windscreen wiper mode. I'd already 'briefed' Lynn over the phone.

'Here she is. All set to play your part in the big surprise?' I checked.

'Sure,' grinned Lynn. 'I've got a lovely spot for her in the meantime.'

We went in to get Dash settled and drop off the stuff. On the way back to the car, I was surprised to see Dash again. The outside part of the pen was right next to the entrance and – despite her torn muscle – she was standing on her hind legs with her forepaws on the bars. So that was what Lynn had meant by a 'lovely spot'. Dash would be in the thick of the action and have a clear view of all arrivals and departures. I stepped up to the bars and scratched her under the chin.

'I'll see you tomorrow, Dash. Best behaviour now, mind you… and get some rest.'

As I drove away, I could see her still standing up at the bars.

'Ladies in the rear; gents up front!'

Sarah's father, Harry, would be our chauffeur to the registry office in central Oxford. I sat alongside him in my grey suit, black shirt and a shockingly bright pink tie. At regular intervals on the tie was the number '69' in little black figures. It was my birth year but, in a pathetically juvenile way, I also liked the naughty allusion. If you can't make mischief at your own wedding then why bother at all? Sarah was also in pink, but her dress was a lighter and more palatable shade. It was warm but she'd thrown a pashmina round her shoulders in case it didn't last.

Our registrar for the day would be Anthony, a camp forty-something with spiky hair and sparkling teeth. He purred slightly when he spoke.

'Andrew and Sarah... welcome. We're all ready for you. This way, please.'

He led us into a ground floor room like a headmaster's office with one large desk and a few straight-backed chairs. There was a small vase of roses on the desk as well as the wedding register itself – already open at the correct page. Sarah and I sat down in front of the desk, with our parents behind us in a neat row.

'Ladies and gentlemen. It's my very great pleasure to have you all here today...'

Anthony launched into his speech with gusto as if the room was heaving with guests. Since we'd opted for the simplest service available and no exchange of rings, he'd have to work fast if he wanted to scale the heights of lyricism.

After checking and double-checking the entry in the register was correct, we were then asked to stand for the vows. This was it. We stood facing each other and held hands. I smiled at Sarah and then, since we were expected to repeat after the registrar, I looked sideways at Anthony. He stopped to grope in his pocket and pull out a packet of tissues. Was he going to sneeze? Or perhaps he'd been so moved his own performance? Instead, he offered them to Sarah. I turned to face her again. Her eyes were wet and a big tear was rolling down one cheek. She was beaming. I squeezed her hands and looked into her eyes. For a moment we were totally lost in each other. This was the woman I'd waited thirty-seven years for. Every minute of every hour of every day. It had been worth it.

'Er, Harry, can you duck down a tad? And if you could all squeeze up.'

Vows and kisses over, we were having a quick photo taken. Anthony had volunteered and was holding the camera at arm's length as if it was a hand grenade.

'How's that?' he asked cheerily, returning the camera. We looked at the screen. The top of Harry's head was missing and my mum's eyes were closed.

'Er, could you do one more... just for luck?' I asked. 'Perhaps you need to move back a touch?'

He obliged and this time cut off Lesley's right arm.

'That's... fine,' I said. 'Thanks.'

I hadn't the heart to insist on him having another crack at it. Besides, we'd have two official photographers at the wedding the next day and between them they'd get just about every blink Sarah and I made. After more smiles and handshakes, he showed us out and along the corridor. The restaurant where we were headed next was behind the registry office so he offered to let us out the rear entrance. He waved and bowed slightly before shutting the door after us. We were standing in a car park with our parents on a sunny Thursday in September... and Sarah and I were married. I had to admit it felt very, very good.

We'd chosen the restaurant since it was close but also because it had a terrace where we could continue to enjoy the sun. We started with some sparkling rosé and sat back to discuss the day's events. Everything was wonderful; everything was going according to plan. We could enjoy lunch before heading off to set up at the theatre and abbey. The furniture was due to be delivered at five, the lights at six. Then my phone rang. I checked the number and saw it was Mark, one of my two best men.

'Mark, hi! Nice timing – I just got married!'

'Congratulations!' Then a pause. 'Listen, it's Claudia – she's just gone into labour. I don't think I can make it tomorrow. I'm gutted. I don't know what to say.'

I didn't either. A rock and a hard place just about summed it up. Mark had already had to skip the stag party since his partner was due on the same date. Now she'd chosen to give birth on my wedding day! It was his first child, he had to be there, absolutely no question about it.

'Don't worry,' I said. 'We'll get round it... I think. Have you spoken to Ben?' Ben was the other best man.

'Yeah – I just rang him. I've sent him my list of duties. He's already got my half of the speech.'

'How's Claudia coping?' I asked, as much to give myself time to think as anything else.

'OK. Sort of. I hope.'

'Listen, she'll be fine,' I said.

'I'll be thinking of you both tomorrow,' he said, his voice wavering with emotion. 'Have a fabulous day, it looks like the sun's going to shine on you after all.'

So that was it. One best man down.

Judging from their expressions, Sarah and the parents had guessed what had happened. I just nodded and gave a big sigh. Perhaps I should have expected it, but it felt like a heavy blow. I'd wanted both best men there for more than just the duties they'd do. Mark, Ben and I had been a close trio ever since college, sharing the ups and downs of our student days and, if anything, becoming closer once life had taken us in different directions. I'd wanted them there as friends and witnesses. I also knew they'd have given a damn good speech between them. Sarah reached across and squeezed my hand.

'Don't worry, sweetheart. You've still got one best man left after all.'

Her eyes sparkled in the sunlight. Mark was right – the sun was going to shine on us after all. It *would* be a fabulous day.

The logistics were getting on top of us. We had five people and two carloads of stuff to take to the abbey in order to set up for the following day. So how many trips did that mean we'd have to make? It was four o'clock. The lounge was full to bursting with boxes, big laundry bags and suitcases. Suit hangers were draped over the back of a chair. It was a good job Dash was out of the way. Harry stood with his arms akimbo.

'I think we can do it with both cars in just one trip,' he said.

I was just about to give in and agree when my phone rang. I answered without checking the screen.

'Yes, hello?'

'Hi, Andrew. It's Mike.'

'Mike, we're a little busy right now… Where are you anyway?'

I'd forgotten my brother, Mike, was coming to the abbey to help us decorate. For once in his life, he'd arrived on time.

'I'm at the abbey already. The guys with the lights are here.'

'What – now? They're two hours early!'

'They say you still owe them half the money.'

'I know. I've got the cheque in my pocket.'

'Are you on your way?'

'Not quite. Well, not at all.'

'Do you want me to pay them in cash?'

'That'd be great,' I said. 'Sorry to land you with this, Mike. We'll be there as soon as we can.'

Twenty minutes later, Harry and I were stuck in heavy traffic on the ring road. Remarkable how many people leave work early on a Thursday. Sarah and the two mums were in a second car somewhere behind us. The rear-view mirror gave a perfect view of nothing but the stuff piled high in the back of the car. I huffed and then my phone rang again. It was Mike, again.

'Hey, how are the lights?' I asked.

'The lights are fine. It's the furniture you've got to worry about. It's here already.'

'You're kidding me!'

'No, some large guy and his mate in a van. They say they need help shifting it. Taking it up a set of stairs wasn't part of the deal or something.'

'Tell them we'll be there in ten minutes, max fifteen,' I said. 'They're early anyway. Everyone's bloody early today!'

We finally pulled into the square next to the abbey. A heavy-looking table was hovering in mid-air. Fingers and feet showed at the edges.

'Mike?' Is that you?'

Mike lowered the table and looked round the side. His forehead was covered in sweat and his face shiny.

'How's it going? You married or what?'

We gave each other a big hug.

'Where's the furniture guy?' I asked.

'Up in the long gallery. So is his mate. We've almost managed it between us – or I have, more like.'

I strode through the abbey gate and raced up the stairs.

The long gallery looked very big and very empty. Six tables were grouped together and surrounded by white plastic chairs, all at different angles as if the room had been evacuated in a hurry. A large man in a collared shirt and pale trousers was wrestling with a chair to get the cover on. Another older but skinny man had stopped for a breather and was leaning on a stack of chairs. I introduced myself to the large man and shook his hand. He had a firm grip.

'You're early,' I said. 'We said five o'clock, didn't we?'

'Just thought we'd get ahead of the traffic,' he countered. He was in his forties but had one of those chubby faces that had barely changed for thirty-five years. Except for the innocence – that was long gone.

'Right. I told you the venue was on the first floor ages ago.'

'There's only two of us today,' he said.

I looked at him and then at his mate. No doubting his maths then.

'We'll help with the rest. It looks like my brother's given you a big hand so far.'

Mike came in with another table and I went downstairs for the last one myself. I was glad it was only the one – it weighed a ton.

'So that's everything then,' the furniture guy said. 'If you sign here, I'll take the balance from you and get off.'

He seemed in a hurry, so I looked round the room carefully.

'We agreed sixty-five chairs, didn't we? There can't be more than forty here. What about the rest?'

'Ah, we couldn't bring them today.'

'What? So when *can* you bring them?' I asked.

'Tomorrow, first thing.' He had all the answers.

'By nine o'clock at the latest?'

'I'll bring them myself. No question.'

I was inclined to give him the benefit of the doubt – I'd got married that morning after all. I gave him the cheque for the balance and watched him leave.

Harry, Mike and I moved the tables into the correct positions and arranged what chairs there were round each. That was more like it. Then we unpacked the table linen, the cloths and napkins, and spread them over each table in the way the caterer had described. After the industrious work of the night before, the napkins were already tied with a pink ribbon and had a name badge attached to each. Sarah and the two mums arrived with bags of fresh green ivy. We'd collected it a few days before and the idea was to wrap it around the long wooden beam which ran down one side of the gallery. I'd been a bit doubtful when Sarah had first suggested the idea but I had to admit that, once in place, it looked stunning and entirely suited the venue.

By eight o'clock, the fairy lights downstairs in the lower hall were twinkling, the bar was in place and a space had been cleared for the cèilidh band. I took one last look, then turned off the power and closed and locked the door. I was exhausted. We were all exhausted.

'That's it,' I said to Sarah and gave her a little kiss behind the ear. 'Are you going to make tracks and head back?' We were keen to preserve the romance of the bride and groom not seeing each other till the last minute on the wedding day, so Sarah would go home while I overnighted at the hotel.

We embraced and looked into each other's eyes.

'Did you have fun today?' I asked.

'Yes… but it'll be more fun tomorrow. I can't believe it's finally come.'

Neither could I.

'Wonder what Dash is up to,' Sarah mused.

'Out like a light, I expect. Dreaming of the track.'

Friday morning, my head was as clear as a bell. Today really was The Big Day. I bounded down the hotel stairs in jeans and a T-shirt, greeted family and friends I'd not yet seen and tucked into a full English breakfast. At just after nine o'clock, I sauntered across to the abbey. No sign of the furniture guy; no sign of the rest of the chairs. I couldn't believe it and called him straight away on his mobile.

'Morning – it's after nine o'clock. Where are the remaining chairs?'

'Ah, yes. I'm on my way over. Just one small job to do first, I'll be there within the hour.'

By half ten, he still hadn't shown and was refusing to answer his phone. What was going on? All my meticulous planning was about to be undone! The meal would be ruined if half the guests had to stand. I tried him again at eleven and still no answer. Time to call in the cavalry. I raced back to the hotel to look for Sarah's dad. He was up in his room. I knocked and Harry came out holding a newspaper – all six foot three of him, in trousers and vest and still with builder's biceps at sixty years old.

'Morning. Everything OK?'

'Not really. The furniture guy said he'd be here at nine with the rest of the chairs and now he's not answering his phone. Must be screening my calls. Could you try him from yours instead?'

'Hmm. Give me the number.'

He called, clearing his throat gruffly before he spoke.

'This is Harry Jennings, father of the bride here at Abingdon Abbey. I believe we're still waiting for some chairs.'

Then the reply which I couldn't hear. I stared out of the window down to the hotel forecourt. Bright sunshine and the Thames was already sparkling. The florist was approaching the entrance with the box of bouquets and buttonholes. Eleven fifteen on the dot.

'You're messing us about is what's happening,' Harry said suddenly. A muscle stiffened in his jaw. 'Let me put it like this. Either you get those chairs here before noon or you'll be picking up firewood instead of your furniture. Understood?'

It was most definitely understood. Harry patted my shoulder and I went to have a cup of herbal tea and tried to relax.

About half an hour before any wedding, there comes a point when there's nothing more to do. Or nothing more that *can* be done. The script is written and everyone has their part to play. I was now at that point, standing in the shower and letting the hot water hit the base of my neck. My suit and shirt were lying on the bed, pressed and ready. In ten minutes, I'd be standing in front of the full-length mirror, my tie tied, my cufflinks linked and my shoes shined. I'd already had texts from best man Ben and the ushers to say they'd arrived and were busy about their duties. Just as I was taking a deep breath and about to leave, Mum knocked and popped her head round the door.

'How do I look?' I said.

'Perfect,' she replied and straightened my tie which I knew for a fact couldn't be straighter.

I grinned; she smiled.

'I'll see you down there, Mum.'

A moment later, there was another knock on the door... but this one was loud and hurried. My brother, Mike. I could see straightaway from his face that something was wrong.

'Aren't you supposed to be on your way to the kennels to pick up Dash?' I asked, concerned.

'My satnav's packed in. I can't believe it! It was fine yesterday but now I can't turn the damn thing on.' Although only ten minutes away, the route to the kennels was too convoluted to explain easily.

'If we go together now, we can be back in twenty minutes,' Mike suggested. 'That's still in time for the ceremony. Just.'

'Are you crazy? Your car's a two-seater – where's Dash going to go?'

Mike hadn't had time to think it through. 'Er, on your lap?' he said lamely.

'She's a bloody greyhound, not a lapdog!'

Having been totally confident in Mike, I didn't even have the phone number or postcode of the kennels handy to give to an usher instead. Even if I did, it would totally ruin Dash's surprise appearance. The only other person who knew the way was Sarah, but asking her to go was absolutely out of the question. She'd be halfway into her wedding dress by now and I wasn't supposed to see her till the ceremony. Of course, I could always forget the whole thing about Dash being ring bearer. Maybe it just wasn't meant to be. Had I spent twelve months trying to turn her from a champion racer into a prize pet only to fall at the last hurdle?

I bit my lip. 'Mike, can I borrow your car?'

The black Triumph Spitfire Mark II gleamed in the sun. From the polished chrome of its bumpers to the plush, open-topped interior, it was faultless and immaculate. I had always wanted a dog; Mike had always wanted a classic sports car. Mike and the Spitfire shared the same birth year and it had been lovingly restored at the cost of much time and considerable effort. On special occasions only, he squeezed his bulky frame into the cockpit, drove it out of the garage and hit the open road.

I started the engine. It sounded like a cross between a lawn mower and a missile. Twenty to three. I'd have to put my foot down if I wasn't to commit the cardinal sin of keeping the bride waiting. Anticipating a breezy ride, I buttoned my suit jacket and put on the spare shades Mike kept in the glove compartment. The Spitfire duly shot off through Abingdon and down the country lanes, shaking a little as I cornered. When I screeched into the driveway of the kennels, Lynn, the owner, rushed out to meet me.

'I was expecting your brother a while ago,' she said, looking confused.

'So was I!' I replied.

I looked towards the kennel nearest the entrance where I'd left Dash the day before.

'Is she ready?'

'She's ready,' confirmed Lynn and ran inside to fetch her.

Hearing my voice, Dash suddenly appeared at the bars, rose up on her hind legs and barked.

'Hello, hello, hello!'

Her black coat had its late summer sheen and her flanks were tense and solid. She licked my fingers and gazed at me as if she'd been stuck in the kennels for a whole year.

I glanced at my watch. Ten to three. With its door open, the Spitfire was low enough for Dash to jump in without being lifted. It was black; it was fast; it was her kind of car. In complete contrast to when I'd first picked her up from the greyhound stadium, she overshot and ended up in the driver's seat.

'Move over, you,' I said as got in and shoved her over to the passenger side. 'Now sit!' Dash hadn't sat like a 'normal' dog since her infamous photo session, but on hearing the command, she promptly sat bolt upright, showing the soft white stripe of her belly. I belted her in – the perfect co-pilot.

On the return journey, I gunned the Spitfire as fast as I dared. Dash was in her element. The wind blasted her fur, her tongue was hanging out like a pink scarf and she grinned from ear to ear. In the town centre, we were stopped by a traffic light on red. I revved the Spitfire and tried to ignore the curious looks from shoppers and passers-by. A cyclist in a full Lycra suit and racing helmet drew up alongside us. He glanced across and then did a double take, removing his shades to stare at Dash.

'She's late for a wedding,' I said casually.

The light turned green and I roared off again.

Back in the hotel car park, I jumped out of the Spitfire and skipped round like a chauffeur to open the door for Dash. It was now three o'clock on the dot.

The first person I saw outside the theatre as Dash and I careered round the corner was my brother and chief usher, Paul. He was standing at the doorway, looking anxious.

'Sarah's not arrived yet, has she?' I asked, gasping.

'Not yet. You cut it a bit fine, didn't you?'

Then fellow usher Charles appeared holding a buttonhole.

'There you are! This last one's got your name on it.'

I watched while he fastened the red rosebud deftly onto my lapel – his fingers threading the needle through the stem.

When I stepped into the theatre with Dash, I was surprised by how full it looked. There were guests in suits, dresses, wraps, fascinators, fancy hats and kilts. There were parents with prams, toddlers and babies; there were couples, singles, my best man and the rest of the ushers, friends and family. There was a flurry of waves and smiles for me; surprised cries of 'Oooh' and 'Aaah' for Dash.

I walked swiftly down the aisle, breathing heavily but smiling at the guests, and plonked Dash on her mat in the front row. Then I tossed Mike his car keys, followed by a gesture of wiping the sweat from my forehead. Ben, my best man, quickly attached the wedding rings to Dash's collar. Finally Rebecca, the celebrant, came over to calm my nerves.

'Don't worry – everything will be fine. It'll all fall into place.'

'As long as it falls into place and not into pieces, I don't mind!'

I looked up at the stage – the table for signing the marriage certificate was on the left, draped in pink silk with a large flower decoration in a terracotta bowl and two chairs behind it. In one corner was a music stand and a gleaming euphonium in its open case. Over to the right were two more chairs where the bride and groom would sit side-by-side. Just like I'd planned it; just like Sarah and I had imagined it.

A minute later, Paul appeared in the doorway again and gave me the thumbs up. As I climbed the steps onto the stage a hush came over the audience. I stood looking at everyone and took another deep breath – I was taking a lot of deep breaths that day. The seven rows were full to bursting. It was exciting to see so many friends who I knew individually sitting together in the same room. It was more exciting to think they were all there for one reason, to see Sarah and me become Mr & Mrs, husband and wife. I suddenly felt more nervous than I'd thought possible. Finally. The moment had come. Then the first few notes of the track we'd chosen as the bridal march, 'Forever Came Today' by Diana Ross & The Supremes. The audience stood up as if on a single command. I listened to the first line of the song as if in a daze.

'There you were, standing there as your eyes reached out to me…'

There she was. Sarah was standing at the door to the theatre, shining in an ivory white dress. It was long and simple and utterly elegant. Sleeveless with a low neckline and sequin-covered shoulder straps. Diamante beads like dewdrops were stitched across the lower half. A puddle train. She was wearing pendant earrings and around her neck, on the most delicate silver chain, was a single pearl. There were pink orchids in her hair and she held a bouquet bursting with aubergine-coloured arum lilies, and red and pink nerines. She was crying… and smiling. As she made her way through the audience on her father's arm, heads turned to follow her like wheat blowing in the wind. She looked down a little – out of modesty or perhaps just concerned not to trip. She didn't trip; she floated. She passed Dash on the front row and beamed. Within a couple of seconds, she was on the stage opposite me. My gaze locked onto hers, a spell only broken by Rebecca the celebrant, who stepped forward and asked everyone to be seated.

'Good afternoon and welcome to our celebration of Sarah and Andrew's wedding. This ceremony, which they have largely written and created themselves, marks a defining moment in their relationship...'

I knew the script off by heart. After the welcome and introduction, came the giving away. Harry was asked if he was happy for his daughter Sarah to be married. He pretended to hold onto her for a second and glanced suspiciously in my direction. Laughter. Then he loosened his arm and Sarah walked towards my outstretched hand. I took it gently and whispered how wonderful she looked. We sat down side by side... and relaxed. Rebecca then continued with some history – how we'd met, the proposal and a few milestones.

'Not least the adoption of their lively, but lovely, greyhound, Dash.'

At the mention of her name, Dash dutifully looked up from her mat and sniffed the air.

Sarah's friend and English toy terrier owner, Soraya, gave the first reading: A Walled Garden. It likened marriage to a 'secret and protected place' where romance bloomed in eternal spring and the blackbirds were our private choir. After seeing Sarah at the registry office the day before, I'd fully expected her to be in tears at some point during the ceremony. What I hadn't expected was that most of the guests would be too. Soraya's voice wavered as she read and her bottom lip trembled. She put her hand on her chest to steady herself and somehow made it to the end of the piece. Then it was the turn of our friend, Harriet, to take to the stage. Harriet played euphonium in a brass band, and the low notes were mellow and soothing. I let my attention wander and gazed out of the window. Bright blue sky; the bobbing twigs of a branch. Autumn leaves danced in the breeze but held fast. Then my brother Paul for the second and final guest reading – the lyrics of the Prince song I'd chosen: 'Forever In My Life'. I'd had it in mind for some time and the chorus even had the words 'I do' in it! Paul duly obliged with a masterclass in deadpan delivery.

Sarah and I were then invited to stand facing each other and recite our promises. A month before the wedding, I'd printed them off and stuck the piece of paper to our wardrobe door at home. I'd read them as I got changed every morning and wanted to say them by heart, but now they'd gone right out of my head. The nerves were beginning to tell. Fortunately, Rebecca the celebrant wasn't about to let us down. We could just repeat them after her. We did so and it felt good that Sarah and I had agreed them together, particularly the last one.

'We have made a home together and that is where I'm happiest, with you. I promise to keep our life there as rewarding as it can be.'

Next the secret words – the part Sarah had been dreading. She read from a slip of paper handed to her by Rebecca.

'Andrew, fortunately for me I discovered early in our relationship you were much more than just your natty dressing and sense of humour. So much so, I can't single out one thing about you – I love the whole package. But I do hope you never stop making me laugh – even on the gloomiest of winter evenings.' Here the tears flowed. She stopped to compose herself and Rebecca handed her a tissue. More tears and applause. Sarah was relieved. Now it was my turn to repay the compliment. I began confidently.

'Sarah, I love your laugh and your smile. They struck me right from the start: our first date at a window table in Oxford Thai. I hope with all my heart that I can keep you laughing and smiling…'

Then I lost it myself and cracked. I cried. Sarah smiled and gave me her tissue – the one that she'd just used. After a few sniffs, I finished the sentence.

'I hope with all my heart that I can keep you laughing and smiling and loving me… I love you.'

Now the exchange of wedding rings… and, at last, the turn of our four-legged ring bearer. Was she up to it? Would she acquit herself as she had on the track? Rebecca beckoned best man Ben and Dash onto the stage.

Ben had never owned a dog or even walked one. He was tall and gangly with girlish good looks. His hair hung down to his shoulders in black curls and in the twenty years I'd known him, he'd never used a comb. Dash, for one, needed no second invitation to take to the stage and tugged Ben up the steps. No sign of a limp even. She immediately stood between us, her tail thumping Sarah's dress. Perhaps it all reminded her of the winner's rostrum? Ben knelt down beside her and unhooked the rings. After handing them to us, he tried to withdraw discreetly but Dash wouldn't shift. She lowered her head and leaned back as I'd seen her do on so many of our winter walks. Ben made a worried face and looked at me. I gestured to the two chairs behind me, ringside seats no less. Ben sat down and pulled Dash towards him. I turned back to Sarah to put on her ring. As soon as I did so, Dash wandered back up and goosed me between the legs with her nose, lifting the back of my suit jacket. This brought the house down.

'I knew we shouldn't have invited her,' I announced ruefully.

Unconcerned, Dash proceeded to shake herself – ears and legs flapping and then her tail in a whiplash to finish. When Ben tried to pull her away again, she leaned against my legs and looked at me with big, hurt eyes. There was nothing to be done, so Sarah reached over Dash to put on my ring. We both finally led Dash off to a round of applause; she'd done her job and stolen the show.

In the riverside garden, the sun continued to shine. Sarah and I greeted and embraced everyone who came within arm's reach. We were happy and proud and relieved and amazed. Two weddings in two days. Yesterday with our parents; today with the world and our dog. It was already more remarkable than I could have wished for… and we still had the meal, speeches and cèilidh to come. The canapés did the rounds but I barely tasted them. I drained my glass of Prosecco and stepped back for a moment. In the space of a year, Sarah and I had come a long way. It'd been A LOT of work. What would the honeymoon have in store, I wondered? Or the next year… or the next ten? Then my brother Paul appeared at my shoulder.

'Time for the photos,' he said, nodding in the direction of Crispin, the photographer.

Crispin was already standing behind the camera on its tripod. He frowned at his copy of the list of shots.

'The first one's down as "Wedding Trio",' he said, 'so that's Sarah, Andrew and… ?'

'… and Dash!' I said, in a sudden panic.

In my post-ceremony trance, I'd completely forgotten about Dash. Where was she? Where was the Bitch of the Year? Had she run off again… or fallen into the river? No. There she was – standing placidly and off the lead in a circle of children. They were busy arranging confetti along Dash's back. A string of flowers hung from her neck like the victory garland of a winner, a born winner.

Afterword

Question: What does nought to forty in five seconds but prefers to nap, has four legs but can't climb stairs and a bumper backside but refuses to sit down?

Well, I guess the answer's clear by now. Don't get me wrong. Adopting Dash was the second best thing I've ever done. She continues to lift my spirits with each passing day and I expect I'll be devastated when she's gone... but that's another story.

Despite my best efforts, I made a few mistakes in our first twelve months together. That said, I'd like to think I've learned from them. If I had to live that year over again, I wouldn't change a thing. OK, maybe I would have consulted a couple of websites more carefully! The Retired Greyhound Trust (www.retiredgreyhounds.co.uk) is great for the basics of what's involved in owning a greyhound and what pitfalls to avoid. There's also a wealth of info and advice to be accessed by joining an online forum like Greyhound Gap (www.greyhoundgap.org.uk).

I would also have reached for three or four books more often. *Retired Racing Greyhounds for Dummies* is an invaluable how-to guide with an American spin. To crate or not to crate, that is the question. *Pet Owner's Guide to Greyhounds* gives a British take, and even has a Dash lookalike on the front cover – right down to the white tip of her tail. *Greyhounds – A Complete Pet Owner's Manual* is also an excellent read, but if anyone understands the section on what determines a greyhound's colour, let me know! Fascinating stuff, however. Another must-have on any greyhound lover's bookshelf is *Retired Greyhounds – A Guide to Care and Understanding*. Some heart-melting photos and particularly good on games and training.

For those who are keen on tracing a greyhound's pedigree, I've already mentioned that there are hours of fun to be had on *Greyhound-Data* (www.greyhound-data.com). From an animal welfare perspective, the world of greyhound racing is a deeply troubling one. The facts and figures on www.greyhounds-uk.org are a necessarily sober reminder that a greyhound's life can be as short as the odds are long.

Finally, I would have taken Dash to socialising or obedience classes after the first month or so of settling in. That way, she would have realised that terriers are dogs too, and not a funny kind of hare. I might also have stuck with a conventional short lead instead of a retractable flexi-lead, which just gave her licence to get into trouble. There you go. No excuse now not to adopt one of the tens of thousands of ex-racers still waiting for a home. And I can almost guarantee that they'll be calmer and more laid-back than my very own 'Bitch of the Year'.

I said adopting Dash was the *second* best thing I've ever done. So what's the very best thing, I hear you ask? Well, I'll leave you to work that one for yourselves. Just don't ask me to plan another wedding!

Have you enjoyed this book?
If so, why not write a review on your favourite website?

Thanks very much for buying this Summersdale book.

www.summersdale.com